S0-BJH-061

ENGLAND WITHOUT RICHARD
1189-1199

By the same Author

JOHN, KING OF ENGLAND

HENRY II

ENGLAND WITHOUT RICHARD 1189-1199

BY

JOHN T. APPLEBY

CORNELL UNIVERSITY PRESS
Ithaca, New York

Published in the United States of America by
CORNELL UNIVERSITY PRESS
1965

Library of Congress Catalog Card Number: 65-22721

PRINTED IN GREAT BRITAIN BY
ROBERT CUNNINGHAM AND SONS LTD., ALVA, SCOTLAND

In memory of

JOHN FITZGERALD KENNEDY

29 May 1917 - 22 November 1963

Reys dels cortes e dels pros emperaire
Foratz, senher, si acsetz mais viscut,
Quar reys joves aviatz nom agut,
E de jovent eratz capdels e paire.

Bertrand de Born, *Mon chan fenisc*

Maps

ACKNOWLEDGMENTS

I am grateful to the staff of the Library of Congress for having made their facilities available to me and for their unfailing courtesy and helpfulness.

I am particularly grateful to Lady Stenton, who kindly read the manuscript, corrected many of my errors, and suggested many improvements. For the remaining errors I am wholly responsible.

J. T. A.

Washington, D.C.

I

1189

IN July 1189 Eleanor of Aquitaine, queen of England, was under confinement at Winchester. Except for a few brief intervals of restricted liberty on ceremonial occasions, she had been imprisoned by her husband, King Henry II, since the spring of 1173, when she had been captured, disguised as a man, whilst fleeing to join her sons in a rebellion against their father that she herself was accused of having inspired.[1]

When Henry died, on 6 July 1189, Richard, his eldest living son and undisputed heir, sent orders to England that his mother was to be released from her captivity and that she was to have authority to order all things as she willed and that all matters were to be disposed of as she directed. Released from her prison and acting on behalf of the son whom she had always loved more dearly than any other of her children, Eleanor assembled her court and made a royal progress 'from city to city and from castle to castle, just as she pleased'.[2]

At Richard's orders, she sent messengers to every county in England to direct that prisoners be released from confinement. She added a personal note to the order by remarking that she had found 'by her own experience that prisons were distasteful to men and that to be released therefrom was a most delightful refreshment to the spirits'.[3] This was not a general and indiscriminate freeing of all prisoners, but an attempt to rectify acts of injustice. The chief beneficiaries of the order were the unfortunate victims of the forest law, which Henry II had enforced with the utmost

[1] Gervase of Canterbury: *Historical Works* (hereafter referred to as Gervase), ed. William Stubbs (2 vols., Rolls Series 73, 1879-80), Vol. I, p. 242; *Gesta Regis Henrici Secundi* and its continuation, *Gesta Regis Ricardi Primi* (hereafter referred to as *Gesta*), ed. William Stubbs (2 vols., Rolls Series 49, 1867), Vol. I, p. 42.

[2] Ralph of Diceto: *Opera Historica* (hereafter referred to as Diceto), ed. William Stubbs (2 vols., Rolls Series 68, 1876), Vol. II, p. 67; *Gesta*, Vol. II, p. 74.

[3] *Gesta*, Vol. II, p. 74.

severity. All those who had been imprisoned for offences against the forest law were to be released, and all sentences of outlawry for those offences were to be quashed.

In a striking anticipation of Chapter 39 of Magna Carta, it was provided that those who had been imprisoned at the king's will or at the will of his justiciars but not by the common decision of the county or hundred courts were also to be released, which indicated that Henry and his agents had been acting in an arbitrary and high-handed way and substituting their arbitrary will for 'the lawful judgment of his peers or the law of the land'. Even those who had been imprisoned by due process of law or on an accusation by another were to be freed if they could find sureties that they would stand their trial.

We are not told who was the author of this document, which admirably sums up the complaints against the arbitrary rule of Henry II in his later days and at the same time anticipates the grievances of the barons against the even more arbitrary rule of John. We do not even know whether it was drawn up by Richard's advisors in Normandy and forwarded to Eleanor for promulgation in England or whether it was composed in England and issued under that all-embracing authority that Richard entrusted to his mother. In any case, it was the work of men who were acutely aware of the abuses of the royal authority under the late king and who were imbued with the idea that even the king must conform to the law of the land.

The minute provisions of the edict make it clear that during Henry's later years the administration of justice, even apart from the tyrannical forest laws, had become arbitrary and corrupt. Many men had been cast into prison at the mere word of the king or his justiciars without having been given a chance to stand their trials, and many more had been imprisoned on appeals, that is, on the accusation of men who offered to prove their charges by doing battle, either in person or by a substitute, against the accused, who had not been given the opportunity of offering sureties that they would stand their trial at the appointed time.

Particularly unjust was the imprisonment of men appealed by known malefactors who hoped to win their own pardon by acting as approvers, that is, by doing battle against those whom they accused of being their accomplices or whom they accused on behalf of the king's officials. It was ordered that these men, who were universally detested, should abjure the realm and leave. Those known malefactors who had accused others of their own free will, without being promised immunity of life and limb, were to be imprisoned till it should be decided what to do with them.

William of Newburgh remarks sourly:

> The prisons were heaving then with multitudes of guilty men awaiting either trial or punishment, but when he [Richard] came to the throne these pests, by his mercy, were released from prison, probably to transgress more confidently in the future.[1]

Finally, Eleanor ordered

> that every free man in the whole realm swear that he would bear fealty to the Lord Richard, lord of England, the son of the Lord King Henry and the Lady Eleanor, in life and limb and earthly honour, as his liege lord, against all men and women who might live and die, and that they would be answerable to him and help him to keep his peace and justice in all things.[2]

Although Eleanor acted, on her son's behalf, with great authority, she was not, properly speaking, regent. The ordinary forms for the government of the country when the king was absent were still observed, and the chief justiciar, Rannulf Glanville, who had been appointed by Henry II in 1180, still exercised the authority committed to him, although now in Richard's name and undoubtedly at Eleanor's direction in matters outside the normal routine.[3]

Richard was in no great hurry to come to England to claim his crown. For the first time since the Norman Conquest the eldest son was undisputed successor to his father's throne. John, Richard's younger brother and the only other possible contender, had joined his brother in rebellion against their father in the last year of Henry's life and was now utterly dependent upon his brother's goodwill.

Richard was acclaimed duke of Normandy at Rouen on 20 July.[4] The English bishops who were in Normandy at the time,

[1] William of Newburgh: *Historia Rerum Anglicarum* (hereafter referred to as Newburgh), in *Chronicles of the Reigns of Stephen, Henry II, and Richard I*, ed. Richard Howlett (4 vols., Rolls Series 82, 1884–9), Vol. I, p. 293.

[2] *Gesta*, Vol. II, p. 75.

[3] H. G. Richardson: 'The Letters and Charters of Eleanor of Aquitaine', *English Historical Review*, LXXIV (April 1959), p. 200.

[4] *Gesta*, Vol. II, p. 73.

Baldwin, archbishop of Canterbury, Hugh of Avalon, bishop of Lincoln, Gilbert, bishop of Rochester, and Hugh of Nonant, bishop of Coventry, crossed over to England in preparation for the coming of their future king. Then came Walter of Coutances, archbishop of Rouen, and two Norman bishops, Henry of Bayeux and John of Evreux.

Duke Richard landed at Portsmouth on 13 August.[1] Although he had been born in England, he had spent most of his life in his duchy of Aquitaine and had returned to England only for two short visits, at Easter 1176 and Christmas 1184.[2] Thus the English people knew little of him by personal experience, but they knew a great deal about him by reputation. Richard had had a hard life. Crowned duke of Aquitaine before his fifteenth birthday, he had been in the saddle and fighting almost continually ever since then both to subdue the unruly barons of Aquitaine and to resist the efforts of his father and his brothers to take his duchy away from him. He had thus gained enormous experience in warfare, and he came to England with the reputation of being one of the best fighters of his time.

As the crowds thronged the road from Portsmouth to Winchester to catch a glimpse of their new ruler, they saw more than a mere fighter. Richard had a softer side to his nature, as his passionate love of poetry and music showed, and he was no mean poet himself. Above all, he had a compelling charm about him that captured men's hearts and imaginations, and a physical presence that caught every eye. Richard, now thirty-one years old and no longer in the first flush of youth, was tall and straight-limbed, with a deep chest and long arms and legs, reddish-gold hair, a pale face, and dazzling blue eyes.[3]

Furthermore, he had the hallowed character of a crusader, for he had taken the Cross in November 1187, the first prince on this side of the Alps to do so.[4] From that moment his projected crusade was the most important thing in his life. Richard came

[1] *Gesta*, Vol. II, p. 75.

[2] Ibid., Vol. I, pp. 115, 120, 319, 333-4.

[3] For Richard's appearance and character, see *Itinerarium Peregrinorum et Gesta Regis Ricardi* (hereafter referred to as *Itinerarium*), Vol. I of *Chronicles and Memorials of the Reign of Richard I*, ed. William Stubbs (2 vols., Rolls Series 38, 1864-5), p. 144; Gerald of Wales: *De Principis Instructione*, ed. G. F. Warner, Vol. VIII of *Opera* (8 vols., Rolls Series 21, 1861-91), pp. 246-50; and Kate Norgate: *Richard the Lion Heart* (London, 1924), pp. 32-7.

[4] Richard of Devizes: *Chronicle*, ed. John T. Appleby (Nelson's Medieval Texts, 1963), p. 5.

to England in order to be crowned king and to drain his realm of as many men, as many supplies, and, above all, as much money as he possibly could.

We are not told what Richard wore when he thus showed himself to his future subjects. With his taste for the magnificent, however, he probably wore clothes fully as striking as those he wore on an occasion of state a couple of years later, the only occasion on which his clothing is described in detail. When he received the submission of the Emperor Isaac in Cyprus in May 1191, he wore a scarlet cap embroidered in gold with birds and beasts, a tunic of rose-coloured samite, and a cape emblazoned with gleaming half-moons and sunbursts of silver, with slippers of cloth-of-gold and golden spurs.[1]

Richard was greeted with wild rejoicing, for the people of England hoped that he would inaugurate a new state of things, undo the injustices and oppressions of the last years of his father's reign, and bring happiness and peace to all men.

> He increased his father's good works and stopped the evil ones. Those whom the father had disinherited the son restored to their original rights; those whom the father had kept in chains the son allowed to go free; those whom the father, for the sake of justice, afflicted with various punishments the son, for the sake of mercy, restored to life.[2]

Richard arrived in Winchester on 15 August and was reunited with his mother. The clergy and people received him with a magnificent procession.

One of his first actions upon arriving in England was to have his father's treasure counted and weighed. According to Roger of Howden, it amounted to over 100,000 marks (a mark, a unit of accounting, not an actual coin, was two-thirds of a pound, 13s. 4d.). The *Gesta Regis Ricardi* gives the incredible figure of £900,000, which Bishop Stubbs reasonably conjectures to be a mistake for £90,000, a more likely figure.[3]

Richard probably paid at this time a debt of honour that considerably diminished his treasure. Henry II, when he made his

[1] *Itinerarium* pp. 197-8. [2] *Gesta*, Vol. II, p. 76.

[3] Roger of Howden: *Chronica* (hereafter referred to as Howden), ed. William Stubbs (4 vols., Rolls Series 51, 1868-71), Vol. III, p. 8 and note 2; *Gesta*, Vol. II, pp. 76-7.

final submission to King Philip II of France, had promised to pay him 20,000 marks to reimburse him for his expenses during the war, and Richard, shortly after his father's death, had agreed to pay an additional 4,000 marks. The Pipe Roll for this year records that 25,000 marks 'were sent across the sea', and it may be assumed that the money was in payment of this debt.[1]

Richard's younger brother, John, who had sailed from Barfleur at the same time as Richard and had landed at Dover, joined his mother and his brother at Winchester. Richard had already, at Rouen, confirmed his father's gifts to John by granting him the county of Mortain in Normandy, unspecified lands to the value of £4,000 a year in England, and the hand of Isabel of Gloucester. He now made the grant of lands in England more specific by giving John the castles and honours of Marlborough, Ludgershall, the Peak, and Bolsover, the honour of Peverell, the town of Nottingham, the castle and honour of Lancaster, the whole of Derbyshire, the honour of Wallingford, 'and many others too numerous to mention'.[2]

Richard also gave John leave to marry Isabel, the daughter and heiress of Earl William of Gloucester, the son of Earl Robert, who was a bastard son of Henry I. John and Isabel were thus second cousins, and Archbishop Baldwin forbade the marriage on the ground of this kinship. John, however, went ahead with his plans, after lodging an appeal to Pope Clement III, and was married to Isabel at Marlborough on 29 August.[3]

Richard could not have been ignorant of John's character. He was treacherous and untrustworthy, as Richard must have known. For no discernible reason other than a desire to be on the winning side, he had deserted his father, whose favourite son he was, and had joined Richard in the rebellion that preceded Henry's death, although, unlike Richard, he had no grievances against the father he had betrayed.

John was now around twenty-one years old. His record up till this time had not been one that would inspire much confidence in his future. His father had named him lord of Ireland in 1177 and had sent him there in 1185. His conduct could hardly have been worse. He succeeded in alienating both the native Irish and the Anglo-Norman settlers and showed himself to be vain,

[1] *Gesta*, Vol. II, pp. 70, 74; Pipe Roll 1 Richard I, p. 5.
[2] *Gesta*, Vol. II, pp. 73, 75, 78. [3] Ibid., Vol. II, p. 78.

capricious, grasping, and utterly lacking in any ability either as an administrator or as a soldier. To be sure, he was only eighteen at the time, but long before he had reached that age Richard was an able fighter and a capable administrator.

Richard had little reason to love John. Encouraged by his father, John, in 1184, had joined forces with his brother Geoffrey, duke of Brittany, and invaded Poitou in a hare-brained effort to wrest it from Richard. Richard had inflicted a sound drubbing on the pair and sent them scurrying back to Brittany. Ever since the death of the king's eldest son Henry, 'the young king', in 1183, Henry II had steadfastly refused to recognise Richard as his heir and had, instead, shown every indication of considering John as his successor to the throne. Richard trusted John so little that he had even refused, in the preceding May or June, to go on crusade unless John went with him, so that he might have him under his eye.[1]

Richard, however, was scrupulous in fulfilling the promises his father had made, in confirming the grants Henry had promised or intended, and in rewarding those who had remained faithful to the old king in his last bitter days of humiliation and defeat. There is no evidence that Richard felt any affection for his father, who had deeply wronged him, attempted to deprive him of his right to the crown, and even seduced the woman to whom he was betrothed, or that he felt any remorse at having accomplished his father's ruin or any regret at his death. He is reported to have gazed impassively at his dead father's face, remained in the church for only a moment, and turned on his heel and strode out.[1]

Richard's adherence to his father's wishes proceeded from prudence and common sense. Henry II, much as his son might have hated him, had been king of England till his death. If Richard was to expect and demand the obedience of his people, it would be as king of England. Out of respect for the office he was to assume and to set an example of obedience to the royal will, he obeyed his father's last wishes. That Richard himself was in rebellion at the time those wishes were expressed was of small moment to him; he no doubt thought of himself not as a rebel but as a wronged son, trying to regain what was rightfully

[1] *Gesta*, Vol. II, p. 66.

[2] *Histoire de Guillaume le Maréchal*, ed. Paul Meyer (3 vols., Paris, 1891-1901), lines 9291-9303.

his, the recognition as his father's heir, a position of which Henry was attempting to defraud him.

With his brother John provided for beyond his deserts, Richard turned to a half-brother who had a more legitimate claim both on their father's gratitude and on Richard's generosity. Geoffrey was born, probably in 1154, of a common whore named Ykenai, according to Walter Map. Henry had given him his father's name and had had him brought up with his legitimate children. He was destined for the Church at an early age and had been educated at the famous schools at Northampton, which at that time were among the best in England.[1]

Geoffrey had been elected bishop of Lincoln in 1172 and sent to Tours by his father to complete his studies. While still bishop-elect, Geoffrey had proved so capable a fighter in his father's defence during the great rebellion of 1173-4 that Henry had declared: 'My other sons are the bastards; this one alone has shown himself my true and legitimate son.' Although the pope had dispensed him from the impediments of illegitimate birth and of being below the canonical age, Geoffrey steadfastly declined to receive the episcopal consecration, which would make it impossible for him to fill any of the great secular positions to which he was aspiring. After the see of Lincoln had been vacant for fifteen years, the pope, in 1181, ordered Geoffrey to make up his mind and either be consecrated or resign. Geoffrey, who felt more attracted to the secular than to the clerical life, chose to resign the bishopric so that he might be 'a soldier in his father's service'.[2]

Gerald of Wales, who knew Geoffrey well, says that he 'aspired to greater things' than a bishopric. This ambition was not unreasonable. William the Conqueror was a bastard; Henry I had provided handsomely for his eldest bastard, Robert, by making him earl of Gloucester and bestowing enormous estates in the west country on him, and to Reginald, another bastard whom his daughter Matilda later made earl of Cornwall, he had given wide lands in the southwest. Henry II, however, was not so prodigal

[1] Walter Map: *De Nugis Curialium*, ed. M. R. James (Oxford, 1914), pp. 238, 246; Pipe Roll 16 Henry II, p. 20; Gerald of Wales: *De Vita Galfridi Archiepiscopi Eboracensis*, ed. J. S. Brewer, in *Opera* (8 vols., Rolls Series 21, 1861-91), Vol. IV, p. 410; H. G. Richardson, 'The Schools of Northampton in the Twelfth Century', *EHR*, LVI (Oct. 1941), pp. 595-605.

[2] Gerald of Wales, op. cit., p. 368; *Gesta*, Vol. II, pp. 271-2.

with lands and titles as his grandfather and his mother had been. He appointed Geoffrey his chancellor, and Geoffrey served him faithfully to the end of the king's life. He was one of the few who stayed with Henry to the end, and the king on his deathbed promised him either the bishopric of Winchester, the richest in England, or the archbishopric of York.[1]

Neither post had any attraction for Geoffrey. 'He hoped that if anything unfortunate should happen to his brother the king on the perilous pilgrimage he might obtain either the whole kingdom or a large part of it.' Richard was well aware of his half-brother's ambitions. It had been reported to him that Geoffrey, when he was amongst his intimate friends, had put the lid of a golden bowl on his head and asked: 'Now isn't this head worthy of wearing a royal crown?' Furthermore, it was said, he was in the habit of trampling underfoot a drawing of his brother, with the remark: 'This is how the worst of kings should be treated.'[2]

Richard determined to scotch his brother's ambitions and at the same time to honour his father's last wishes. Before Geoffrey returned to England, Richard ordered the canons of York to elect him archbishop, a post that had been vacant since the death of Roger of Pont l'Évêque in 1181. Some of the canons met in York on 10 August and obediently elected Geoffrey. Immediately Hubert Walter, dean of York, and Hugh of Le Puiset, bishop of Durham, protested against the election on the ground that they, as well as many of the canons, had had no voice in it, and they appealed to the pope. Neither protest, although legitimate, was disinterested. Hubert Walter coveted the archbishopric for himself, and Bishop Hugh wanted the post for his son, Bourchard. Queen Eleanor, who had no love for her husband's bastard, and Rannulf Glanville, the chief justiciar and Hubert Walter's uncle, opposed the appointment, but Richard did not heed their protests.[3]

While Richard was making a leisurely progress towards London, he learned that the Welsh had raided the border and laid waste several towns. With characteristic impetuosity he wanted to go at once and subdue the rebels, but Queen Eleanor persuaded him to postpone action till after he was crowned.[4]

[1] Gerald of Wales, op. cit., pp. 368, 371. [2] Ibid., pp. 368, 379.
[3] Gerald of Wales, op. cit., p. 373; *Gesta*, Vol. II, pp. 77-8.
[4] Gervase, Vol. I, p. 457.

Richard arrived at last in London and was greeted by a great procession. On Sunday, 3 September 1189, he was crowned in Westminster Abbey. The writers of the time give a minutely detailed account of the ceremony, which perhaps indicates that a new order was introduced; at any rate, the rite of 1189 has been closely followed in all subsequent coronations.

The clergy, dressed in copes of purple silk, went in procession, preceded by acolytes carrying a cross, candles, and thuribles of incense, to Richard's chamber in Westminster Palace and escorted him to the Abbey, over linen cloth laid the whole way, with 'glorious song'. The procession was led into the Abbey by clerks carrying holy water, crosses, candles, and thuribles. Then came the clergy in due order, first the priors, next the abbots, and then the bishops. In the midst of them walked four barons carrying golden candelabra.

Next came the king's regalia. Godfrey of Luci carried the cap of state, John Marshal the golden spurs, William Marshal, newly married to the great heiress of the earl of Pembroke, the golden sceptre surmounted by a golden cross, and William, earl of Salisbury, the golden verge with a golden dove at its end. Three earls, David of Huntingdon, the brother of the king of Scots, John, Richard's brother, and Robert, earl of Leicester, carried swords with golden scabbards. Next came six earls and barons carrying a chest on the top of which were the royal insignia and garments, and after them William of Mandeville, earl of Essex, carried the golden crown, studded with rich gems.

Richard walked with Hugh, bishop of Durham, at his right and Reginald, bishop of Bath, at his left. Four barons carried a silken canopy over them, held aloft on lances. A crowd of earls, barons, knights, and various laymen and clergy brought up the rear.

When the procession reached the high altar and everyone knelt, Richard took the threefold oath before the Gospels and the relics of many saints. He swore that all the days of his life he would show peace and honour and reverence to God and Holy Church and the clergy; that he would exercise right justice over the people committed to his rule; and that he would blot out all evil laws and wrongful customs, if any existed in his realm, and would preserve good laws and customs.

At his throne Richard was then undressed, except for his shirt, which was open at the shoulders, and his drawers. He was shod with slippers embroidered with gold. Archbishop Baldwin placed the sceptre in Richard's right hand and the verge in his left. Then the archbishop anointed Richard on the head, the shoulders, and the chest. Since the see of London was vacant through the death of Gilbert Foliot on 18 February 1187, the dean of London, Ralph of Diceto, acting in his stead, handed the oil and chrism to the archbishop.[1] A linen cloth and the cap of state were placed on Richard's head, and he was dressed in a tunic and dalmatic. The archbishop handed him the sword of justice, two earls put the golden spurs on his feet, and the mantle was placed about his shoulders.

Richard was led back to the altar. The archbishop adjured him, in the name of Almighty God, not to take upon himself the kingship unless he fully intended to keep the oaths he had sworn. Richard replied that with God's grace he intended to keep them. He then took the crown from the altar and handed it to the archbishop, who placed it on Richard's head. The archbishop gave him the sceptre and verge, which presumably the bishops of Durham and Bath had been holding, and, thus crowned, King Richard went to his throne, preceded by the barons holding the golden candelabra and the three earls carrying the swords and with the bishops of Durham and Bath, one on each side. The king sat on his throne while the archbishop celebrated the Mass of the Sunday. The king's crown was so heavy that two earls held it over his head. At the offertory the two bishops led the king to the altar, and Richard made the customary offering of a mark of gold.

After the Mass the king returned in procession to his chamber, where he laid aside the heavy crown and vestments and put on lighter ones for his comfort during the coronation feast. During the banquet, which the chroniclers describe as of the greatest profusion, richness, variety, and plenty, the clergy, in due order of rank, sat at the king's table. The earls, barons, and knights sat at separate tables 'and feasted splendidly'. One may gain some idea of the size of the banquet from the fact that 1,770 pitchers, 900 cups, and 5,050 dishes had been bought in preparation for it.[2]

[1] Diceto, Vol. II, pp. 47, 69.

[2] *Gesta*, Vol. II, pp. 80-3; Howden, Vol. III, pp. 9-11; Pipe Roll 1 Richard I, pp. 21, 30, 216.

Richard had ordered that no woman or Jew should be allowed at his coronation feast. While the king and his court were feasting in masculine splendour, several of the leading Jews of the country, in a desire to present their respects and their gifts to the new king, attempted to enter the palace. A great crowd had gathered at the gates, and when they saw the Jews they fell upon them and beat them severely, killing some of them and leaving others half-dead. The riot spread to the city. The mob besieged the Jews in their houses, killed many of them, and set the houses on fire. Since almost all the buildings of London were of wood, with only the churches and the houses of the greatest being of stone, the fire spread, and great damage was done.

When the king heard the uproar he sent the chief justiciar, Rannulf Glanville, to subdue the mob. Rannulf was powerless before the fury of the Londoners, who had embarked upon an orgy of looting and plundering that lasted all through the night. What had begun as an outburst of anti-Semitism turned into a general demonstration of lawlessness.

The Jews had been introduced into England by William the Conqueror, but they had remained a minute minority, confined largely to the greater towns. They could not be fitted into the feudal system, and hence they enjoyed the dubious privilege of being directly under the king's protection. Although Christians engaged in money-lending under various stratagems to avoid the Church's prohibition of usury, as all lending at any degree of interest was considered, the majority of the money-lenders were Jews. When a Jewish money-lender died, the king, as sole lord and protector of the Jews, either inherited both his money and the bonds that witnessed the borrowings of Christians from the Jew or else forced the Jew's heirs to pay heavily to acquire their inheritance. When Aaron of Lincoln, the richest Jew in England, died in 1186, Henry II seized his bonds, which represented such vast wealth that later on a special department of the Exchequer had to be set up to deal with them.[1]

Although not all Jews were money-lenders by any means, the opprobrium in which money-lenders were held was visited upon the whole Jewish community. Furthermore, outbreaks of anti-Semitism were one of the darker concomitants of the crusading

[1] H. G. Richardson: *The English Jewry under Angevin Kings* (London, 1960), pp. 1-14, 115-18.

movement. In the pitch of enthusiasm to which people had necessarily to be raised in order to embark upon such a perilous enterprise, their hatred of the distant enemies of Christ, as they termed the Saracens, might easily be deflected to the Jews nearer at hand. Atrocious massacres of the Jews had occurred at Rouen and in Germany at the outset of the First Crusade.[1]

Richard was furious when he learned the extent of the riot. Not only had he been insulted by this breach of his peace on the very day of his crowning; his Jews, who were under his protection and who represented a potential source of wealth to him, had been plundered. He ordered that the criminals be apprehended and punished, but, as is usual in affairs of this sort, the criminals were a nameless mob, impossible to identify. Only three men were hanged: one because he had stolen from another Christian and two because they had set fires that had spread to Christians' houses. Richard sent stringent orders to every sheriff to prevent such uprisings in the rest of the country.[2]

The king, on 5 September, received the homage of the bishops, earls, and barons who had gathered for his coronation. Then, says Roger of Howden baldly, 'he put up for sale everything he had'. 'I would have sold London itself if I could have found a buyer,' Richard later remarked.[3] His avowed object was to raise money for the crusade, and he went about it in the most direct way possible. He could have levied a tax on the whole country, but the yield would have been uncertain and, more important, the collection would have been slow. Richard wanted all the money he could lay his hands on, and he wanted it immediately.

In addition to the sale of lands, offices, and privileges upon which he now embarked, Richard had been given a further means of raising money. Pope Clement III had sent him letters patent by which he was authorised to free from their vows to go to the Holy Land any of his subjects whom he wanted to leave in England to carry on the government during his absence. Henry II in 1188 had forced many men to take the Cross who had no real desire to go on the crusade, and others who had taken the crusader's

[1] Cecil Roth: *A History of the Jews in England* (Oxford, 1941), p. 6; Steven Runciman: *A History of the Crusades* (3 vols., Cambridge, 1951-5), Vol. I, pp. 134-40.

[2] *Gesta*, Vol. II, p. 84; Newburgh, Vol. I, p. 297.

[3] Howden, Vol. III, p. 13; Richard of Devizes, p. 9.

vow in the enthusiasm of the moment had later repented their rashness. These men now purchased from the king permission to remain at home. Richard thus acquired 'an inestimable sum

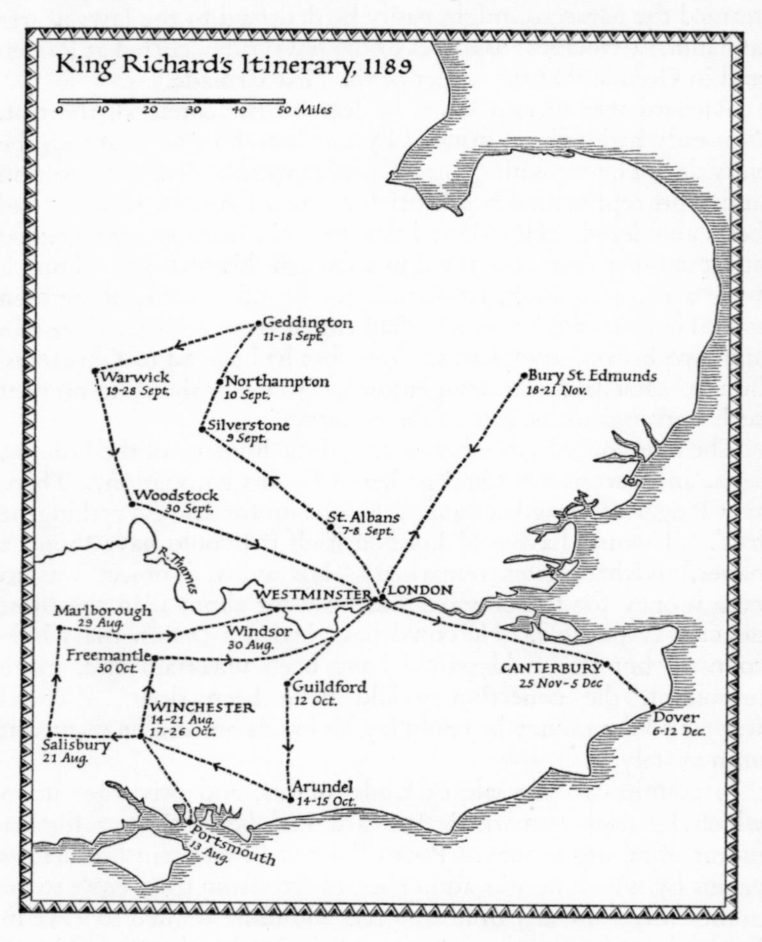

of money' and at the same time provided for the continuity of the administration.[1]

The king went to Geddington in Northamptonshire and summoned the Great Council of all his bishops and barons to meet at Pipewell Abbey nearby on 15 September. In addition to the

[1] Howden, Vol. III, p. 17; Gerald of Wales: *De Principis Instructione*, p. 251.

archbishopric of York, to which Geoffrey had been elected, four bishoprics were now vacant. Richard, on the first day of the council, appointed Godfrey of Luci, the son of one of his father's most trusted and capable servants, Richard of Luci, to Winchester, which had been vacant since the death in the previous December of Richard of Ilchester. Godfrey made a triple bargain with the king: he bought the manors of Meon and Wargrave for his church for £3,000, secured the possession of his inheritance for 1,000 marks, and obtained the sheriffdom of Hampshire and the custody of Winchester Castle.[1]

Richard's second appointment rewarded a faithful official who had also stood high in Henry's favour. Richard, treasurer of the kingdom and archdeacon of Ely, was the son of Nigel, bishop of Ely, who had been treasurer under Henry I and was recalled by Henry II early in his reign to reorganise the Treasury. When Nigel retired from the king's service around 1158 he bought the post for his son Richard for £400.[2] Richard is best remembered as the author of the *Dialogus de Scaccario*, an invaluable explanation of the workings of the Exchequer. The king now appointed him bishop of London, a see that had been vacant since the death of Gilbert Foliot in the spring of 1188.

It should be understood that the king did not have the right to appoint bishops directly. He merely ordered the chapter of the cathedral to elect the man of his choice as bishop. The chapter of course complied, and the king then gave him the lands attached to the bishopric as a temporal fief, for which the bishop-elect, before his consecration, did homage like any other baron. Thus the outward forms of the freedom of the Church, which Richard had sworn to uphold, were observed.

On the following day the king completed his episcopal appointments. He nominated William Longchamp, who had been his chancellor in Aquitaine, to the see of Ely. Geoffrey Ridel, bishop of Ely since 1173, had come to meet Richard at Winchester, fallen ill, and died there on 21 August. He died intestate, and Richard therefore confiscated his enormous fortune of 3,000 marks in coin, as well as 'gold, silver, horses, precious clothes, grain, and stock' of an immense value. In addition to naming

[1] Richard of Devizes, pp. 7–9; Pipe Roll 2 Richard I, pp. 138, 151.

[2] Richard son of Nigel: *Dialogus de Scaccario*, ed. Charles Johnson (Nelson's Medieval Texts, 1950), p. xv.

Longchamp bishop of Ely, Richard also made him chancellor of England at a price of £3,000, although Reginald, bishop of Bath, bid £4,000 for the post.[1]

The last appointments were made with a view to easing the situation at York, where both the dean, Hubert Walter, and the bishop of Durham, Hugh of Le Puiset, had opposed the appointment of Geoffrey as archbishop. The king now named Hubert Walter bishop of Salisbury, a see that had been vacant since 1184, and Bishop Hugh's son Bourchard treasurer of York, an office that had been occupied by Geoffrey till his election as archbishop. Hubert Walter and Bishop Hugh then withdrew their objections to Geoffrey's election, and it was confirmed by the Great Council. As dean of York, to replace Hubert Walter, Richard nominated Henry Marshal, the brother of the faithful William Marshal.[2]

No sooner had the king made peace amongst the clergy at York, however, than Geoffrey, perhaps in desperation when he saw approaching the episcopal consecration that would bar him from the high secular station on which he had set his heart, gave vent to that quarrelsome and obstinate disposition that was henceforth to disfigure his career. He was now archbishop-elect of York, and as such he objected loudly and violently both to his brother's appointments to the chapter of York and to some of the other nominations, concerning which he claimed to have a voice. 'He swore that the king's grants should not stand, except by his own will and consent.' Richard, at the end of his patience with this most difficult brother, in a swift fit of anger then and there stripped him of all his lands on both sides of the sea.[3]

On the final day of the council, 17 September, the king turned his attention to the government of the realm during his intended absence. Rannulf Glanville had been Henry's chief justiciar since 1180. He had had a long and distinguished career. He had been sheriff of Yorkshire from 1163 till he lost that post as a result of the Inquest of Sheriffs in 1170. During the great revolt of 1173-4 he had distinguished himself at the Battle of Alnwick, where he had captured the king of Scots. Henry had rewarded him by re-appointing him sheriff of Yorkshire and by naming him as one of the itinerant justiciars and employing him on

[1] Diceto, Vol. II, p. 68; Richard of Devizes, p. 7.
[2] Gerald of Wales: *De Vita Galfridi*, p. 368; Howden, Vol. III, pp. 15-16.
[3] Howden, Vol. III, p. 17.

various embassies. As chief justiciar he was the king's most trusted servant, occupying a position of the highest importance and serving as the king's vice-regent when he was out of the country.

There seems to have been some trouble between him and Richard, but the exact relationship between the two after Richard's arrival in England is not clear. Richard of Devizes says that Richard imprisoned him and forced him to purchase his release for £15,000. That Rannulf could pay such a sum is ample evidence that, as Richard of Devizes says, he took advantage of the king's confidence. Official evidence of Rannulf's misdeeds is found in the Pipe Roll, in an entry in which he admits that he and his servants had taken more than £1,600 in cash, in addition to a vast store of booty. Rannulf's steward, Reiner, who acted as his deputy in Yorkshire, was implicated in his shady doings, and he, too, had to promise a thousand marks to regain Richard's goodwill.[1]

Rannulf, however, was still in a position to oppose the election of Geoffrey as archbishop of York; he was present at the coronation feast and took a leading part in suppressing the riots against the Jews, and he was present at the council at Pipewell.[2]

Richard probably used Rannulf for his own purposes, to ensure the continuity of government during his first weeks in England, but made it clear that his days of power were over. Although Richard in general followed the policy of rewarding his father's trusted servants, the post of chief justiciar was of such great importance that he would bestow it only on a man whom he knew well and trusted fully. He had previously in Aquitaine followed the policy of forcing those whom he distrusted to promise to accompany him on the crusade, so that he might have them under his eye, and it may well be that such motives accounted for his treatment of Rannulf, who in any case, thanks to his military experience and administrative ability, would be a good man to have at hand during the crusade.

William of Newburgh, however, says that Rannulf, because he was already an old man and because he did not approve of the new king's actions, solemnly resigned his office in order to go to

[1] Richard of Devizes, p. 5; Pipe Roll 23 Henry II, pp. 81-2; Pipe Roll 2 Richard I, p. 67.

[2] Gerald of Wales, op. cit., p. 373; Newburgh, Vol. I, p. 296.

Jerusalem, for he had taken the Cross during King Henry's reign. This is confirmed by the author of the *Gesta*, who says that Rannulf, 'worn out by old age and hard work', begged the king's leave to go to Jerusalem.[1]

Whether he resigned or was deposed, Rannulf at any rate ceased to be chief justiciar. At the council at Pipewell Richard appointed Bishop Hugh of Durham and William of Mandeville, earl of Essex and count of Aumale, as joint chief justiciars. Probably at the same time that he made him justiciar, Richard created Bishop Hugh earl of Northumberland for £10,000, according to Richard of Devizes, of which sum 2,000 marks were still owing at Michaelmas 1190, and gave him complete jurisdiction over the county, which was now united, for administrative purposes, to Hugh's county palatine of Durham and was no longer accounted for at the Exchequer. The king also sold Bishop Hugh the manor of Sadberge for a further 600 marks. All this seemed a wonderful joke to the king, who remarked: 'What a clever workman am I, to make a new earl out of an old bishop!'[2]

The post of chief justiciar was the most important secular position in the realm. When the king was in the country, the chief justiciar acted as the head of the judiciary and presided both over the meetings of the king's court of justice at Westminster and over the sessions of the Exchequer. When the king was out of the country, the chief justiciar stood in the king's place and was responsible for the government of the realm.[3]

Henry II had spent a little more than half his time in his domains across the Channel, where he could be in close touch with English affairs and whence a steady stream of letters and orders directed his officials in England in the performance of their duties. Richard, however, was planning to embark on a most hazardous venture that would lead him almost to the other end of the known world. Communication with his island realm would at best be so slow as to be almost useless. When crises arose they would have to be dealt with by the men on the spot; there would be no time to appeal to the king.

[1] William of Newburgh, Vol. I, pp. 302–3; *Gesta*, Vol. II, p. 87.

[2] *Gesta*, Vol. II, p. 87; Richard of Devizes, p. 6; Pipe Roll 2 Richard I, p. 21; Howden, Vol. III, p. 13; Newburgh, Vol. I, p. 305.

[3] H. G. Richardson and G. O. Sayles: *The Governance of Mediaeval England from the Conquest to Magna Carta* (Edinburgh, 1963), pp. 157, 159, 165–6, 173.

The men whom Richard chose to share this post were both well advanced in years. Hugh of Le Puiset, bishop of Durham since 1153, was one of the richest and most powerful men of the North.[1] He had reigned almost as an independent monarch in his county palatine of Durham for over thirty-five years. Although they were related, King Henry seems to have been on rather distant terms with Bishop Hugh. The king did not visit Durham, and the bishop did not often frequent the court. Hugh had not made any effort to help Henry, while he was still only duke of Normandy, to win the throne. When the king of Scots invaded the North in 1173, Bishop Hugh, although he did not actively support him, did not try to defend the country against his depredations.

In his favour it may be said that he had administered his bishopric and his county palatine wisely and efficiently and that he was on terms of friendship and mutual respect with most of the great men of the North. Above all, he was a gentleman of the old school, grave, stately, and courteous in his bearing, a patron of the arts, a notable builder, and a lover of the good things of life. None of this, however, indicates that he was particularly well fitted for the post to which Richard had assigned him.

In order to pay off some of his debts to the king, Bishop Hugh had to use the money he had collected for the crusade. He therefore sent messengers to the pope to beg to be released from his vow. He was not honest enough, William of Newburgh charges, to say: 'I have bought an earldom, and therefore I cannot go to Jerusalem: I beg you to hold me excused.' Instead, he pleaded his advanced age as an excuse for laying aside the Cross.[2]

William of Mandeville, earl of Essex, had married Hadwisa, the heiress of the count of Aumale, and had assumed that title in his wife's right. He had gone on crusade with Count Philip of Flanders and had helped to win the great victory at Ramleh in 1177. King Henry's closest friend, he had accompanied him on his last wild flight from Le Mans in June 1189. Richard liked and trusted him, and shortly after appointing the earl as one of the chief justiciars he sent him on a mission to Normandy.[3]

[1] See G. V. Scammell: *Hugh du Puiset, Bishop of Durham* (Cambridge, 1956).
[2] William of Newburgh, Vol. I, p. 305.
[3] *Gesta*, Vol. II, p. 91.

That neither of these two men seemed to have the qualities that would be needed to govern a turbulent realm for an indefinite period apparently did not occur to Richard, who in any case had little appreciation of the complexity of the work they would have to do. What disposed him in their favour was probably the fact that both were men of the highest honour, whose integrity had never been questioned. Richard prized honour and valour above all other qualities, and he was particularly repelled by the double-dealing and financial unscrupulousness that had characterised many of his father's actions.

Richard named William Marshal and four of the principal judges of the King's Court, Geoffrey son of Peter, William Briwerre, Robert of Whitefield, and Roger son of Reinfrey, as associates of the two chief justiciars. He intended, no doubt, that Queen Eleanor, in whom he had the utmost confidence, should exercise a guiding influence over them all. Both Geoffrey son of Peter and William Briwerre had taken the Cross, and Richard freed them from their obligations in return for an unspecified sum of money.[1]

Further sums were realised at the Michaelmas session of the Exchequer, when the sheriffs made their final accounting for the year. Of the thirty-one sheriffs who rendered their accounts, only six were left in office. Even amongst these six there was some juggling of counties. Robert Delamere kept Oxfordshire and was given Berkshire as well, upon his promise to pay £100. Henry of Cornhill retained Surrey and was given Kent in exchange for 100 marks. Oger son of Oger, who was shifted from Buckinghamshire and Bedfordshire to Hampshire, promised 200 marks for the exchange and for the privilege of marrying his daughters to whomever he chose.[2]

Rannulf Glanville, the former chief justiciar, relinquished or was deprived of the sheriffdom of Yorkshire, which was given to John Marshal, William's brother. Rannulf's son-in-law, Ralph of Arden, was ousted from Herefordshire, which was given to Henry Longchamp, William Longchamp's brother. Ralph was also convicted of having deprived Franco de Bohun, by force, of lands in Sussex and had to offer 1,000 marks for the king's good will. William Marshal received the sheriffdom of

[1] Howden, Vol. III, p. 16; Richard of Devizes, p. 6.
[2] Pipe Roll 2 Richard I, pp. 14, 155, 116.

Gloucestershire in exchange for 50 marks, and Earl William of Salisbury became sheriff of Wiltshire, a post for which he promised 60 marks.[1]

Robert Marmion was not only deprived of Worcestershire; he was fined £1,000 into the bargain. Bishop Hugh of Coventry bought the sheriffdoms of Warwickshire, Leicestershire, and Staffordshire for 200 marks. Richard Engaigne, who evidently wanted some security of tenure amidst all this upheaval, promised 300 marks for the sheriffdom of Northamptonshire for three years. The largest single sum was promised by Gerard of Camville, who offered 700 marks for the sheriffdom of Lincolnshire and for the custody of Lincoln Castle, which belonged by right of inheritance to his wife, Nicholaa of La Haye.[2]

All the sums mentioned above are taken from the Pipe Rolls, which, it should be remembered, record only the financial accountings of the sheriffs. They are by no means a complete record of all the money that the king received. If a man could pay cash on the spot, and Richard of course preferred transactions of this nature, the payment would not be recorded in the Pipe Roll. In this general sale of 'powers, dominations, earldoms, sheriffdoms, castles, manors, booty, and the like',[3] a great deal of money was paid directly to the king. Only when a man could not pay cash for his purchase was his debt entered in the Pipe Roll for future collection by the sheriff.

Although one may question the wisdom of this general replacement of sheriffs when the king was on the verge of leaving the country, the extraction of money from the new sheriffs was a legitimate transaction. The office was a profitable one. A major source of the king's regular revenue was the income from the royal manors, the king's demesne land. The sheriffs did not act as agents simply to collect the income and then turn it in to the Treasury. They paid a fixed fee every year as the 'farm' of the counties. The farm had been fixed long ago, at a sum low enough not only to allow for fluctuations in income from the manors, dependent upon the year's crops, but also to guarantee the sheriff a reasonable profit for his trouble, since he was officially unpaid. Prices had risen considerably since the farm had been

[1] Pipe Roll 2 Richard I, pp. 58, 45, 111, 122; Richard of Devizes, p. 7.
[2] Pipe Roll 2 Richard I, pp. 24, 43, 29, 89; Richard of Devizes, p. 30.
[3] *Gesta*, Vol. II, p. 90.

fixed, and the king tried to compensate for the increase either by demanding a payment in addition to the farm as a 'surplus' or by selling the office, as in these cases, for whatever he could get for it. In addition to his income from the royal manors and from such windfalls as occasional wardships and the custody of escheats, the sheriff had almost boundless opportunities for peculation, and few failed to take advantage of them.

If a man was willing to pay 100 marks a year for the sheriffdom of Northamptonshire, as Richard Engaigne was, one may be certain that he counted on making more than that out of the office. That Rannulf Glanville could pay £15,000 to the king, as Richard of Devizes says he did, and still have enough left over to journey to the Holy Land is ample evidence that the sheriff of Yorkshire, at any rate, did not lose money on the job.

Geoffrey, the king's brother, meanwhile began to consider the position in which he had contrived to place himself by his ambition and his obstinacy. Richard had made it plain to him that his aspirations to hold high secular honours were vain, and, by stripping him of all his lands, both those he held of his own right and those belonging to the archbishopric of York, that even the career in the Church that he had hitherto scorned depended on his brother's goodwill.

Geoffrey's plan apparently was to enjoy the revenues of the see of York and the power and position of the archbishop-elect, just as he had at Lincoln, without committing himself irrevocably to the clerical life by accepting consecration. Richard understood what Geoffrey's intentions were, and he determined to quash them.

Richard despatched some of his household knights to Geoffrey with the order that he have himself ordained immediately, and when Geoffrey put off the ceremony that would separate him from his worldly ambitions, Richard sent a group of clerks and bishops to him with an even stronger command. The pope, on the earlier occasion of his election to the see of Lincoln, had already dispensed him from the impediment of illegitimacy. Geoffrey therefore, on 23 September, at his manor of Southwell, had himself ordained priest, 'unwilling and complaining', by his suffragan, John, bishop of Whithorn.[1]

When Richard learned that his brother had thus at last cut

[1] *Gesta*, Vol. II, p. 88; Gerald of Wales: *De Vita Galfridi*, p. 374.

himself off from the possibility of succeeding to the throne, he exclaimed: 'Now at last we are safe from that quarter, and henceforth our worries and care are laid to rest in that respect.'[1]

Geoffrey went to his cathedral city early in October and was received by the clergy and people in a solemn procession. Henry Marshal and Bourchard of Le Puiset then demanded that he install them in their offices, but Geoffrey refused to do so until his election should have been confirmed by the pope. This repeated refusal to install his nominees made Richard all the more enraged against Geoffrey. When Geoffrey sent Adam of Thornover, one of the canons of York, and several other messengers to ask the pope for his pallium, the symbol of his authority as archbishop, Richard would not allow them to leave the realm.[2] Although King Henry had ostensibly renounced the Constitutions of Clarendon in 1172, he nevertheless continued to enforce such of its provisions as represented in his eyes 'the ancient customs of the realm'. One of these, which had been in force at least since the Conquest, was the requirement that 'archbishops, bishops, and parsons of the realm' should ask the king's leave in order to go outside the kingdom. Richard was thus following an established precedent in exercising control over the movements of Geoffrey's emissaries.

Richard had sent messengers, shortly after he landed in England, to all the ports in England, Normandy, and Aquitaine, to select the biggest and best ships for his service on the crusade. He had these ships distributed amongst the men whom he had chosen to lead his fleet and ordered that they be amply laden with arms and provisions. Enormous supplies of beans, salt pork, and cheese were laid in, together with 10,000 horse shoes.[3]

The Account of Ships in the Pipe Roll for the year ending at Michaelmas 1190 shows some of the king's expenditures on his fleet. He bought 33 ships from the Cinque Ports, paying two-thirds of the cost, the remainder of which was probably met by the towns, and three ships from Southampton and a like number from Shoreham. He paid the whole cost, £56 13s. 4d., of a ship that belonged to Walter son of the Boatswain, and £66 13s. 4d. for a ship that he gave to the Hospitallers.

[1] Gerald of Wales, op. cit., p. 375.
[2] *Gesta*, Vol. II, pp. 91-2.
[3] Pipe Roll 2 Richard I, pp. 53, 104, 112-13.

Shortly before the fleet set sail, in all probability, he paid the wages of around 1,100 sailors for a year in advance, each sailor receiving 2d. per day and the steersman 4d. The crews ranged from 25 for the smaller vessels to 61 for the king's own ship, the *Esnecca*. 45 ships are mentioned in this passage, which is only a partial accounting of how Henry of Cornhill spent the sum of £5,023 6s. 8d. More ships were acquired, both in England and the king's continental domains and in the Mediterranean. When Richard sailed from Sicily on 10 April 1191, he had a fleet of 219 vessels.[1]

Whilst these preparations were under way, Richard had not forgotten the insults offered to him, as he saw the matter, by the Welsh earlier in the summer. Although their raids seem to have been nothing more than the usual outbreaks of lawlessness, Richard called together 'a great army' in order to punish Rhys ap Gruffyd and the other chieftains of South Wales. The Pipe Roll, however, records none of the laying in of great stores of arms and provisions that would accompany the assembling of a large force, and it would seem that this was more in the nature of a limited expedition to restore order.

Richard put John in command of the army, which in itself is a good indication that no extensive military operations were intended; otherwise, one may be certain that no other duties would have prevented the king himself from leading the army and engaging in the occupation that he knew and loved best of all. Although John had shown no military ability whatever, now that he had the honour of Gloucester he had a particular interest in seeing that these border raids were stopped.

To accompany John, whom Richard had learned not to trust, the king sent his chancellor, William Longchamp, bishop-elect of Ely, a man who enjoyed his highest confidence.

The Welsh were impressed and subdued by this display of force, and there is no record that any fighting took place. The chieftains of South Wales came to John at Worcester and made peace, swearing not to trouble the king's lands whilst he was on crusade. Rhys ap Gruffyd, prince of South Wales, came to Oxford under John's safe-conduct to render homage to the king, but Richard sent word that he was too busy to come to meet him, as King Henry had done in the past. Rhys was highly

[1] Pipe Roll 2 Richard I, pp. 8-9; Richard of Devizes, p. 28.

offended at this slight to his dignity and went back to Wales without having seen the king.[1]

Richard used this expedition, which could hardly be considered a war, as an excuse for levying a scutage on those barons who had not taken part in it, at the rate of 10s. on each knight's fee. This gave rise to the famous entry in the Pipe Roll, one of the few places in that series of accounts in which the clerks who compiled it gave free rein to a sense of humour:

> The bishop of Ely [William Longchamp] owes £20 of that scutage on account of his knights. But he had them and a great many more in that same army in the king's service. And therefore with angels and archangels he is quit.[2]

The bishops of England assembled at Westminster on 22 October for the consecration, by Archbishop Baldwin, of Godfrey of Luci as bishop of Winchester and of Hubert Walter as bishop of Salisbury.[3] After the ceremonies were completed, Hugh of Nonant, bishop of Coventry, brought up a matter that closely touched his fellow bishops and particularly the archbishop. Many of the English cathedrals had an unusual constitution in that their chapters were not bodies of secular canons, as normally, but were the monks of the monasteries attached to the cathedrals. At Canterbury, for instance, the chapter was composed of the monks of Christ Church. Since the bishop was the titular abbot of the monastery, the monks of Christ Church claimed and usually exercised the right of electing the archbishop of Canterbury, who was also their abbot.

This might have worked well enough had it not been for two factors that arose in the course of time. One was that the bishop, the titular abbot, was usually so busy either with the king's affairs (for a bishopric was usually the reward, in the twelfth century, for a loyal servant of the king) or with the administration of his diocese that he had no time to devote to the supervision of the monastery, which then devolved upon the prior.

The second factor was that a division was made between the lands belonging to the bishopric and those belonging to the monastery. This was done because the king took over the lands when the bishopric was vacant, in order to enjoy the revenues

[1] *Gesta*, Vol. II, pp. 88, 97; Howden, Vol. III, p. 23; Richard of Devizes, p. 7.
[2] Pipe Roll 2 Richard I, p. 116.
[3] Diceto, Vol. II, p. 71.

from them, just as he took over a lay fief when the owner died and the heir was under age. As long as the bishop and the monks held their lands in common, during a vacancy the monastery had to subsist on whatever sums the king was pleased to dole out to it. The king, furthermore, often prolonged the vacancy in order to increase his revenues, thus adding to the difficulties of the monastery. In order to avoid this situation, the lands were so divided that during a vacancy only those belonging to the bishopric fell into the king's hands and the revenues of the monastery continued uninterrupted.

Practical and necessary as these measures were, they led to an almost complete separation of the bishop from his chapter, over which he had no control, either disciplinary or financial. In spite of this separation, however, the monks still claimed and usually exercised the right of electing the bishop, although their choice was usually dictated by the king. In addition to having no control over his chapter, the fact that it was made up of the monks of the monastery meant that the bishop could not provide for his officials, who helped him in the administration of the diocese, by appointing them canons of his cathedral chapter.

Just as the papacy, at this period, was greatly enlarging the sphere of its jurisdiction and evolving a body of canon law that strove to define that jurisdiction, so too were the bishops seeking to extend their influence over their dioceses, to exercise a more thorough control over them, and to define their powers by means of charters and in synods. Monasteries that were exempt from episcopal visitation or control were thorns in the bishops' sides, and the sharpest thorn of all was a monastic chapter that claimed to be independent of the bishop, its nominal head. There were, naturally, periods of great friction between the bishop and the monastery attached to his cathedral.[1]

The situation came to a head when Archbishop Baldwin, a Cistercian and a scholar of some note, disgusted by the recalcitrance of the monks of Christ Church, determined to found a college of secular canons in a suburb of Canterbury, to be made up of the clerks of his household, who would be amenable to his control, who would pursue those studies that he thought were neglected by the slothful monks, and who would assist him in the

[1] See Dom David Knowles: *The Monastic Order in England* (Cambridge, 1940), pp. 313-30.

discharge of his duties as archbishop. In so doing Baldwin brought on the most bitter ecclesiastical quarrel of the time.[1]

Hugh of Nonant, bishop of Coventry, was faced by the same problem that troubled Archbishop Baldwin, but he proposed a more direct solution. Of a noble Norman family, the nephew of Bishop Arnulf of Lisieux and a friend of Henry II, who had employed him on a number of diplomatic missions, Hugh was elected bishop of Coventry in 1186 and consecrated on 31 January 1188. Just how the quarrel between Hugh and the monks of Coventry arose it is difficult to determine, for the writers of the period are such violent partisans either of the monks or of the bishop that there is no impartial account of the matter. Gervase of Canterbury, a monk who hated Hugh bitterly, says that he was 'elected or, rather, intruded' into the see, which probably means that the monks of Coventry elected him against their wishes, at the king's command. William of Newburgh says that Hugh sowed or fostered discord between the prior and the monks so that he might use the ensuing scandal as a pretext for ejecting the monks. At any rate, Hugh was faced by the not uncommon situation of finding the monks and the prior at loggerheads, and, as their titular abbot, he determined upon drastic measures.[2]

In addition to buying the post of sheriff of Warwickshire and Leicestershire for 200 marks, Bishop Hugh promised King Richard 300 marks 'to have the priory of Coventry', which had long been free from the bishop's jurisdiction, with the intention of replacing the monks by secular canons. Having thus gained the king's permission, the bishop, on 9 October 1189, 'invaded the priory with an armed band, drove out the prior, had the monks, who had fled to the church, beaten, disabling and wounding some of them, throwing others into prison in chains, and driving out the rest, stripped of all they owned. He broke open all the chests of the church and burned the charters and privileges', according to Gervase.[3]

Gerald of Wales, whose sympathies were with the bishop, makes Hugh the injured party and says that the monks of Coven-

[1] See the introduction to *Epistolae Cantuarienses*, ed. William Stubbs, Vol. II of *Chronicles and Memorials of the Reign of Richard I* (2 vols., Rolls Series 38, 1864-5).

[2] Gervase, Vol. I, p. 326; Newburgh, Vol. I, pp. 394-5.

[3] Pipe Roll 2 Richard I, pp. 37, 43; Gervase, Vol. I, p. 461.

try assaulted the bishop and his clerks and threw them out of the cathedral. Whether or not Hugh was the aggressor, it is certain that the bishop and his clerks on the one hand and the monks on the other came to blows.

Hugh now appeared before the assembled bishops at Westminster and with that eloquence for which he was famous described the insults, humiliations, and violence to which he had been subjected. His stirring words and the sight of the bruises and wounds that he and his clerks displayed moved the whole assembly to tears. As a climax to his speech, the bishop prostrated himself with outstretched arms in the form of a cross before the archbishop and his fellow bishops and begged them to avenge this insult, not to himself or even to their episcopal order, but to the honour of God and His Holy Church.

The bishops raised Hugh to his feet. Putting on full pontificals and with lighted candles, the archbishop and the bishops solemnly excommunicated both those who had committed this outrage and those who had encouraged them. Gerald adds that the assembly spent the next three or four days in discussing ways and means of correcting this and similar situations, which, together with the sentence pronounced by the whole group, would indicate not only that the bishops thought that Hugh was in the right but also that many of them were faced by the same problem.

Hugh, a practical man of affairs who had already made several trips to Rome on King Henry's behalf, realised that the final decision in this vexing matter lay with the pope, and he knew that trips to Rome and gifts to the papal court required money. He therefore proposed that they build up a war-chest. If his fellow bishops, and here he named in particular those in the same situation as himself—Canterbury, Rochester, Winchester, Bath, Worcester, Ely, Norwich, and Durham—would contribute two thousand marks, he would add another thousand 'in order to free himself and his poor church of Coventry', and thus they could carry the matter through in proper style.

This proposal greatly pleased all the bishops. The only one who would not agree to it was the one most nearly concerned, the archbishop himself, and his veto of course killed the scheme. Baldwin had been a monk, although a Cistercian, whereas the monks against whom the measure was aimed were black monks, or Benedictines, as they are now called. He was not willing, he said, that in his time such a great change, to the detriment of the monks' honour, should be made. Gerald, who knew him well, for he had accompanied the archbishop when he preached the crusade in Wales in 1188, describes Baldwin as a man of great gifts and industry, vastly learned, but wholly lacking in vigour and boldness: two qualities, one may note, however, that Baldwin displayed to a high degree in his bold and vigorous dealings with his monks of Canterbury.

Although they would not help to defray his expenses, the bishops provided Hugh with letters indicating their support, and he promptly sent them off to Rome. Since both Gerald of Wales, who detested the black monks, and Richard of Devizes, a black monk to whom Bishop Hugh was the Devil incarnate, agree concerning the bishops' letters, one may believe that the bishops at any rate felt that active measures should be taken to correct the anomalous situation.[1]

King Richard determined to put an end to the quarrel between Archbishop Baldwin and his monks, which had been dragging on for more than three years. Baldwin's original purpose had been to found a college of secular canons at Hackington, just outside Canterbury. The monks, however, declared that he intended to take away all their rights and give them to the canons. They accused him of planning to deprive them of the right to elect the archbishop; they said that his new foundation would replace the church of Canterbury as the mother and head of the Church in England; they fancied that he planned to steal the body of St. Thomas from them; and they asserted that he had deprived them of revenues that were rightly theirs so that he might build this new foundation. Since Baldwin had prudently associated the king and all the bishops of the province in his venture by promising to allot the gift of a stall to each of them, the monks declared that he intended to set himself up as pope in England, with the canons of the new foundation as a college of cardinals.

Baldwin, for his part, was not a tactful man, although it is difficult to see how he could have carried out his plan in a tactful manner in the face of the opposition of the monks, on whom tact would have been wasted. He soon came to the end of his small

[1] Gerald of Wales: *Speculum Ecclesiae*, ed. J. S. Brewer, in Vol. IV of *Opera*, pp. 64-7; Richard of Devizes, p. 8.

supply of patience in dealing with them, and then he proceeded to violence. When the monks refused to obey him, he shut them up in their monastery and, so the monks claimed, cast some of them into prison.[1]

Both parties to the dispute appealed to Rome, and successive popes favoured first one side and then the other. In the spring of 1189 Pope Clement III sent a legate, John of Anagni, who had been made a cardinal by Pope Hadrian IV in 1158, with full powers to settle the matter. The cardinal reached Normandy in May, but King Henry forbade him to cross over to England. Henry had little use for papal legates, and he had no intention of turning one loose in England whilst he was out of the country and unable to supervise his actions.

Cardinal John had perforce to cool his heels in Normandy whilst Henry fought out the last stages of his struggle against Philip II of France and his ally, Henry's own son Richard. After Henry's death the legate proposed to Duke Richard that he be allowed to proceed on his mission and go to England, but Richard refused to give him permission. He was going to England to be crowned, he said, and he would not allow the legate to be present at his coronation, 'lest the Roman Church might afterwards claim to have some rights in it'. The papacy at this time was expanding its powers in every possible sphere. If Richard allowed a papal legate to be present at his coronation, he feared that the papacy would end up by claiming the right not only to send a legate to future coronations but perhaps even to confer the crown of England, as it did that of the Empire.[2]

To nip such a possibility in the bud, Richard sent the cardinal off to collect the Saladin Tithe in the dioceses of Poitiers and Limoges, to raise money for the crusade. He then ordered the monks of Canterbury, after he had arrived in England, to send a delegation, empowered to act on behalf of the entire community, to appear before him at a meeting of the Great Council. Fourteen monks, amongst whom was the sacristan and historian, Gervase, went to Westminster and laid their case before the king on 8 November. The hearing was a stormy one. The monks, who wanted to read all their charters to the assembly, were obstinately unyielding. The session dragged on all day. The

[1] Introduction to *Epistolae Cantuarienses*, pp. xxxv-lxi.
[2] Ibid., pp. 280, 290, 296, 300.

king several times lost his temper with the monks, and Bishop Hugh of Nonant remarked to him: 'Now, what did I tell you about the monks? If you would listen to me, there wouldn't be a single monk in any of the cathedrals of England within two months. To the Devil with the monks!'[1]

On the second day of the hearing the king induced the delegation to agree to abide by the decision of a group of eight bishops, four abbots, and the priors of the Austin Canons at Merton and Waltham. The archbishop also said that he was willing to leave the whole matter to the king and his council. The monks then returned to Canterbury whilst the committee considered the case.

Richard meanwhile went to Bury St. Edmunds, the site of one of the greatest abbeys in England, to celebrate the feast of the martyred king of the East Angles on 19 November. Abbot Samson had recently acquired the king's goodwill by purchasing from him the manor of Mildenhall for a thousand marks. Richard now gave the abbey fifteen marks to provide two candles to burn day and night before the martyr's shrine.[2]

While the king was on this pilgrimage, the legate, Cardinal John of Anagni, landed at Dover on the 20th. For him to come to England without the king's permission and indeed contrary to his express wishes was an act of gross discourtesy. Queen Eleanor, acting on her son's behalf, promptly ordered him to stay where he was or else go back where he came from, until such time as the king should make his wishes known to him.[3]

Richard and his court arrived at Canterbury on the 27th. Planning to leave England shortly, the king had summoned all the great men of the realm to meet him and to help him make the final dispositions for the government of his realm whilst he was on crusade. He was also determined to settle the quarrel between the archbishop and the monks of Canterbury without the legate's interference. He applied all his powers of charm, persuasion, and, finally, firmness to force the monks to accept the compromise that he, with the advice of the archbishop of Rouen and the English bishops, had determined upon.

The negotiations went on for two days. On the 29th Arch-

[1] *Epistolae Cantuarienses*, pp. 310, 318.

[2] Howden, Vol. III, p. 18; Pipe Roll 2 Richard I, p. 101; Jocelin of Brakelond: *Chronicle*, ed. H. E. Butler (Nelson's Medieval Texts, 1949), pp. 45-6; Ralph of Coggeshall: *Chronicon Anglicanum*, ed. Joseph Stevenson (Rolls Series 66, 1875), p. 97.

[3] *Epistolae Cantuarienses*, pp. 321-2; Diceto, Vol. II, p. 72.

bishop Baldwin and the monks accepted the terms. The archbishop agreed to move the college of canons to another place, to demolish all the buildings at Hackington except the chapel, to depose the prior whom he had installed against the wishes of the monks, and to give back to them the estates he had taken to provide for his new foundation.

On the face of it, this was a great victory for the monks, but the chapel at Hackington, although it was to be served by only one priest and was not to be considered a parish church, still remained, and the archbishop still clung to his project, now fortified by Richard's approval, of founding a college of canons, even though it was not to be at Canterbury.[1]

Now that he had made peace between the archbishop and the monks, Richard summoned the legate from Dover and had him received with a solemn procession. This mark of honour, however, did little to salve the cardinal's pride, and he was greatly incensed that peace should have been made without his help, for it was to accomplish that end that the pope had sent him on his mission.

Although he was closely watched by the archbishop, Cardinal John contrived to have an interview with the monks, who induced him to draw up a deposition stating that the agreement with Archbishop Baldwin had been extorted from the monks by force and through fear of the king; that it had been drawn up without their knowledge and consent, and that it therefore was not binding on them. Thus the cardinal contrived to undo whatever good the king had done.[2]

As papal legate the cardinal had extraordinary powers, and Count John appealed to him to use those powers in his behalf. Archbishop Baldwin had laid his lands under interdict in the preceding August because he had married his cousin, Isabel of Gloucester, without a dispensation. Flattered, no doubt, that the king's brother should pay him that attention and respect that the king had singularly failed to show, the cardinal at once lifted the interdict.

Geoffrey's opponents also approached the legate and protested against his election as archbishop of York. Bishop Hugh of Durham and Hubert Walter, formerly dean of York and now

[1] Gervase, Vol. I, pp. 474–81.

[2] *Epistolae Cantuarienses*, p. 323.

bishop of Salisbury, declared that the election was invalid because they, who had the right of casting the first and therefore decisive votes, had not been present. Henry Marshal, the new dean, also accused Geoffrey of not having been canonically elected because he was a murderer, conceived in adultery and born of a whore. Cardinal John nevertheless confirmed the election by his authority as legate.

Richard meanwhile had ordered Geoffrey and Bishop Hugh of Durham to meet William, king of Scots, at the River Tweed and escort him to Canterbury. William travelled in royal style, with Geoffrey and Hugh, accompanied by John Marshal, sheriff of Yorkshire, and all the barons of the county in attendance. When he arrived at Canterbury, William made an agreement with the English king that swelled Richard's coffers, guaranteed the peace and tranquillity of the North, and at the same time restored King William's self-esteem.

As a punishment for his invasion of northern England during the great rebellion of 1173 and 1174, King Henry had forced King William, whom he was holding prisoner at the time, to do homage to him for his kingdom of Scotland and to surrender five of his most important castles. In exchange for a payment of 10,000 marks, Richard now freed him from these humiliating terms, gave him a charter of release from his fealty and allegiance, and restored his castles to him. Of all of Richard's actions in England, this was the wisest and most statesmanlike.

Geoffrey in turn struck a bargain with his brother on the only terms that would be acceptable to the king. Geoffrey promised him £3,000 'in order to have his love', and Richard gave him a charter confirming his election as archbishop of York and returning to him the lands that the king in his anger had confiscated. Richard also applied pressure on Geoffrey's detractors and forced them to withdraw their appeal against his election. Geoffrey then confirmed Henry Marshal and Bourchard of Le Puiset in their offices in the chapter of York. Now that all the parties were reconciled, at least for the time being, they despatched letters to the pope requesting that he confirm Geoffrey's election, as his legate had just done.[1]

Richard had already provided handsomely for John. At the same meeting of the Great Council that witnessed the treaty with

[1] Howden, Vol. III, pp. 25–8.

the king of Scots, Richard gave a princely endowment to his brother. In addition to the territories already entrusted to him, the king now gave him the counties of Cornwall, Devon, Dorset, and Somerset.[1] Henceforth these four counties, together with Nottinghamshire and Derbyshire and the honour of Lancaster, formed a separate jurisdiction entirely under John's control and rendered no accounts at the Exchequer.

John now had a virtually independent principality embracing all the southwest of England and a broad band through the Midlands. At no time since the Conquest, probably, had a subject been allowed to exercise control over so vast a territory; certainly no-one had had jurisdiction over a solid block of territory of such an extent. Men had occasionally been granted enormous fiefs, to be sure, but the king had always taken care that the lands should be widely scattered rather than contiguous.

Neither the king nor any chronicler assigned any reason for this extraordinary grant, made at a time when the king needed and would certainly continue to need every penny he could lay his hands on to finance his crusade. Richard seems to have had a half-contemptuous affection for his younger brother, but that would hardly explain his more than lavish generosity to him. Nor would motives of prudence explain it. John had to be provided for, both because Richard scrupulously carried out his father's last promises and because he could not afford to leave behind him a discontented brother who might be tempted to seize what he felt to be his due, but hardly to this extent. If the grant was intended as a bribe to keep John quiet during Richard's absence, it was a bribe munificent beyond any need.

The truth of the matter may be that Richard simply had no idea of the value of money. He was accused of being avaricious because he squeezed every penny possible from his subjects, but he did this, not from motives of avarice, but because he needed enormous sums of money to meet his unprecedented expenditures. Richard did everything on the grandest and most extravagant scale possible. His coronation was the most magnificent that England had ever seen; his grants to his brother were generous far beyond both John's expectations and his deserts, and his expenditures whilst on crusade were staggering. As far as Richard was concerned, money existed only to be spent, and the

[1] Howden, Vol. III, p. 27.

only check on his spending was the amount of money available.

His provision for his mother was almost as generous as his grants to John. He not only confirmed the dower that Henry had settled on her; he gave her, as well, all the lands that both King Henry I and King Stephen had given to their queens.[1]

After these settlements, Richard went to Dover on 5 December and prepared to cross over to Normandy. Earl William of Mandeville, whom the king had named as one of the two chief justiciars to govern the kingdom in his absence, had died at Gisors of an acute semi-tertian fever. The king gave his widow, Countess Hadwisa, whom Richard of Devizes describes as 'a woman almost a man, lacking nothing virile except the virile organs', to his friend William of Fors. Hadwisa showed her mettle by refusing to marry him, whereupon the king caused her estates in Yorkshire to be seized and had stock to the value of £114 1s. 4d. sold from them. The countess gave in and married the man of the king's choice.[2]

To replace Earl William, Richard appointed William Longchamp as joint chief justiciar with Bishop Hugh of Le Puiset. Longchamp's importance was increased by the king's giving him one of his seals and ordering him 'by means of it to have his orders carried out in the kingdom'. Bishop Hugh was given the custody of Windsor Castle, but Longchamp received the Tower of London, a vastly more important fortification. The chancellor spent over £1,200 in the course of the year in strengthening and repairing the castle.[3]

Taking Cardinal John of Anagni and Walter of Coutances, archbishop of Rouen, with him, Richard sailed from Dover on 11 December and landed at Calais. Many men said that the king was leaving England, never to return.

> It was said that the premature and immoderate use of arms, in which he had indulged more strenuously than was fitting from the very onset of adolescence, had so broken and weakened him that he would soon be wasted away by his expedition to the East. Others, however, said that he was so corrupted and wasted away by a quartan fever from which he had long suffered that he would not be able to survive such a great and difficult undertaking: an argu-

[1] Howden, Vol. III, p. 27.
[2] Richard of Devizes, p. 10; Pipe Roll 6 Richard I, p. 163.
[3] Howden, Vol. III, p. 28; Pipe Roll 2 Richard I, p. 1.

ment that was proved groundless by the paleness of his face and the corpulence of his limbs. Still others said that he had over a hundred ulcers in his body, through which the corrupt humours drained.[1]

Men might well believe that Richard planned never to return, for during his four months' stay in England he had done almost everything possible to break up the firm and orderly government that his father had imposed on the country. He had discharged Rannulf Glanville, who, corrupt though he may have been, was the most efficient administrator in the kingdom. He had disturbed the financial and judicial administration by discharging almost all the experienced sheriffs and substituting new men in their stead. He had prevailed upon many of the most capable barons to accompany him to the Holy Land at a time when England would most need their services. He had placed in a position of high trust and responsibility William Longchamp, a man who knew little about England and English ways and who did not trouble to hide his contempt for the English. He had intruded his bastard brother into the second highest ecclesiastical position in the land, in the face of the determined opposition of almost everyone concerned and against the protests of the oldest and most experienced bishop in the hierarchy. Although he had the power to release him from his crusading vows, he allowed the first subject in the realm, the archbishop of Canterbury, the one man in a position to enforce peace in Church and State, to continue with his plans to go on crusade.

At a time when the country was groaning under the heavy exactions of his father, Richard had squeezed from his English subjects every penny he could wring from them. No-one of his time attempted even to guess how much money Richard extracted from the country, but everyone agreed that it was a far greater sum than any of his predecessors had ever succeeded in raising.

Finally, although he was not even married, he set off on his perilous adventure without designating an heir, and he left behind him his brother John, ambitious, treacherous, and untrustworthy, exercising regal powers over a compact territory embracing six counties.

[1] Newburgh, Vol. I, p. 306.

II

1190

THE hasty and ill-considered measures that Richard had improvised for the government of England during his absence led to trouble almost as soon as he had crossed the Channel. By associating William Longchamp with Hugh of Le Puiset without defining exactly the extent either of their powers or of the powers of the justiciars who were to work with them, Richard laid the foundations for trouble. Henry II, it is true, had used the device of joint chief justiciars early in his reign, but he had ensured the success of the expedient by choosing men of proven worth and ability and by supervising closely their actions till he was certain that they would work well together.

Richard, on the contrary, had selected two men neither of whom had had experience on a large scale, although both had had, the one as bishop and ruler of the palatine county of Durham and the other as Richard's chancellor in Poitou, considerable experience in administration. Regardless of how much experience they might have had individually, the important consideration was how well they would work in double harness. Richard took no pains to see that they could work together, and since he chose two men who had in common only a great pride, an intense ambition, and a vast fund of self-importance, he might have been certain that there would be trouble.

Immediately after the king left England, dissension broke out between the two 'as to which of them should be considered the greater, and what pleased the one displeased the other'.[1] News of the falling-out reached Richard in Normandy. Soon after Candlemas, 2 February 1190, the king summoned a meeting of his council to try to arrange for a more stable delegation of authority. His mother, Eleanor, crossed over to Normandy, taking with her the hapless Alice of France, to whom Richard

[1] Howden, Vol. III, p. 29.

had been betrothed for twenty-one years. They were accompanied by the king's two brothers, John and Geoffrey, and by an imposing escort of prelates: Archbishop Baldwin, the bishops of Durham and Ely, whose quarrels were the major occasion for the meeting, and Bishops John of Norwich, Godfrey of Winchester, Reginald of Bath, Hubert Walter of Salisbury, and the redoubtable Hugh of Coventry.

After conferring with them and with such of his bishops and barons as were already with him, Richard, early in March, provided a solution that clarified the situation only slightly without at the same time removing the basis of the difficulty. He appointed William Longchamp chief justiciar of England, but at the same time he named Hugh of Le Puiset as justiciar from the Humber to the Scottish border. These appointments, which again failed to specify the powers of the two men, show both Richard's indifference to the welfare of his realm and his inability to realise the complexity of the task he was imposing on the two bishops. The administration of Aquitaine, with which alone Richard was familiar, was rudimentary compared with that of England, and Richard's chief responsibilities as duke of Aquitaine had been largely military, confined to putting down almost endless rebellions amongst his nobles and keeping some semblance of order amongst them. Richard had none of his father's interest in administrative problems and none of his genius at solving them. As far as he was concerned, England might govern itself as best it could whilst he was away, provided always that it furnished him with money and supplies for his crusade.

After thus designating the two bishops as chief justiciars, Richard sent messengers to Pope Clement III to ask him to make William Longchamp papal legate in England, since Archbishop Baldwin, the head of the hierarchy, would be absent on crusade.

Richard's next measure was the only one that shows that he had any grasp of the realities of the situation he was leaving behind or any knowledge of the characters of his brothers. He forced both John and Geoffrey to swear that they would not return to England within the next three years without his permission. He quickly undid most of the good of this act, however, by releasing John from his promise and giving him leave to return. He did this at his mother's request, which shows that he and Eleanor had different views of the situation that was likely to arise.[1] John was the most likely candidate for the throne in the event of his brother's death. The only other prospective claimant was the infant Arthur, born on 29 March 1187, the posthumous son of their brother Geoffrey, duke of Brittany. Eleanor seems to have taken the view that since John was the logical heir apparent, it was better for him to be in England, so that if it came to the worst an orderly succession would be secured, than for him to be out of the country and exposed to the wiles of Richard's enemies.

Richard, on the other hand, distrusted the ambitions of both John and Geoffrey and was afraid that one or the other of them would stir up trouble in England and possibly attempt to seize the crown. Each view, of course, had its drawbacks. Richard combined the drawbacks of both of them by permitting John to return to England and enjoy a princely jurisdiction over a large portion of the country whilst at the same time he refused to recognise John as his heir and set up as his vice-gerent such a violently ambitious man as William Longchamp.

Geoffrey, meanwhile, after his reconciliation with his brother at Dover, had returned to York, probably with King William on his way back to Scotland. No sooner had Geoffrey reached York than his quarrel with the dean and the treasurer, in spite of the apparent truce that the king had imposed on them, broke out with renewed fury.

On the eve of the Epiphany, 5 January 1190, Geoffrey announced his intention of hearing vespers in his cathedral that afternoon. When he entered the church, accompanied by the precentor, Hamo, and a number of the canons, he found that Henry Marshal and Bourchard of Le Puiset had refused to wait for him and had ordered the canons to begin the office. Geoffrey, angered by this insult and supported by the precentor and the canons in his train, commanded that the choir cease their chant and take it up again at the beginning of vespers. The canons chose to obey their archbishop-elect. Geoffrey began the first vespers of the Epiphany at the first psalm. The treasurer, Henry Marshal, had all the candles extinguished. When the office was finished in darkness, Geoffrey denounced the dean and the treasurer for their disrespectful behaviour and ordered all services suspended in the cathedral until they made satisfaction to him.

[1] *Gesta*, Vol. II, p. 106.

On the next day the people of York gathered in the cathedral to hear Mass and the divine office. The archbishop-elect, the dean, the treasurer, and all the canons took their places in the choir. When Geoffrey demanded that Henry and Bourchard atone for their actions, they not only refused to make amends; they used such insulting language to him that the people, siding with their archbishop, started to attack them with the intention of beating some respect and obedience into them. Geoffrey intervened and stopped the people, whilst the dean and the treasurer fled in terror. Geoffrey then and there excommunicated the contumacious pair, and there was no service in the cathedral that day.[1]

When Geoffrey arrived in Normandy in obedience to Richard's summons and met him at Lion-sur-Mer, the king at first greeted him amicably and with the respect due to an archbishop. On the next day he enquired concerning the money Geoffrey had promised him. Geoffrey had been trying to raise money in England, but Hugh of Le Puiset had retained custody of the lands belonging to the archbishopric and had refused to allow him to collect any of the revenues. Geoffrey was forced to admit to Richard that he had come empty-handed. The king's smiles turned into frowns, and he would accept no excuses from his brother.

Richard now determined to have Geoffrey's election quashed. Since the papal legate had confirmed the election and all of Geoffrey's erstwhile opponents had written to the pope to request that he repeat the confirmation, the only avenue open to Richard was to appeal directly to Clement III. He therefore sent Reginald, bishop of Bath, and Bourchard of Le Puiset to Rome to ask the pope to annul the election. Bourchard had been excommunicated by Geoffrey on 6 January, and when he reached Rome he persuaded the pope to absolve him.[2]

To be on the safe side, meanwhile, Richard issued orders to all the archbishops in his lands on both sides of the Channel that they were not in any circumstances to consecrate Geoffrey. Finally, as has been told, he forced his brother to swear that he would stay out of England for a period of three years from that date.

Geoffrey now had no recourse except to beg his brother to re-

[1] Howden, Vol. III, pp. 31-2.

[2] Howden, Vol. III, p. 74.

turn him to his favour, since he had no money with which to buy his goodwill. Richard meanwhile had been forced again to postpone his starting out on the crusade. The queen of France, Isabella of Hainault, had died in childbirth on 15 March, and so Richard and Philip agreed to meet on Midsummer Day. Geoffrey seems to have followed Richard about during the remainder of the king's stay in his continental domains. He was with him at Tours, where Richard solemnly received his pilgrim's staff and scrip towards the end of June, and then accompanied him to Vézelay, where Richard and Philip met early in July for their formal setting out.

Geoffrey had managed to scrape together some 800 marks, which he now gave his brother, and he promised to pay the remainder of his debt into the Exchequer in England. So many different agreements were made, Richard changed his mind so often, and such divergent figures are mentioned by the various chroniclers that all one can be certain of is that at Michaelmas 1190 Geoffrey still owed £2,000 'to have the king's goodwill and the custody of the castle of Baugé' in Anjou.[1]

Geoffrey accompanied the crusading host for two days' journey beyond Vézelay and then took leave of his brother, apparently restored to his good graces. When they parted, Richard kissed him and said: 'Brother, what I love do you likewise love, and what I hate do you likewise hate; and thus we shall be of one heart and one mind.'

Geoffrey then went back to Tours, where he had studied after his election to the see of Lincoln. Bartholomew, archbishop of Tours, was an old friend, and Geoffrey hoped to be consecrated by him. By this time Geoffrey's messengers had returned from Rome bearing the pope's confirmation of his election, in a letter dated 7 March 1190. In the face of Richard's orders prohibiting his consecration, this letter was of little immediate use. Geoffrey settled down in Tours and went to work to induce his brother by letters both to revoke his prohibition and to release him, as he had Count John, from his oath not to return to England.[2]

Archbishop Baldwin meanwhile was putting his affairs in order so that he too might set out on the crusade. On 31 December 1189 he consecrated Richard son of Nigel bishop of

[1] Pipe Roll 2 Richard I, p. 67.
[2] Gerald of Wales: *De Vita Galfridi*, pp. 380–2; Diceto, Vol. II, pp. 78–9.

London and William Longchamp bishop of Ely. Although he had agreed to abandon his design to establish a college of secular canons at Canterbury, he merely changed the site of the establishment. He acquired some land at Lambeth from the bishop and monks of Rochester and proposed to set up his foundation there. He had the buildings at Canterbury, except the chapel, dismantled and the materials moved to Lambeth. Meanwhile he had the tents that he intended to take with him to the Holy Land set up on the Lambeth site on 13 January, to make his possession secure by occupation. To keep his rebellious and contumacious monks of Canterbury under control, he appointed Osbern, who was detested by them all, as prior.

The archbishop summoned the bishops of England to meet at Westminster on 19 February. With their advice and consent he appointed Richard, bishop of London, his deputy in governing the province and Gilbert Glanville, bishop of Rochester, his vicar both in the archdiocese of Canterbury and in the churches of the manors belonging to the archbishopric. From London he went to Canterbury, and there, on 24 February, he received his pilgrim's staff and scrip. On 6 March he sailed from Dover to Normandy to join the king and set forth with him on the crusade. A large part of Richard's English fleet, which had spent the winter in fitting out and gathering supplies, sailed for Marseilles, where it was to meet the king, later in the month.[1]

While Archbishop Baldwin was at Rouen he suspended Hugh of Nonant, bishop of Coventry, from his episcopal office because he had obtained for himself the post of sheriff of Warwickshire, Leicestershire, and Staffordshire. Although Canon XII of the Third Lateran Council (1179), which forbade clerics to hold secular office,[2] was interpreted extremely loosely, so that even bishops served as castellans and justiciars and, as in the case of William Longchamp, chancellors, not even the most elastic conscience would allow them to serve in such a completely secular office as that of sheriff.

Hugh, when taken to task by the archbishop, promised to resign his sheriffdoms within a fortnight of the approaching Easter and never again to undertake such offices, 'which were degrading

[1] Gervase, Vol. I, pp. 483-5; Diceto, Vol. II, p. 75.

[2] *Conciliorum Oecumenicorum Decreta*, ed. J. Alberigo *et al.* (Freiburg, 1962), p. 194.

to the episcopal dignity'. Baldwin wrote to his deputy, Bishop Richard of London, to inform him of Hugh's promise and to ask him to make sure that Hugh kept it. And keep it he did, after a fashion, for he resigned as sheriff at the following Michaelmas, although he had paid in full for the office.[1]

After the uprising against the Jews in London during the coronation feast, the king had issued such strict orders for their protection that they were not molested again as long as Richard was in England. Shortly after he crossed over to Normandy, however, a fresh outbreak began that culminated in a bloody and shameful massacre.

There was at this time a sizable colony of Jews at Lynn, a prosperous port much frequented by foreign traders. William of Newburgh, who heartily deplores the whole business, places the blame for the initial outburst on the Jews themselves. In January 1190, he says, they attacked a Jewish convert to Christianity, calling him a traitor and a liar. The convert sought refuge in a church, and his cries for help were answered both by the Christian inhabitants and by some young foreign traders. In the general uprising that followed, the townspeople were somewhat cautious out of fear of the royal officials, but the foreigners were not deterred by any such thoughts.

The mob set to work killing Jews and sacking and burning their houses. The last man to be murdered was a Jewish physician, high in the regard of the Christian community, who on the day following the outburst 'somewhat immoderately' deplored the slaughter and prophesied God's vengeance on the killers. The foreigners loaded the loot in their ships and sailed away. The townspeople, left to face the questions of the royal officials, blamed the whole affair on the young traders.

From Lynn the fever spread to Norwich, where on 6 February a number of Jews were killed. The majority of the Jewish community sought refuge in the castle, however, and thus escaped the mob.

The next outburst, at Stamford on 7 March, revealed more clearly the motives behind the killings. The town was thronged with people who had gathered there for the Lenten Fair and with a group of young men about to set forth on the crusade. When these crusaders saw 'that the enemies of Christ's Cross living there

[1] Diceto, Vol. II, pp. 77-8; Pipe Roll 3 & 4 Richard I, pp. 128, 248.

possessed so much, whilst they themselves had so little for such a journey', they began plundering the Jews on the pretext of raising money to pay their expenses whilst on the crusade.

Some of the townspeople and visitors to the fair joined in. A number of the Jews were murdered; the others fled to the castle for safety, and the houses of all of them were looted. One of the crusaders, a young man named John, fled to Northampton, where he took refuge with a friend, to whom he entrusted part of his loot. The friend, however, killed John for the sake of his money and threw his body outside the town that night. When the body was discovered it was promptly reverenced as that of a martyr, with the encouragement of some of the local clergy. The unofficial cult was reported to Bishop Hugh of Lincoln, a man outstanding both for his holiness of life and for his commonsense. The bishop immediately came to Northampton, delivered a scathing sermon against the simple-mindedness of those who had started the cult and the cupidity of those who had encouraged it in the hope of profiting from the presence of a martyr's tomb in their midst, and threatened with excommunication anyone who continued the superstitious practices.

Speeding northward, the fever next reached Lincoln, where had lived the famous Aaron of Lincoln, the wealthiest Jew in England and one of the richest men in the country. The fact that little damage was done there was probably due to the vigilance of Bishop Hugh and of the sheriff of Lincolnshire, Gerard of Camville, who also had the custody of Lincoln Castle. Forewarned by the happenings to the south, at the first signs of trouble the Jews of Lincoln took all their possessions into the castle, and the sheriff and his officers quickly brought the situation under control.

In York the outburst reached its height. The Jewish community there was a particularly wealthy one, and two of the leading Jews, Benedict and Joyce, had built houses that William of Newburgh describes as royal palaces. Envy, avarice, and religious intolerance drew together two groups, those who were heavily in debt to the Jews and those who were preparing to set out on the crusade, in a conspiracy against the Jews. During a stormy night in March, under cover of the excitement generated by a fire that may have been set for that purpose, an armed band attacked the house of Benedict, who had died during the previous autumn of injuries received in the course of the riot during the coronation feast. They killed Benedict's widow and children and everyone else in the house, sacked it, and set it afire.

Most of the Jews of York, to the number of five hundred adults, together with their children, fled to the castle, taking their possessions with them. The mob, now completely out of control, seized all the Jews they could find outside the castle and offered them the choice of baptism or death. The warden of the castle, meanwhile, had to go out for some reason or other. When he returned from his errand, the Jews, 'already uncertain as to whom they could trust', refused to admit him.

The warden then called on the sheriff of Yorkshire, John Marshal, for help. The sheriff and the warden encouraged the mob to attack the tower in which the Jews had barricaded themselves, and a Premonstratensian hermit, clad in white, stirred up the mob to an even higher pitch of fury. The townspeople were now reinforced by the knights of the shire, whom the sheriff had summoned, and all the young men of the city and the surrounding countryside.

The sheriff realised too late the magnitude of the evil forces he had stirred up and tried to restrain their fury. The mob stormed the tower with all the means at their command. The Jews could fight back only by demolishing some of the interior walls of the tower and hurling the stones thus obtained at their assailants. Although a lucky shot struck the hermit in the forefront of the attackers and killed him, the outcome of the siege was evident. The Jews managed to hold out for several days, but they had no illusions as to what their fate would be.

When the Christians set up regular siege engines as though for a military operation, the Jews realised that their end was at hand. On the night of 16 March, in despair, many of them destroyed their treasures, slit the throats of their wives and children, set fire to the castle, and then killed themselves.

Those who did not have the courage for this desperate expedient fled from the castle and threw themselves on their besiegers' mercy, promising to be baptised if their lives would be spared. The Christians promised them safety and then massacred the whole lot of them on the following day, 17 March. When this bloody work was done, the mob marched to the cathedral and made a bonfire in the middle of the church of the bonds recording the debts owing to them, deposited there for safekeeping by the Jews. Thus the mob showed that their religious intolerance was well mixed with a desire to escape repaying the money that some of them had borrowed from the Jews.

Such crusaders as were in the mob slipped quietly away, whilst the people of the town and the county cooled off and began to consider the punishment they knew to be imminent.

The final act of this bloody drama was played out on the following day, Palm Sunday, at Bury St. Edmunds, where fifty-seven Jews were slain.[1]

[1] Newburgh, Vol. I, pp. 308-23; Diceto, Vol. II, pp. 75-6; *Gesta*, Vol. II, p. 107.

A messenger was sent on Easter Monday, 26 March, to the chancellor, who was with the king in Normandy, to tell him of the massacre at York. When Richard learned that the peace and safety he had decreed for the Jews had been broken in so flagrant a fashion, his wrath knew no bounds. As William of Newburgh points out, the king was angry on two accounts: that his orders should have been disobeyed as soon as his back was turned and that the Exchequer should have been defrauded of the income that it would normally have received from the Jews. He therefore ordered William Longchamp to go to England and punish the perpetrators of this double insult.[1]

Longchamp's brother Osbert had crossed over to Normandy at the beginning of Lent in charge of a shipment of money from the Exchequer to the king. He probably accompanied his brother back to England. As soon as the chancellor landed he summoned a large army, led by another brother, Henry Longchamp, sheriff of Herefordshire, and went to York to punish the guilty ones. He deprived the castellan of York Castle and the sheriff of Yorkshire, John Marshal, of their offices because they had not acted with sufficient vigour in trying to put down the uprising, and he appointed his brother Osbert as sheriff in John Marshal's place.[2]

With the departure of Archbishop Baldwin on the crusade and the indefinite postponement of Geoffrey's consecration as archbishop of York, the Church in England was without a head, save for the bishop of London, acting as Baldwin's deputy. King Richard had asked the pope to appoint William Longchamp papal legate, but the pope did not issue the commission till 5 June.[3] It was characteristic of Longchamp, however, that upon his arrival at York and on the strength of the king's request to the pope he should demand that the clergy receive him with a procession and the ringing of all the church bells, a mark of honour paid to only the highest figures in Church and State. The clergy of York replied, properly enough, that as far as they knew William Longchamp was bishop of Ely and one of the chief justiciars and nothing more, and that in neither capacity was he entitled to such a singular mark of honour and respect.

[1] Pipe Roll 2 Richard I, p. 3; Newburgh, Vol. I, p. 323.
[2] Pipe Roll 2 Richard I, pp. 2-3, 8.
[3] Diceto, Vol. II, p. 83.

Longchamp, 'by the authority of his office as legate', which he had not yet received, suspended all the clergy of the cathedral, placed the cathedral under an interdict, and had the bells removed from the towers and placed on the ground, until such time as the clergy should humbly come before him and make satisfaction.[1]

From York the bishop of Ely probably went to Lincoln to punish the leaders of the abortive uprising there, for the Pipe Roll records the expenditure of 15s. for 60 pairs of iron fetters sent to Lincoln at the chancellor's order, and Richard of Devizes mentions his being at Lincoln at this time.[2]

On his way south Longchamp was met by his fellow justiciar, Bishop Hugh of Le Puiset, to whom King Richard, in Normandy, had given a commission as justiciar north of the Humber and sent back to England. When Hugh arrived in London, however, he found that the barons of the Exchequer refused to let him join their deliberations, no doubt at Longchamp's orders. The frustrated bishop then set out to meet his colleague and encountered him at Blythe, in Nottinghamshire. Bishop Hugh handed Longchamp the king's commission and attempted at once to take an active part in the conduct of the government, as though nothing could be done without his consent.

The wily Longchamp deceived him with fair words, promising fully to obey the king's command. According to Richard of Devizes, Longchamp then asked the bishop to meet him at Tickhill, about five miles from Blythe, a week later, and at that meeting he produced a mandate from the king bearing a later date than Bishop Hugh's commission and giving the chancellor supreme authority in the realm. Roger of Howden says that Longchamp took Bishop Hugh with him to Southwell and there made him prisoner, which is confirmed by Gerald of Wales. Yet a third authority states that Longchamp took Hugh with him to London and then seized him.[3]

All agree, at any rate, that there was an appreciable interval between their first meeting and Longchamp's violent action against Bishop Hugh. Caution and delay were foreign to Longchamp's impetuous and arrogant nature, and one may hazard the

[1] *Gesta*, Vol. II, pp. 105-9; Howden, Vol. III, pp. 34-5.

[2] Pipe Roll 2 Richard I, p. 3; Richard of Devizes, p. 11.

[3] Richard of Devizes, pp. 11-12; Howden, Vol. III, p. 35; Gerald of Wales: *De Vita Galfridi*, p. 428; *Gesta*, Vol. II, p. 109.

guess that during the interval between their first meeting, at which he greeted Bishop Hugh with great respect and promised to obey the king's mandate, and his subsequent violent seizure of the bishop, the wily Longchamp made the most of the opportunity and forged a mandate from the king, giving it a later date than Bishop Hugh's and incorporating into it the powers that he needed to override the bishop's authority as associate justiciar. Such a course of action would be quite in keeping with Longchamp's character as his contemporaries report it, and since he had possession of one of the king's seals it would probably not be difficult for him to prepare a document with all the marks of authenticity.

Whether at Tickhill, Southwell, or London, Longchamp turned suddenly and violently on the bishop and took him prisoner. 'I seize you,' he said, 'not as a bishop seizing another bishop, but as the chancellor seizing a castellan.' Longchamp forced Bishop Hugh to surrender Windsor Castle and the forest appertaining to it, the custody of which had been given to him by the king; Newcastle-upon-Tyne, which was turned over to Osbert Longchamp; the county of Northumberland, over which William Longchamp appointed William of Stuteville as sheriff, and, finally, the manor of Sadberge, which Bishop Hugh had bought, in the preceding September, for six hundred marks. As Richard of Devizes puts it, Longchamp scarcely left Bishop Hugh the bare sword with which the king had girded him as earl of Northumberland.[1]

As though the unfortunate bishop were a convicted traitor rather than his fellow justiciar, Longchamp forced him to turn over his son Henry and Gilbert of Leya as hostages to ensure that he would keep 'the king's peace and the peace of his realm'.[2]

Utterly defeated, crushed in all his ambitions and stripped of his newly acquired honours and lands, Bishop Hugh retired to his manor of Howden, in Yorkshire, to nurse his shame and disappointment. After he had been there a few days, the obnoxious Osbert Longchamp and William of Stuteville, accompanied by an armed band, arrived and threatened to arrest the bishop again, at the chancellor's command. Hugh was able to dissuade them by giving securities that he would not leave Howden

[1] Richard of Devizes, pp. 10–12; Pipe Roll 2 Richard I, p. 18; Roger of Howden, Vol. III, pp. 13, 35.

[2] *Gesta*, Vol. II, p. 109.

except with the permission of the king or the chancellor. He at once sent messengers to the king to inform him of how he had been treated.

The bishop's messengers overtook King Richard at Marseilles, where he was waiting for his fleet to arrive, at the beginning of August. The king was, or at least pretended to be, angry when he heard how the chancellor had treated Bishop Hugh. He issued a charter confirming Hugh in his possession of Sadberge and threatening with God's wrath and curse and his own anyone who attempted to take the manor away from the bishop. According to the author of the *Gesta*, he also ordered that Newcastle-upon-Tyne be restored to him; Roger of Howden says that the whole county of Northumberland was to be given back. That both are correct is shown by the fact that neither the castle nor the county appears in the Pipe Roll for 1191, which would indicate that they were restored to the bishop around Michaelmas 1190.[1]

Having thus defeated and ousted from his post the man with whom he was supposed to work in close harmony, Longchamp next turned his attention to William Marshal, one of the associate justiciars by whose advice and counsel King Richard had ordered the chancellor to be guided. Unlike the others, William had had no experience as a professional administrator. As a landless knight, he had been the faithful friend first of Henry, 'the young king', Richard's elder brother, till his death in 1183, and then of Henry II, whom he had served to the very end. Richard had rewarded him by giving him the hand of one of the richest heiresses in England, Isabel, the daughter of 'Strongbow', Richard of Clare, earl of Striguil or Pembroke. William enjoyed all the lands that had belonged to Earl Richard, but he was not formally made earl of Striguil till John ascended the throne.[2]

William had purchased the sheriffdom of Gloucestershire and the custody of Gloucester Castle for 50 marks.[3] Now that he had the Tower of London and Windsor Castle firmly in his grasp, with the castles of York and, for the time being, Newcastle-upon-Tyne in the custody of his own men, Longchamp turned to the west, where his chief rival, Count John, was supreme. Long-

[1] *Gesta*, Vol. II, p. 110; Howden, Vol. III, pp. 35, 38-9.

[2] For William Marshal's career, see Sidney Painter: *William Marshal* (Baltimore, 1933).

[3] Pipe Roll 2 Richard I, p. 58.

champ did not yet dare openly to proceed against the king's brother, but he knew that sooner or later he would have to cross swords with him if the chancellor pursued his plans, undoubtedly already formed, of eliminating his rivals one by one. To secure an advance base for future operations against John, Longchamp decided to take Gloucester Castle, even though it had been entrusted to William Marshal.

While Longchamp was engaged in besieging the castle, Godfrey of Lucy, bishop of Winchester, arrived unexpectedly on the scene. Godfrey, it will be remembered, had been summoned to Normandy by the king for the council held in March. He had then fallen ill and was unable for the time being to return to England. During his absence, Longchamp had seized the county of Hampshire, the castles at Winchester and Porchester, and even Bishop Godfrey's patrimony, for all of which the bishop had compounded with the king at the price of £3,000.

Godfrey returned to England to find himself arbitrarily stripped of everything except his bishopric. The only reason that can be assigned for Longchamp's high-handed action is the one given by Richard of Devizes: 'All power always has been, always is, and always will be jealous of anyone sharing it.' Although Godfrey at that time had no power beyond that of his office as bishop, Longchamp may have seen in a man so well versed in public affairs a possible rival to the power that he had determined should belong only to him.

Godfrey, however, was not one to take such treatment lying down. He set out to find the chancellor and encountered him before Gloucester Castle. When Godfrey arrived, Longchamp attempted to enlist his aid.

'You have come at an opportune time, my dearest friend,' said the chancellor, embracing Godfrey warmly. 'Should I go on with the siege, or should I leave off?'

'If you want peace, lay down your arms,' said Bishop Godfrey coldly. The chancellor, taken aback by this display of firmness, had the retreat sounded and discontinued the siege. Godfrey succeeded in forcing him to restore his patrimony to him, but he could get nothing more.[1]

In spite of this temporary set-back, Longchamp now seized complete power. He made no pretence of consulting the other

[1] Richard of Devizes, pp. 11-13.

justiciars, who were, at the king's orders, to be associated with him in the government, but he scorned their council and acted in an arbitrary and tyrannical manner. 'He oppressed the clergy and the people, confounding right and wrong, and there was no-one in the realm who dared resist him, either in word or in deed.' His injustices and exactions aroused a storm of protest, and those who had been injured and insulted by him sent messengers or went in person to complain to the king. Richard, as seems to have been habitual with him, 'gave each one whatever letters he wanted and sent them all back to the chancellor'.[1] Longchamp either disregarded these letters or, as in the case of the bishop of Durham, produced later and contradictory ones approving his course of action. The chancellor's position was made impregnable by two letters that conferred on him, beyond any challenging, supreme power in both Church and state in England.

> Clement the pope, to William, bishop of Ely: greetings. In compliance with the praiseworthy desire and wholesome request of our dearest son in the Lord, Richard, the illustrious king of the English, we are led to confer upon you, by apostolic authority, the office of legate in all England, in the archbishopric both of Canterbury and of York, in Wales, and in those parts of Ireland in which that noble man, John, count of Mortain and the king's brother, has jurisdiction and dominion.
>
> Given at the Lateran, on 5 June, in the third year of our pontificate [1191].

The second letter, whilst it did not clear up the question as to whether or not Longchamp was formally appointed sole chief justiciar, certainly conferred upon him all the authority the king could give him.

> Richard, king of the English, to all his faithful men: greetings. We order and command you, as you have faith in us and as you love yourselves and all that is yours, to be wholly obedient to our dear and faithful chancellor, the bishop of Ely, in everything that pertains to us and that you do for him everything he tells you on our behalf as you would do for us.
>
> Myself as witness, at Bayeux, on the 6th day of June.[2]

Armed thus with supreme authority, Longchamp surrounded

[1] *Gesta*, Vol. II, p. 108; Richard of Devizes, p. 11.
[2] Diceto, Vol. II, p. 83.

himself with a thousand followers and made royal progresses through the realm, bringing catastrophe and ruin wherever he went. When he quartered himself and his great train, like a swarm of locusts, on a monastery, the establishment was reduced to the utmost poverty for years to come. 'Lay folk found him to be more than a king, and the clergy more than a pope; and to both he was an unbearable tyrant.'[1]

Gerald of Wales, the best hater of his time, has left an unforgettable picture of this monster of arrogance and ambition:

> He was short and contemptible in stature and crippled in both haunches, with a big head and with the hair on his forehead coming down almost to his eyebrows, like an ape. He was very dark, with little sunken black eyes, a flat nose, a snarling face. His beard below his eyes and his hair above them were all shaggy; his chin was receding, and his lips were spread apart in an affected, false, and almost continual grin, which he very suitably used as a disguise. His neck was short, his back was humped, and his belly stuck out in front and his buttocks at the back. His legs were crooked, and although his body was small his feet were huge.

According to Gerald, the inward man was as foul and unattractive as the outward. In addition to greed, cupidity, inordinate ambition, and complete unscrupulousness, Gerald accuses him of being sexually perverted. To make his conduct even more offensive and unbearable, Longchamp openly professed his contempt for the English and let no occasion pass when he might express his hatred in the foulest terms. He brought over a troupe of French jugglers and minstrels to sing his praises in public places, and in Longchamp's presence they were accustomed to sing his favourite couplet:

> You do such great things so easily and so well
> That whether you are god or man one cannot tell.[2]

William Longchamp reached the height of his glory when as papal legate, chancellor, and the king's representative in England he held a council at Westminster on 13 October, more to satisfy his vanity and display his power than to provide for any pressing need of the Church. He and Hugh of Nonant were on friendly terms at this time. When Bishop Hugh had appealed to the

[1] *Gesta*, Vol. II, p. 143; Newburgh, Vol. I, p. 333.
[2] Gerald of Wales: *De Vita Galfridi*, pp. 420-7.

pope for permission to substitute secular canons for the monks at Coventry, he had wisely promised to use the endowment of the monastery to set up prebends, a certain number of which he proposed to settle in perpetuity upon some of the cardinals of the Roman curia. Since the monks of Coventry were unable to send any of their number to Rome to present their side of the case, the pope, after waiting in vain for six months to hear from them, decided in favour of the bishop.

At the pope's direction, Longchamp at this council decreed that the monks were to be expelled from Coventry and that Bishop Hugh might proceed with his plans. The monks were accordingly cast out on Christmas Eve and dispersed amongst other houses, and the bishop set to work demolishing the monastic buildings and putting up houses for the future canons. Moses, the prior, then set out for Rome at this late date to lodge his complaint.[1]

As though he had not dealt the monastic order a severe enough blow, Longchamp, apparently at this same council, accused the black monks of wandering all over the country on the pretext of making pilgrimages to the shrines of St. Thomas at Canterbury and St. Edmund at Bury. Furthermore, although one of the chief complaints against the legate was that he travelled about with an escort of over a thousand horsemen, Longchamp declared that the abbots themselves kept too many horses.

Abbot Samson of Bury St. Edmunds, a stout-hearted East Anglian, would not submit to such dictation from a low-born Frenchman, papal legate and chancellor though he might be. 'We will not accept', he declared, 'any decree that is contrary to the Rule of St. Benedict, which permits abbots to have free disposal of their monks. As for me, I serve the barony of St. Edmund and his realm. Thirteen horses are not enough for me, as they might be for certain other abbots; I must have more, in order to carry out my duty of keeping the king's justice.'[2]

Although William Longchamp contrived to create a vast amount of confusion and dissatisfaction, the ordinary course of the government seems to have been little affected by his rise to power. Henry II and his advisors had succeeded in devising a

[1] Gervase, Vol. I, pp. 488-9; Newburgh, Vol. I, pp. 331, 395; Diceto, Vol. II, p. 85; Richard of Devizes, pp. 13, 69-70.

[2] Jocelin of Brakelond: *Chronicle*, p. 54.

system so efficient for its day and in staffing it with men so well versed in its procedures and so devoted to its aims that it continued to function in its usual way even though the king was far from the country and apparently indifferent to its government and even though the government was headed by a man who knew almost nothing of its procedure.

The highly complex functions of the Exchequer in accounting for the sheriffs' receipts of money continued with their normal efficiency, although the sheriffs had the added burdens of collecting and accounting for the great sums of money promised the king in exchange for the lands, honours, and offices with which he had been so prodigal. The fact that most of these men were new to their offices is not apparent from the accounts they rendered, which would indicate that even within the counties there must have been a fairly permanent staff of minor officials to keep the accounts, collect the monies owing, and follow up the fines and amercements levied in the courts of justice.

The power and authority of the king's government were represented in most men's eyes by the itinerant justiciars, who periodically visited the counties in order to hear both the pleas of the Crown, the cases, that is, that were reserved to the royal judges rather than the local officials, and all other pleas, both civil and criminal. Although the chroniclers represent the country as being in a disturbed condition, the itinerant justiciars conducted their eyres with unusual thoroughness. In the course of the year ending at Michaelmas 1190 the justiciars visited every county except Oxfordshire and Berkshire and, of course, the counties directly under Count John's administration.[1]

The heaviest share of the work seems to have fallen to the party headed by Geoffrey son of Peter, the most capable and experienced of the associate justiciars, and Abbot Benedict of Peterborough. They visited Lincolnshire, Buckinghamshire and Bedfordshire, Warwickshire and Leicestershire, and Northamptonshire, the largest of the six circuits into which the country was divided for the purposes of this eyre.[2]

[1] Doris M. Stenton: Introduction to Pipe Rolls 3 & 4 Richard I, pp. xx-xxii.
[2] Pipe Roll 3 Richard I, pp. 12, 110, 128, 158.

III

1191

SUPREME now in Church and state, the king's chancellor and chief justiciar of the realm, bishop of Ely and papal legate, William Longchamp had only one rival in sight, John, count of Mortain, the king's brother. Although he is not mentioned during the year following the meeting of the council in Normandy in March 1190 at which the king released him from his vow to stay out of England for three years, one may be certain that John lost little time in returning to England. The county of Mortain in Normandy, from which he took his title, was small and could offer no such attractions to him as could his vast holdings in England, where he set himself up in almost regal style.

John of course could not fail to observe Longchamp's rise to power and authority, and as the chancellor seized control of one castle after another on various pretexts John took alarm at his unbounded ambition. The first mention of any relations between the two is the statement by Richard of Devizes that they had their first conference 'concerning the custody of certain castles and the money granted from the Exchequer' at Winchester on 4 March. It may have been at this meeting that Longchamp lent John the sum of £200, for which Roger Bigot and Gilbert son of Renfrey stood sureties.[1]

John's suspicions and distrust were increased when he learned that Longchamp had made a secret treaty with William, king of Scots, concerning the succession to the throne in the case of Richard's death. Except for the statement by the author of the *Annals of Winchester* that Richard had designated his nephew Arthur as his heir before he left Normandy, no English chronicler records any provision that Richard made for the succession, although all of them emphasise that he was departing on a most

[1] Richard of Devizes, p. 26; Pipe Roll 3 Richard I, pp. xv, 50, 77.

perilous undertaking from which it was possible and even probable that he would not return.[1]

In November 1190, however, Richard, in Sicily, had made a treaty with King Tancred, one of the provisions of which was an agreement that Arthur should marry Tancred's daughter. In reporting this treaty to Pope Clement III, who was to have the power of enforcing its provisions, and in the text of the treaty, Richard referred to Arthur as 'our nephew and, if we perchance should die childless, our heir'.[2] News of the treaty would have reached England by the spring of 1191, and for the first time John may have realised the insecurity of his position. That insecurity was increased by the fact that his mother had set out, in the previous winter, to escort Berengaria of Navarre to Richard as his bride.

Arthur, the posthumous son of Geoffrey, duke of Brittany, was only four years old, having been born on 29 March 1187. Although he was the only son of the king's elder brother, succession by strict primogeniture was not yet the established rule and John, Henry's son and Richard's brother, was generally thought to be nearer the throne than Arthur, Henry's grandson and Richard's nephew, although Arthur's father, now dead, had been older than John. The fact that he would be a minor for many years weighed heavily against any claim that he might have. The very fact that he was a minor, however, recommended him to Longchamp, for if Arthur were to become king, Longchamp, firmly entrenched in power, might hope to rule in the name of Richard's successor as he was now ruling in Richard's.

The chancellor therefore sent two of his brothers to King William to arrange a treaty with him whereby the king of Scots agreed to recognise Arthur, who was, incidentally, his nephew also, as heir to the throne. Longchamp's ambassadors advanced the further argument that he had received letters from Richard, in Sicily, written perhaps at the time when the treaty with Tancred was made, designating Arthur as his successor and directing that he employ Longchamp as his chief advisor until he reached manhood.[3]

[1] *Annales de Wintonia*, in *Annales Monastici*, ed. H. R. Luard (5 vols., Rolls Series 36, 1864-9), Vol. II, p. 64.

[2] *Gesta*, Vol. II, pp. 135, 137; Howden, Vol. III, pp. 63, 65.

[3] Newburgh, Vol. I, p. 335-6.

Count John learned of these negotiations and recognised that they constituted a powerful threat to his future prospects. From one of watchful and suspicious neutrality his attitude changed to one of determined hostility.

Both John and Longchamp now began to prepare for the inevitable conflict, yet neither of them was confident enough of his position and strength to resort to open hostilities. Longchamp strengthened the defences of the castles under his control and began to employ large numbers of mercenary soldiers; Count John courted those whom the chancellor had offended, a group that included some of the most important and powerful men in England.

Longchamp's position was somewhat weakened by the receipt of the news that Pope Clement III had died late in March or early in April, for his office as legate came to an end with the death of the pope who had appointed him. He immediately, however, drew up a petition to the new pope, Celestine III, asking that he be re-appointed. Surprisingly enough, most of the bishops of England signed the petition. In view of the almost universal detestation in which Longchamp was held, one can only assume that the bishops did so, not because they approved of Longchamp, but because they feared him. Although his post as legate gave him great authority in ecclesiastical matters, he relied much more upon his power as chief justiciar, a power sufficient to tie the hands of any other bishop if he should happen to be appointed legate in Longchamp's place.

About this time, however, Longchamp began to picture an even brighter future for himself. Archbishop Baldwin, Bishop Hubert Walter of Salisbury, Rannulf Glanville, and some other crusaders had gone directly to the Holy Land from Marseilles. Rannulf Glanville had died in October, and Archbishop Baldwin died before the besieged city of Acre on 19 November 1190. News of his death, however, did not reach England till the following March. It was confirmed by the receipt of a letter from the king, dated 25 January, at Messina, to the monks of Canterbury, informing them of Baldwin's death and ordering them to elect as their new archbishop William, archbishop of Montreale, whom Richard had probably met in Sicily. The monks, who had no intention of electing an unknown foreigner, declined to act on what they professed to believe was no more than an unsubstantiated rumour, although they had sufficient faith in it to eject immediately their hated prior, Osbern, whom Baldwin had forced on them, and to elect in his place the subprior, Geoffrey, who had been one of the leading spirits in their quarrel with Baldwin.[1]

The chancellor, who had the responsibility of seeing that the king's commands were carried out, did not insist on obedience to this one, for he had already begun to hope that he himself might be elected archbishop of Canterbury. He seized the temporal possessions of the archbishopric, which reverted to the Crown as long as the see was vacant. He already had possession of the temporalities of York.[2]

The arrival of Walter of Coutances, archbishop of Rouen, at Shoreham on 27 June with a variety of letters from the king placed Longchamp's position in England under a different light. Ever since he left England Richard had been receiving complaints about his chancellor's conduct. Although he pretended to hear each petitioner sympathetically and gave him whatever letters he asked for, he always followed up these letters with others ordering that the chancellor was to be obeyed in all things.[3] Longchamp of course took advantage of these contradictory orders to carry out only the ones that suited him.

When Queen Eleanor joined her son in February, however, she gave him such alarming reports of the situation in England and of his chancellor's conduct that Richard began to realise the explosive nature of the situation. The measures that he then took, probably with Eleanor's advice and counsel, were intended to curb his vice-gerent's power in both Church and state. When the queen and Archbishop Walter of Coutances left the king at Messina on 2 April, Eleanor was charged with the mission of stopping in Rome and inducing the pope to disregard all of Richard's previous requests and to order the consecration of Geoffrey as archbishop of York.[4] This abrupt reversal of Richard's continued refusal to permit Geoffrey's consecration could have proceeded only from the king's determination to send his brother back to England as archbishop of York and thus able

[1] *Gesta*, Vol. II, p. 115; Diceto, Vol. II, p. 84; Gervase, Vol. I, pp. 490, 493–6.
[2] Newburgh, Vol. I, p. 333.
[3] Richard of Devizes, pp. 11, 29.
[4] Howden, Vol. III, p. 100.

to curb the powers of the bishop of Ely in matters affecting the Church.

At the same time the king released Archbishop Walter from his crusader's vow, taking from him all the money he had brought along for the journey, and sent him back to England armed with a number of letters, suitable for a variety of occasions, addressed to William Longchamp and the other justiciars. One of the letters, to Longchamp and his four associate justiciars, ordered them to act in all things with the advice of Archbishop Walter, who was to be joined with them in governing the country. Two other letters, however, the one addressed to William Marshal alone and the other to all four of the associate justiciars, directed that if the chancellor refused to follow their advice and that of the archbishop of Rouen, to whom 'we have opened our heart and entrusted our secrets', they were to override Longchamp and follow the archbishop's advice in all matters.[1]

Although Longchamp received Archbishop Walter with every mark of honour and respect, he nevertheless refused to obey these orders, on the ground that he best of all knew the king's mind and that the king's known wishes were more binding than letters that might be either false or obtained by fraud. No matter how flattering a reception he may have given the archbishop or what reasons he may have given for refusing to recognise his commission, at any rate Longchamp declined to associate Archbishop Walter with him in the government and continued to act as though he were the sole ruler of England.[2]

Walter of Coutances, a Cornishman by birth, was a learned man of literary tastes. He had been archdeacon of Oxford, treasurer of Rouen, and seal-bearer to King Henry II. He was consecrated bishop of Lincoln in 1183 and then elected archbishop of Rouen in the following year.[3] He had been employed on many diplomatic missions by King Henry and was a man of considerable administrative ability. When Longchamp refused to recognise Walter's commission from the king, he was not only armed with his overwhelming arrogance but was also backed up by the possession of many important castles and the command of

[1] Richard of Devizes, p. 28; Diceto, Vol. II, pp. 90-1; Gerald of Wales: *De Vita Galfridi*, pp. 400-1.

[2] Richard of Devizes, p. 29; Newburgh, Vol. II, pp. 336-7.

[3] Gerald of Wales, op. cit., p. 408.

an army of mercenary soldiers, whereas the archbishop had only the king's letters, whose very authenticity Longchamp professed to doubt.

No-one who had worked with Henry II for any length of time could have failed to learn that there are other weapons than mere brute force with which to meet brute force. Count John already had the sympathy of many of the leading men of the realm, not because he was an attractive figure that would inspire confidence in his abilities but because he was the only person of a rank high enough to offer any resistance to the overweening chancellor. The archbishop of Rouen, whilst preserving the appearance of friendship with Longchamp, encouraged John to send letters throughout the country soliciting the support of the barons and clergy in case open conflict should arise between him and the chancellor. The barons responded favourably to John's overtures, whilst the clergy, 'more timid by nature', declined to commit themselves.[1]

Matters came to a head when Longchamp demanded that Gerard of Camville surrender Lincoln Castle to him. Gerard, 'a rich and noble man', whose younger brother Richard was one of the commanders of King Richard's fleet, had married Nicholaa of La Haye, the daughter and heiress of the hereditary constable of Lincoln Castle. Even before Richard was crowned, Gerard had sought him out in Normandy and obtained from him a charter confirming to himself and Nicholaa his wife and their heirs 'all the right and inheritance that they should have in England and in Normandy, with the custody and the office of castellan of Lincoln Castle'. At the great sale of lands and offices after Richard's coronation, Gerard had promised the king 700 marks in order to be appointed sheriff of Lincolnshire and to have his office as castellan confirmed.[2]

Longchamp seems already to have deprived Gerard of his position as sheriff, probably at the preceding Michaelmas, and to have installed William of Stuteville in his place. Longchamp did not trust Gerard, 'a factious man, prodigal of his allegiance', and he was eager to add Lincoln to the castles under his immediate

[1] Richard of Devizes, p. 30.

[2] Newburgh, Vol. I, p. 337; Doris M. Stenton: Introd. to Pipe Roll 3 & 4 Richard I, pp. xxv-xxvi; *Ancient Charters*, ed. J. H. Round (Pipe Roll Society 10, 1888), pp. 91-3; Pipe Roll 2 Richard I, p. 89.

control. When he demanded that Gerard surrender the castle and swear allegiance to him, Gerard fled to Count John, leaving the castle in the capable hands of his wife, Nicholaa.

Longchamp was hindered in the execution of these designs for a short time by the necessity of subduing an uprising on the Welsh border, where Roger of Mortimer, one of the most powerful of the Marcher barons, was suspected of having allied himself with his Welsh neighbours. Longchamp quickly assembled an army, reduced Roger's stronghold of Wigmore, and sent Roger, who was accused of cowardice by his allies, into exile for three years.[1]

The chancellor then turned immediately to Lincoln and laid siege to the castle, which Nicholaa stoutly defended like a man. The Pipe Roll shows that Longchamp assembled 30 knights at 2s. per day, 20 mounted soldiers at 4d. per day, and 300 foot-soldiers at 2d. per day for the siege, and that he put a force of 40 miners to work undermining the walls of the castle.[2]

This was the very opportunity that John and his friends had been waiting for. He forced Robert of Crockston and Eudes of Deville, the constables of Nottingham and Tickhill respectively, to surrender those castles to him, thus giving him strong bases from which to control the Midlands. Flushed with this success and with the knowledge that he had the support of many of the barons, he demanded that Longchamp lift the siege of Lincoln immediately and threatened 'to visit him with a rod of iron'.[3]

For the first time Longchamp seems to have realised the extent of the opposition he had aroused. He learned at last that many of the barons who he had thought were his chief supporters favoured Count John instead. Putting up a brave front, however, he in turn ordered John to surrender the two castles he had just taken, and, ignoring the fact that Richard had released John from his promise to stay out of England almost as soon as it had been given, he demanded that John stand trial before the king's court for having broken his oath to his brother.[4]

Archbishop Walter, whom Longchamp thought he had still under his thumb, served as intermediary in these demands and played a part that reflected more credit on his cunning than on his honesty. Bearing messages from one side to the other, he

[1] Richard of Devizes, pp. 30-1.
[2] Pipe Roll 3 Richard I, p. 1.
[3] *Gesta*, Vol. II, p. 207.
[4] Newburgh, Vol. I, p. 338; Richard of Devizes, p. 32.

praised the chancellor's determination when he was with Longchamp and fanned the count's ambitions when he was with John, urging him to 'venture great things, worthy of Gyaros and of prison', if he wanted to take his rightful place in the realm. Publicly, however, he urged that, rather than resort to open conflict, which would in the end plunge the country into civil war, the two parties submit their differences to arbitration and arrive at a peaceful compromise. Urged on by their advisors, John and Longchamp at last agreed to meet for a conference at Winchester on 28 July. Longchamp, checked for the first time since he had seized power, abandoned the siege of Lincoln and took refuge in the Tower of London, which he had kept fully stocked with men and supplies.

On the appointed day both parties met at Winchester with their supporters. John had already sent word to all who favoured him to come to the conference armed as if for war, and he took the added precaution of stationing 4,000 Welsh mercenaries in the vicinity, so that they might rescue him in case of treachery. Longchamp for his part had summoned a third of the feudal levy of England, which would produce around 2,000 knights, and he also brought a number of Welshmen, paid out of the Exchequer. Each side was prepared for war, but the chancellor, for all his bluster and brave show, knew that if it came to open hostilities John would have the support of the majority of the barons.

An elaborate procedure for reaching a compromise was set up. Although the archbishop of Rouen kept discreetly in the background, it is possible, in view of his previous role as intermediary, that he took a leading part in the arrangements. Three bishops, Godfrey of Winchester, Richard of London, and Reginald of Bath, in whom both sides had full confidence, were named, and these three, in turn, named the arbitrators who were to set the terms of the compromise. The bishops chose as spokesmen for the chancellor the three earls who had consistently supported Longchamp: William of Albini, earl of Arundel, the son of one of the staunchest friends of King Henry II; Richard of Clare, who had married one of the three daughters of Earl William of Gloucester; and Hamelin of Warenne, a bastard half-brother of Henry II; and eight other men of lesser rank. On John's side they named Stephen Ridel, his chancellor, William of Wenneval, Reginald of Wasseville, and eight others.

These arbitrators swore on the Holy Gospels that they would settle the disputes between the count and the chancellor 'to the honour of each party and the peace of the realm, and that if any differences should arise between the two in the future they would faithfully bring them to an end'. The count and William Longchamp, for their part, swore to abide by whatever settlement the arbitrators might agree upon.[1]

The text of the treaty, as given by Roger of Howden, provided first that Count John was to surrender the castles of Tickhill and Nottingham, which he had seized shortly before this, to Archbishop Walter, who in turn was to entrust Nottingham to William Marshal, who seems to have been neutral throughout the conflict, and Tickhill to William of Wenneval, one of John's principal supporters, to hold 'to the honour and fealty of the lord king until his return. And if perchance the lord king (which God forbid!) should die on his pilgrimage, let them give back these castles to the count without any holding back or delay.' It was provided furthermore that if the chancellor exceeded his lawful powers in dealing with Count John or if he acted contrary to the advice and counsel of the archbishop of Rouen, the justiciars appointed as his associates, and the members of the king's court, and did not quickly mend his ways when he was warned to do so, then those two castles were to be given back to John immediately.

The great castles of Wallingford, Bristol, the Peak, Bolsover, Eye, Hereford, Exeter, and Launceston, which lay within the lands and honours assigned to John, were to be held for the king by men of proven loyalty, but with the provision that if the king should die they were to be turned over immediately to John.

To put a stop to Longchamp's high-handed behaviour, it was provided that 'bishops and abbots, earls and barons, vavassors and freeholders are not to be disseised of their lands or chattels at the pleasure of the justiciars and ministers of the lord king, but they shall be dealt with by the judgment of the lord king's court according to the legitimate customs and assizes of the realm or the order of the lord king'. John was to observe these same provisions in his territory.

This section is especially interesting because it shows that the power of arbitrary disseisin, an unquestioned prerogative of

[1] Richard of Devizes, pp. 32-4.

Henry II and Richard,[1] had been taken over by the justiciars as part of the regular machinery of government. From being an arbitrary and extraordinary function of the king's *vis et voluntas* in dealing with his barons, it had become such an accepted supplement to the regular proceedings of the courts that not Longchamp alone in his assumption of his master's powers but the king's 'justiciars and ministers' as a body used it as an ordinary method of punishment when the courts would be too slow or, perhaps, reluctant to disseise a baron for the reasons on which the justiciars acted.

Against this assumption, by mere justiciars and ministers, of a power that was assumed to be a unique attribute of kingship, the barons protested, and protested effectively. It had not yet occurred to them to protest formally against the power itself, bitterly though they must have resented it, when it was wielded by the king in person, for they acquiesced in disseisins made at 'the order of the lord king'. They were undoubtedly turning the matter over in their minds and in discussions amongst themselves, however, and their resentment, fanned by the excessive and tyrannical misuse of the power by Richard's successor, led to the formulation of Chapter 39 of Magna Carta.

If any of the provisions of this treaty were violated, at John's complaint the archbishop of Rouen, the king's justiciars, and the guarantors who had sworn to enforce the treaty were to remedy matters, and John, in his territory, was to do likewise if they complained to him. This section emphasises John's complete independence in governing the lands assigned to him and reads almost as though it were referring to a foreign land.

In a provision reminiscent of the civil war in King Stephen's reign, when evil men built castles over the land, from which they spread out to burn, destroy, and kill, it was agreed that any new castles begun or completed since the king left England were to be torn down and that no new ones were to be built henceforth except at the king's direct order.

A clear defeat for Longchamp lay in the provision that Gerard of Camville was to be reinstated as sheriff of Lincolnshire, but it was agreed that he was to stand trial in the king's court, although the nature of his offence was not specified.

[1] See J. E. A. Jolliffe, *Angevin Kingship* (2nd ed., London, 1963), Chap. III, pp. 50 et seq.

Apparently John's territory had been serving as a haven for malefactors, for it was provided that he was not to shelter outlaws or the king's enemies. He might, however, receive those who had been accused of 'offences against the lord king', so long as the accused man offered to stand his trial in the king's court: a curious provision that seemed to provide immunity for anyone who wanted to take refuge in an area that the royal justiciars did not visit.

Both John and the chancellor swore before the archbishop of Rouen to keep this treaty 'in good faith and without evil intent', and fourteen guarantors, seven on each side, swore likewise.

The treaty concluded with the astonishing provision that if the king, before his return, were to order that the treaty was not to be kept and its provisions were thus to become void, the castles of Nottingham and Tickhill were to be turned over to John, 'no matter what the lord king may order concerning the matter'.[1]

Richard of Devizes, who gives a summary of the treaty that agrees in the important particulars with the text as found in Roger of Howden, adds the provision that if the king should die the chancellor would not seek the count's disinheritance but would do everything in his power to advance him to the throne.[2] While there is no mention in the treaty of the succession to the throne, the provision that some of the most important castles in the realm were to be turned over to John in the event of his brother's death would ensure that John would have control of the country and an easy path to the throne. Richard's marriage to Berengaria in Cyprus on 12 May[3] perhaps made the matter of the succession less controversial, for it would be assumed that the king would provide his kingdom with an heir as soon as possible, since it was presumably for that purpose that his mother had arranged the match.

The fact that Richard of Devizes gives a summary of the treaty that does not agree in every particular with the text as given by Roger of Howden and that he carelessly dates it 25 April, although he has just stated that the agreement was reached at the conference held on 28 July, together with the fact that William of Newburgh[4] dates these early stages of the struggle between Count John and William Longchamp in a way that cannot be

[1] Howden, Vol. III, pp. 135-7.
[2] Richard of Devizes, p. 34.
[3] Diceto, Vol, II, p. 110.
[4] Vol. I, pp. 337-9.

reconciled with the other contemporary accounts, led Bishop Stubbs, in an attempt to reconcile Newburgh's account with the others, to believe that there were two sieges of Lincoln, three conferences at Winchester, and two separate treaties, of which the first, summarised by Richard of Devizes, was dated 25 April and the second, given in full by Roger of Howden, 28 July.[1]

There seems little reason, beyond a desire to establish the credibility of William of Newburgh's account in every detail, to postulate such a multiplicity of sieges, conferences, and treaties, which none of the contemporary writers mentions. The summary given by Richard of Devizes, who of all the chroniclers was closest to the scene, agrees in its main provisions with the text in Roger of Howden. Although Richard, a monk of St. Swithun's at Winchester, was in an excellent position to know of these matters and no doubt either saw a text of the treaty or was told of its main provisions, he is summarising, from memory, the important points of a long and complicated document, and it is hardly to be wondered at that he should make a few mistakes on such unimportant points as whether William of Wenneval was to have the custody of Nottingham Castle or of Tickhill. His mistake in dating the treaty is obviously sheer carelessness, a fault that afflicts the best of historians at times.[2]

Regardless of its exact date, the Treaty of Winchester is one of the most valuable documents of Richard's reign for the insight it gives into conditions in England at the time and particularly into the growth of a vigorous spirit of responsibility amongst the very class of men who, less than fifty years before this, would have unhesitatingly plunged the country into civil war on far less provocation. Two opposing parties, both under violent, headstrong, and ambitious leaders, after a show of strength on both sides and with an impressive array of accusations against each other, met in circumstances that would seem to be certain guarantees of open warfare, since each leader was backed up by an imposing army, each could make a convincing claim for the rightness of his position and the validity of the powers he was attempting to exercise, and each was stubbornly determined to maintain his right.

[1] Howden, Vol. III, p. 134, n. 2.

[2] For a fuller discussion of this matter, I venture to refer the reader, if I may, to Appendix F, 'The Treaty of Winchester', in my edition of Richard of Devizes, pp. 90–8.

The wonder of it all is that when John, with his army of Welshmen and with his friends in arms, and William Longchamp, with the knights who had answered his summons and with his mercenary soldiers, met at Winchester, open warfare did not break out. That it did not is due to the wisdom and prudence of those men who took upon themselves the task of promoting a peaceful settlement that both sides would accept. Who those men were we shall probably never know, considering how scanty are the records of the event. It may have been Walter of Coutances, archbishop of Rouen, although Richard of Devizes, at least, assigns him a rather discreditable part and accuses him of dishonesty and double-dealing. It may have been the bishops of Winchester, London, and Bath, who had all had a great deal of experience in affairs of government and who enjoyed the confidence of both sides. It may have been, finally, the sound good sense of the whole assembly of bishops, barons, and knights, who had been trained in the hard but salutary school of Henry II to a growing sense of responsibility for the orderly conduct of the government and who succeeded in averting civil war.

That William Longchamp had outraged the sense of propriety of many of them is obvious from the provisions of the treaty. Although the chancellor had the technical right on his side, armed as he was both with the king's letters directing that he was to be obeyed in all things and with his double office of chief justiciar and papal legate, he had sadly abused that right, and some of the most important provisions are those in which his powers were curtailed and the orderly process of consultation with his associates insisted upon. The most eloquent tribute to the good work of Henry II is found in the importance given to the due processes of law, 'the judgment of the lord king's court according to the legitimate customs and assizes of the realm'.

John's hand was greatly strengthened both by the curbing of Longchamp's excessive powers and by the provisions assuring him of control of many important castles and hence, in the last analysis, of the country, if his brother should die. One of the clauses that perhaps gave him the greatest satisfaction was that restoring his faithful man, Gerard of Camville, to his offices and ejecting William of Stuteville, whom Longchamp had intruded as sheriff of Lincolnshire.

When order had been restored, Roger of Lacy, the hereditary

constable of Chester, to whom William Longchamp had given the castles of Nottingham and Tickhill, set out to punish Robert of Crockston and Eudes of Deville for having turned them over to Count John. Forewarned, the two fled and refused to stand their trial. Roger turned then to Alan of Leek and Peter of Bovencourt, who had been associated with the constables. Peter had already gone to London and declared before Count John, the chancellor, and the king's court that 'the castle of Tickhill had been given up to Count John against his will and against his orders, and that if he had had helpers who were of one mind in defending it against Count John, as he had wanted to, it would not have been surrendered to the count'.

Longchamp would not listen to Peter. 'Go to your lord, the constable of Chester,' he told him, 'and purge yourself in his court of the crime of which he has accused you.' Count John gave Peter a letter supporting his statement, but when Peter presented himself before Roger of Lacy and offered to prove his innocence in any way that he directed, Roger would not hear him.

Without giving them any sort of a trial, Roger had both Peter and Alan of Leek hanged on a gallows with iron chains. On the third day a certain squire was discovered driving away the birds that were feasting on the two corpses. Roger had him hanged beside the bodies of his friends. Count John promptly took away from Roger all the lands that he held of the count to punish him for this barbarous behaviour.[1]

With Longchamp's temporal powers curbed and both parties constrained to keep the peace, John and his adherents bided their time, certain that the chancellor's arrogance would eventually deliver him into their hands. Lonchamp's powers as papal legate had expired with the death of Clement III, and as soon as he learned of the pope's death he had petitioned the new pontiff, Celestine III, for a renewal of his office. The date at which Celestine re-appointed him is uncertain, but he was so confident of his office that he apparently continued to act as legate in the interval before he received the confirmation.

A threat to his position now arose from an unexpected quarter. At King Richard's request, conveyed by Queen Eleanor in April, the new pope confirmed the election of Geoffrey as archbishop of

[1] *Gesta*, Vol. II, pp. 234-5.

York, ordered Archbishop Bartholomew of Tours to consecrate him, and, as a singular mark of his favour, sent the archbishop-elect the pallium, the badge of his power of jurisdiction, even before he was consecrated.[1] The usual procedure was for a new archbishop, after his election had been confirmed and he had been consecrated, to go in person to Rome to receive the pallium from the pope's hands, although in exceptional cases, such as that of Archbishop Thomas of Canterbury, the pope had allowed a new archbishop to request the pallium by messengers rather than in person.

Longchamp of course learned of Geoffrey's impending consecration, and he realised that the presence of the archbishop of York in England would greatly curtail the despotic control that he was exercising over the Church and would detract from the eminent position he held, which is no doubt what King Richard had intended when he had reversed his decision and asked that Geoffrey be consecrated. Longchamp furthermore was enjoying the revenues from the possessions of the see of York and had so wasted and squandered its resources that he could look forward with dread to the accounting that would follow when Geoffrey came to claim his see.

In the face of the pope's express command Longchamp could hardly prevent Geoffrey's consecration, but he could at least exert all his powers to keep him out of England. On 30 July he ordered the sheriffs of the counties bordering on the Channel to arrest Geoffrey if he should land at any port within their jurisdictions. To make sure that no unwelcome orders arrived in the country, he added that any letters from 'the lord pope or any other great man' should be held up and not allowed to enter England. He also sent a messenger, probably his friend the earl of Arundel, to the countess of Flanders, whose husband had died before Acre on 1 June 1191, to ask her not to allow Geoffrey to cross over to England from any port in Flanders, and he attempted to ingratiate himself into the favour of a certain Hugh, one of the Countess's officials, by giving him six marks with which to buy a silver cup as a gift.[2]

Longchamp's control over the Church in England was threat-

[1] Newburgh, Vol. I, p. 339.

[2] Gerald of Wales: *De Vita Galfridi*, pp. 388-9; Diceto, Vol. II, p. 96; Howden, Vol. III, p. 111; Pipe Roll 3 Richard I, pp. xvii, 141.

ened from another quarter with the arrival of Walter of Coutances, archbishop of Rouen. No-one, least of all the monks of Canterbury, had taken seriously the king's order that they elect Archbishop William of Montreale as their new archbishop, and William Longchamp had apparently connived at their refusal to act. He had a convent of monks at his cathedral of Ely and seems to have been on good terms with them, a fact that would further recommend him to the monks of Canterbury.

When Walter of Coutances arrived in England with a pouch full of letters from the king and enjoying the king's confidence and the trust of Count John and many of the leading men of the kingdom, Longchamp recognised that Walter not only openly threatened his supremacy as chief justiciar but also was a powerful and dangerous rival to his ambition to be archbishop of Canterbury. Longchamp therefore wrote Walter a sharp letter on 25 August, forbidding him to go to Canterbury on any pretext whatever. Longchamp aroused great indignation by using in his letter the royal formula, 'If you presume to cross the Thames, we shall not be able to hide the anger and wrath that we shall feel against you.'[1]

At about this same time, Count John learned that Longchamp was plotting to have himself elected archbishop of Canterbury. In John's eyes, of course, Longchamp was the worst possible candidate for the position, and the count immediately wrote to the monks and strictly forbade them to proceed with the election.[2]

Geoffrey meanwhile was consecrated archbishop by Archbishop Bartholomew at Tours, on 18 August, with Bishop Henry of Bayonne and six suffragan bishops assisting. Immediately after his consecration Geoffrey took the threefold oath of obedience to the Roman see: that he would receive papal legates with due respect, that he would forward appeals to the pope, and that he would visit Rome every three years, either in person or by a proper envoy. Bartholomew then vested him with the pallium.[3]

The new archbishop went to Guines in Flanders and tried to arrange for his passage to England. When he learned that he was not to be permitted to cross, he sent to the countess and asked

[1] Gerald of Wales, op. cit., pp. 399-400; Diceto, Vol. II, pp. 92-3; J. E. A. Jolliffe, op. cit., p. 98*n*.

[2] *Epistolae Cantuarienses*, p. 346.

[3] Diceto, Vol. II, p. 96

her by whose orders he was denied passage. The countess replied that she was acting at the request of the English chancellor. She generously added, however, that since the prohibition applied only to him, there was no reason why his servants and companions should not cross over. Geoffrey took the hint and sent all his household to Dover, where they landed on Friday, 13 September. By exercising a little cunning, he found a small English vessel that carried him across the Channel on the following day.

Geoffrey landed at Dover before the middle of the morning and was immediately surrounded by guards, who ordered him to go without delay to the castle to report to the castellan's wife, Richeut, a sister of the chancellor. Geoffrey contrived to escape on horseback from the guards and fled to St. Martin's Priory, a dependency of Christ Church Convent at Canterbury. The guards, following hot on his heels, surrounded the monastery.

After hearing Mass, the archbishop sent a messenger to Richeut to ask her by whose authority she had attempted to apprehend him. She replied that she was acting on behalf of her brother, the chancellor, whom, she added, she would obey with such faithfulness that if he were to order her to set fire to Dover Castle or to burn down the whole city of London she would do so unhesitatingly. She also sent William of Auberville and a number of other Kentish knights to him to demand that he take an oath of fealty to the king and the chancellor and that he offer reliable securities for keeping the peace.

Geoffrey indignantly replied that he had already taken the oath of fealty to his brother and that he would take no other oaths at their direction. The knights then placed an armed guard about the monastery, with men watching every exit, and began a regular siege.

On Sunday morning, after celebrating Mass, Geoffrey solemnly and publicly pronounced the sentence of excommunication upon Richeut by name and upon all others, in general, whether armed or unarmed, who either ordered the siege or took part in it. The besiegers thereupon stationed guards within the church itself to keep Geoffrey from leaving it, even to go to the chamber in the priory in which he had spent the previous night.

Late in the afternoon the constable of Dover Castle, Matthew of Clare, Richeut's husband, came to the church and demanded that the archbishop take the oath of fealty to the king and the chancellor. Geoffrey repeated his previous denial, but he added that when he appeared before a meeting of the bishops and barons of the realm and of men faithful to the king his brother, he would gladly submit to their counsel, if it appeared to them that he should take any oath to the king beyond the one he had already taken. With this, the constable allowed Geoffrey to go from the church into the priory, but he kept the guards stationed before all the doors.

Geoffrey remained a prisoner in the priory till Wednesday, 18 September. Late in the afternoon of that day two knights, Aubrey of Marney and Alexander Puintel,[1] who were counted amongst Longchamp's most faithful servants, arrived with a band of around fifteen armed men. They beat on the door of the church, which had been barricaded against them, and threatened to break it down unless it was immediately opened to them. At their assurance that they had come to talk to the archbishop peacefully, the monks opened the door to the knights, who entered with their band of mercenaries, all armed in coats of mail under their cloaks.

They found the archbishop seated near the altar, with a white stole around his neck and his processional cross, with an ivory figure on a cross of gold, in his hands. Into the minds of all beholders leaped, as no doubt the archbishop intended that it should, the memory of St. Thomas, who had sat thus, holding his cross before him, at the Council of Northampton.

'The chancellor orders you,' they told him, 'because you have entered this land contrary to the king's prohibition and his own, to go aboard a ship and make haste to cross back again.'

The archbishop replied that he would do nothing at the chancellor's order, but that he had come peacefully into the realm, as was evident from the fact that he had brought no soldiers with him, although he might easily have collected a large band of mercenaries if he had wanted to do so. He had come to England with the king's leave and friendship, as was plainly shown by the king's letters, which Geoffrey had already forwarded to the chancellor.

'If you have nothing more to say,' the knights told him, 'we must do what we have been ordered to do.' When the archbishop did not answer, they went outside the church, threw off

[1] Pipe Roll 3 Richard I, pp. xvii, 136.

their cloaks, and came back armed and in coats of mail. Again they asked the archbishop to obey the chancellor's order, and again he refused.

With a fine show of piety the knights first genuflected to the altar and struck their breasts three times. Then they seized the archbishop by the arms and shoulders and drew him to the door of the church. 'As soon as he was past the threshold he excommunicated those who had laid hands on him.' They then took him by the arms and legs and dragged him out of the church, with his head banging on the pavement.

The knights offered him a horse so that he might ride with them to the castle, but he refused, for the horse belonged to excommunicated men with whom he would have no dealings. Geoffrey went on foot, half pushed and half dragged through the mud, clinging firmly to his processional cross and wearing his stole, to Dover Castle, accompanied by the clerks of his household, a number of the clergy who had come to him at the news of his arrival in England, and a throng of townspeople.

Matthew of Clare, the constable, was not made of such stern stuff as was his wife. When the archbishop was dragged into his presence, Matthew fell on his knees before him and burst into tears at the thought of the predicament in which his brother-in-law's orders had placed him. He imprisoned Geoffrey with three of his clerks and four servants to wait on them, but in an effort to mitigate the severity of the chancellor's orders he sent his prisoners food from his own table. Geoffrey indignantly refused it. To keep himself free from all dealings with his excommunicated warders he had his servants bring him food, water, and fire from the town.

On the third day of Geoffrey's imprisonment the chancellor confiscated all his horses and had them brought to him as though they were the spoils of war. Almost every day he sent messengers to the prisoner, now offering to furnish him with ships if he would return to the Continent and again ordering him to swear fealty to the king and to him. Geoffrey would reply to none of them. Matthew of Clare, meanwhile, as he realised the enormity of the sacrilege in which he shared, came again and again to kneel before the archbishop and protest that he was innocent of all evil intent and that he was merely obeying orders, however unwillingly. Although Geoffrey, like his father, had a fiery temper and was quick to take offence, he was too big-hearted to harbour a grudge when his pardon had been asked, and he absolved Matthew.[1]

The news of Geoffrey's imprisonment spread through England more quickly than the wind.[2] His case was too closely parallel to that of St. Thomas for it not to arouse horror. That the chancellor in his arrogance should dare thus to treat an archbishop was regarded as an intolerable sacrilege. In addition to being the king's half-brother, Geoffrey was known and respected for his unswerving loyalty to his father; alone of Henry's sons he had stayed with him to the end, comforting him in his agony, pillowing his head on his breast as the king lay dying, and whispering words of love to him as his tormented soul fared forth. Geoffrey had spent a considerable part of his life in England, where he had shown his courage in fighting the Scots in 1173-4, and the English seem to have liked and admired him. That an arrogant foreigner whose grandfather was said to have been a runaway serf should treat such a man in such a manner united the English nation against Longchamp.

The monks of Canterbury, being the nearest, were among the first to learn of how Geoffrey had been treated. Invoking 'the blood of our glorious martyr Thomas', they wrote at once to Longchamp to demand that he explain why the innocent archbishop had been dragged by an armed band from the very altar of their church at Dover and hauled through the filth and mud, carrying his cross, to prison.

Longchamp in his reply bade them not to be disturbed because the archbishop of York was being held at Dover. It was not at his order, he explained, that Geoffrey had been seized in the church and held in prison. He had merely directed that if the archbishop should happen to land in England and refused to swear that fealty to the lord king that Geoffrey, he said, had never sworn, he should be sent back to Flanders, for the archbishop had taken an oath that he would not come to England as long as the king was on his pilgrimage.[3]

That most of the leading men were united in Geoffrey's de-

[1] Gerald of Wales: *De Vita Galfridi*, pp. 387-93; Diceto, Vol. II, p. 97; Richard of Devizes, pp. 40-2.

[2] Newburgh, Vol. I, pp. 340-1; Richard of Devizes, p. 42.

[3] Gervase, Vol. I, pp. 505-6; *Epistolae Cantuarienses*, pp. 344-5.

fence is shown best of all by the fact that the saintly Hugh of Avalon, bishop of Lincoln and the most highly respected member of the episcopate, as soon as he heard the news of the archbishop's imprisonment, publicly, at Oxford, excommunicated Richeut and Matthew of Clare by name and laid a general sentence on all the authors and promoters of the outrage. Bishop Richard of London, upon receipt of the news, sought out the chancellor, who was then at Norwich, and threatened to lay the whole province of Canterbury under interdict unless the archbishop were set free immediately. John of Oxford, bishop of Norwich and St. Thomas's old enemy, added his protests to the general outcry.

Hugh of Nonant, bishop of Coventry, had been one of Longchamp's supporters, probably because the chancellor had sided with him in his dispute with his monks. At some time previous to this, however, he had switched his allegiance to Count John, for it was clear that John would in the end triumph over the chancellor. Hugh now took the leading part in organising the opposition to Longchamp.

John was at Lancaster when his brother was seized. Bishop Hugh bore the news to him and urged him to take immediate steps to avenge the insult. John was not content merely to send messengers to the chancellor to protest against his actions and to write to those who had stood as guarantors of the Treaty of Winchester to rouse them to action. He promptly sent two knights to Dover to order the castellan to set the archbishop free at once. If his brother had been guilty of any offence, John's messengers said, the count would stand surety for him. Although the knights used much violent language, Matthew refused to obey the orders of anyone save his master the chancellor. The knights then returned to John to report their failure.[1]

The chancellor was now overwhelmed by protests from bishops, barons, clergy, and people alike over his treatment of the king's brother. At first he attempted to excuse himself, as he had to the monks of Canterbury, by saying that it was not at his orders that the archbishop had been treated with such violence, but this transparent lie deceived no-one.

At last, when the whole realm was turned against him and all his opponents were united in denouncing him, he began to

[1] Gerald of Wales, op. cit., pp. 393-5; Richard of Devizes, p. 45.

realise the seriousness both of his actions and of the predicament in which they had landed him. He had beaten down the bishop of Durham, the justiciars whose advice the king had ordered him to follow, and the archbishop of Rouen, and he had emerged from the struggle with Count John with most of his powers and all of his arrogance intact. Now by his final act of folly and pride he had united them all against him. If he had made an alliance with any one of his previous opponents he might have weathered this storm, but he would share his power with no-one. Longchamp was determined to be supreme in England in Church and state, and his very jealousy of the power that the archbishop of York might presumably wield led him into his fatal blunder.

Seeing that almost everyone of any importance was against him, Longchamp sent Hamelin, earl of Warenne, to Dover to order that Geoffrey be released. Earl Hamelin required that the archbishop swear 'as a bishop and a priest' that he would go to London and appear before the bishops and barons of the realm and abide by their decision as to what he should do. Since that was what he had been intending to do ever since the trouble with the chancellor first arose, it was an easy oath for Geoffrey to take.

He was released on Thursday, 26 September. Offered horses for himself and his servants, he refused them, saying that he would go out of prison in the same way that he had come in. Wearing his white stole around his neck and carrying his cross, Geoffrey returned to St. Martin's Priory on foot, accompanied by a rejoicing throng.

On Saturday Geoffrey set out for London. He stopped at Canterbury and prayed for a long time at St. Thomas's tomb. Then he was greeted with 'a most beautiful procession' by the monks of St. Augustine's, where he spent the night. William of Albini, earl of Arundel, and Henry of Cornhill, sheriff of Kent, at the chancellor's order met him at Canterbury and escorted him to London.

The archbishop arrived in London on Wednesday, 2 October. The clergy and people turned out almost in a body to conduct him in a solemn procession to St. Paul's, where he was welcomed with every mark of honour and respect by Richard, bishop of London.[1]

[1] Gerald of Wales, op. cit., pp. 395–6; Diceto, Vol. II, pp. 97–8; Gervase, Vol. I, p. 507.

Count John meanwhile had sent a summons to all the bishops and barons in the following terms:

> As you love God's honour and the Church's and the lord king's and the realm's and mine, be at Loddon Bridge on the Saturday next after Michaelmas, between Reading and Windsor, because, God willing, I will meet you there, so that we may deal with certain great and arduous matters concerning the lord king and the realm.[1]

He sent two messengers to London to bear his summons both to William Longchamp and to Archbishop Geoffrey, who had been presenting his case so effectively to the leading citizens of London that the city was thrown into an uproar. Conditions were so disturbed that the Michaelmas session of the Exchequer apparently opened at Oxford.[2] Longchamp was so afraid of the citizens that he gave Geoffrey, who had pledged himself to remain in London, leave to go to the conference, under the condition that he return after the third day. Longchamp himself went to Windsor Castle with an imposing guard.

Count John and his friends and supporters meanwhile were gathering at Reading, about fifteen miles west of Windsor. Geoffrey arrived there on Friday, 4 October, and was greeted by his brother with kisses and embraces. On the morning appointed for the conference, Saturday, 5 October, after Mass, the assembly gathered at Reading. Geoffrey, in a room where 'the greater and more honourable men' had met, explained his case and told how the chancellor had treated him. Then he fell on his knees before them and with tears in his eyes begged them to avenge the injury that had been done to Christ and His Church by the insults he had received. His audience in turn knelt before him and promised to do so as one man.

The crowd then set out for the meeting place at the bridge over the Loddon some three miles from Reading. William Longchamp had also started from Windsor, accompanied by Richard, bishop of London, William, earl of Arundel, Hamelin, earl of Warenne, Roger Bigod, earl of Norfolk, and a crowd of hangers-on. When they had proceeded about four miles, however, the chancellor's courage deserted him at the thought of meeting all his enemies assembled in one body. Turning back to the safety of Windsor Castle, he sent the party on without him.

Present at the meeting were two archbishops, Walter of Rouen

[1] Diceto, Vol. II, p. 98. [2] Pipe Rolls 3 & 4 Richard I, pp. xviii, 99.

and Geoffrey of York; five bishops, Richard of London, Hugh of Lincoln, Godfrey of Winchester, Reginald of Bath, and Hugh of Coventry; Count John, and the leading barons of the realm. Geoffrey spoke to the assembly first and had the king's letter read aloud that authorised him to return to England with the king's leave, favour, and friendship and to take part in the justiciars' deliberations as the king's brother and faithful supporter.

Walter of Coutances, archbishop of Rouen, spoke next and had the king's letters read to the assembly whereby he was ordered to join in the direction of public affairs and particularly, as one to whom the king had revealed the secrets of his heart, to take charge of the election of the archbishop of Canterbury. Since these letters were in Latin, Bishop Hugh of Nonant translated them into French for the benefit of the laymen present. Archbishop Walter then told the assembly that when he attempted to follow the king's orders and arrange for an election at Canterbury the chancellor forbade him so much as to cross the Thames from London. Furthermore, he asserted, the chancellor had never once asked for or followed his advice in any matter whatever.

Three of the justiciars, William Marshal, William Briwerre, and Geoffrey son of Peter, also testified that the chancellor had likewise ignored them, contrary to the king's orders. Although Hugh of Le Puiset, bishop of Durham, was not present, it seems likely that he had sent someone to recite the story of the wrongs he had suffered at the Chancellor's hands. The earl of Arundel, who acted as Longchamp's spokesman, was unable to make any reply to these accusations.[1]

After all these men had made their charges against the chancellor, Walter of Coutances had the king's commission, which Longchamp had ignored in such a contemptuous fashion, read to the assembly. This document clearly authorised the archbishop and the justiciars to depose the chancellor if he failed to follow their advice. Acting on the strength of the king's orders, Archbishop Walter urged his hearers, 'both Count John and the others, on the king's behalf, to rise up as one man against the chancellor, deprive him of his power because he was useless to the king and the realm, and install someone else who would pay more attention to their advice'.

[1] Gerald of Wales, op. cit., pp. 397-400; *Gesta*, Vol. II, pp. 212.

The assembly immediately decided to summon the chancellor to hear the charges against him and sent the bishops of Lincoln, Winchester, and Coventry and a number of barons to bring him to them. Longchamp, however, pleaded that he was too ill to attend the conference on that day. The bishops and barons, upon receipt of this news, returned to Reading, where they spent the night.

Early on Sunday morning the chancellor sent William of Braose and a number of knights from his household, accompanied by a band of foreign mercenaries, to Count John to offer him bribes if he would support him. The chancellor must have taken a dim view indeed of his own position to be forced to solicit the support of Count John, whom he had rightly considered the chief threat to his power. John was never one to be offended by the offer of money, but matters had gone too far now for him to be able to change sides even if he had wanted to. Furthermore, he was rejoicing in the thought that the chancellor's downfall was now imminent, and he was unwilling to jeopardise his own position by siding with him.

At noon Bishop Reginald of Bath celebrated Mass. In the course of the ceremony the two archbishops and the bishops, wearing their mitres and holding their pastoral staffs, with lighted candles 'laid a dreadful curse on all who gave counsel or help or orders that the archbishop of York should be dragged out of church, treated unworthily, and cast into prison, and they cut them off from the fellowship of Holy Mother Church, mentioning by name Aubrey of Marney and Alexander Puintel'. Bishop Hugh of Nonant explained the proceedings to the congregation and gave the reasons for the sentence that was being pronounced.

Late in the afternoon Longchamp's messengers went back to their master in Windsor Castle, accompanied by two knights sent by Count John and the barons. The knights bore not only John's refusal of the bribes offered him but also a stern summons to the chancellor to come to the meeting at a safe place near Windsor on the next day to hear the judgment that had been pronounced on him. If he did not come, they warned him, 'he could henceforth have no trust in them'.

On Monday morning, 7 October, the bishops and barons left Reading and crossed the Loddon. Count John, who proposed to spend the night in Staines, had his baggage sent on ahead of him under a strong guard, and those of the assembly who planned to go on to London after the conference did likewise. The party then rode on towards Windsor. The chancellor meanwhile had ventured forth from Windsor Castle with an armed escort. Before he had ridden far, one of his knights, Henry Bisset, who had been spying on the opposing party, dashed up with the news that Count John had set out to capture London.[1]

The chancellor was filled with terror by these tidings, and 'sparing neither horse nor spurs' he fled back to Windsor. He made hurried arrangements for the defence of the castle, crossed the Thames, and set out for London in the greatest confusion, in pursuit, as he thought, of Count John and his party.

When the bishops and barons learned of the chancellor's sudden flight they were at first thrown into confusion. 'And what shall we do now?' asked Bishop Reginald of Bath. 'Shall we go back to Reading?'

'Certainly not,' Bishop Hugh of Nonant replied, with a wit that was much admired. 'Let's go to London and buy some winter clothes.' Largely on the advice of the bishop of Coventry, the whole party set out on the road to Staines.[2]

Just outside London, where the two roads met, some of Count John's men encountered part of the chancellor's escort, and spirited fighting broke out. Ralph Beauchamp, whom the chancellor had knighted, wounded Roger of Planes, John's justiciar, so gravely that he died at the end of the month. John's men, however, won the fight, and the chancellor's party fled to the Tower.[3]

As soon as he reached the city Longchamp had Henry of Cornhill, his loyal supporter, summon the leading citizens to the Guildhall. The chancellor urged them to shut the gates in the face of Count John, who, he assured them, was planning to seize the realm. The citizens burst into violent arguments, Henry of Cornhill siding with the chancellor and Richard son of Reiner, who, with Henry, had been joint sheriff of London and Middlesex in the year ending at Michaelmas 1189, declaring that they might do great damage to the city if they shut the gates against the old

[1] Gerald of Wales, op. cit., pp. 400–3; Diceto, Vol. II, pp. 98–9; Richard of Devizes, pp. 45–6.

[2] Gerald of Wales, op. cit., pp. 403–4.

[3] Diceto, Vol. II, p. 99; *Gesta*, Vol. II, pp. 212–13.

king's son and the new king's brother and heir. Rather, he said, they should go out to meet him and find out what his intentions really were.

Archbishop Geoffrey had not wasted his time whilst he was in London immediately after his release; he had presented his case so effectively to the Londoners that he had succeeded in stirring up a great deal of enthusiasm for himself and of hatred for the chancellor. This now bore its fruit. The party favouring Count John prevailed, and the whole assembly turned upon the chancellor, calling him a disturber of the realm and a traitor.

Longchamp and his followers took refuge in the Tower and prepared for a siege, while the citizens went out with lanterns and torches to welcome Count John, who arrived with his party after nightfall. John was escorted in triumph to the house of Richard son of Reiner, where he spent the night.

The support of the Londoners was essential if either side was to gain its objective, and no doubt his host explained to Count John that evening what the price of their support would be. The citizens meanwhile set a close guard over the Tower, both by land and by water, to prevent the chancellor's escape.

On Tuesday morning the bells of St. Paul's were rung to summon the citizens, and a meeting of all the bishops, barons, and leading citizens was held in the cathedral. Again the archbishop of York described his ignominious treatment at the hands of the chancellor; again the archbishop of Rouen told how the chancellor had scorned the king's orders and refused to listen to the archbishop's advice; again the representative of Bishop Hugh of Le Puiset told how the chancellor had ousted the bishop of Durham from his place amongst the justiciars and from his earldom; and again the other justiciars told how the chancellor had ignored them in his conduct of the government. Hugh of Nonant summed up all the complaints so effectively that the assembly declared with one voice: 'We will not have this man to rule over us!'[1]

Archbishop Walter and William Marshal then exhibited the king's letters directing them to depose the chancellor if he should refuse to be guided by their advice and should do harm to the realm. Acting on the authority of these letters, the assembly deposed William Longchamp and declared that Walter of

[1] Richard of Devizes, pp. 46, 48; Diceto, Vol. II, p. 99.

Coutances was chief justiciar in his stead. Going beyond their instructions, they gave Count John the title of 'governor of the whole realm' (*rector totius regni*), according to Richard of Devizes, and the custody of all the castles he wanted.

Assuming that this report is correct, it is difficult to see just what John's title meant. Authority to govern in the king's name was vested in the chief justiciar, acting with the advice of his fellow justiciars, and John's title probably meant no more than that as the king's brother and presumptive heir he was to have a general and intentionally vague oversight over the course of affairs. He took precedence over the chief justiciar, however, for in a final concord made before the King's Court on 30 November 1191 he was listed before the archbishop of Rouen.[1] Richard of Devizes also says that new itinerant justiciars, keepers of the Exchequer, and castellans of castles were put in office, but this probably means only that Longchamp's avowed partisans were deprived of office.

Eleven sheriffs changed office, but one cannot be sure that in every case the displaced man was a partisan of the chancellor. His brother Henry, of course, was replaced as sheriff of Herefordshire by William of Braose, and Osbert Longchamp was replaced in Yorkshire by Hugh Bardolf, who in turn relinquished Warwickshire and Leicestershire to Hugh of Nonant. Bishop Hugh evidently felt that his previous renunciation of secular office was no longer binding, since Archbishop Baldwin, to whom he had made the promise, had died. All the custodies that Bishop Godfrey of Winchester had bought and paid for were given back to him, and Bishop Hugh of Le Puiset was again recognised as earl of Northumberland.

As the price of their support the citizens of London exacted from the magnates the recognition of their commune, which the nobles and even the bishops were forced to swear to support. Exactly what form the commune took at this particular time we are not told, but it was essentially a revolutionary form of government whereby the burghers freed themselves from the control of the king and his justiciars and set up an independent government. The citizens not only elected their mayor and alderman, but presumably chose all their other officers as well. They would thus administer their own law in their own courts, without any

[1] *Rotuli Curiae Regis*, ed. Sir Francis Palgrave (2 vols., London, 1835), Vol. I, p. cv.

supervision by the justiciars, who would normally hear all cases beyond the competence of the folk-moot.

Society was organised at this time primarily on the basis of land-holding and the obligations arising therefrom. Three classes of men, however, did not fit into that scheme, which looks so orderly at first glance: the Jews, whose position has already been discussed; the merchants, many of whom either lived in London or used it as their base of operations; and the artisans, craftsmen, and labourers in towns and cities. Trade was expanding rapidly at this period, and the merchants felt that their wealth and importance entitled them to a voice in the government. It seems fairly clear that the establishment of a commune was obtained primarily by the merchants, perhaps with the help of the workmen dependent upon them.

The granting of corporate liberties was directly contrary to the policy of Henry II, who had insisted on keeping cities under his immediate control, both so that he might exercise a closer supervision over them and so that he might wring more money from them in the form of tallages and gifts. Not for a million marks, Richard of Devizes says, would either Henry or Richard have granted this commune or, rather, conspiracy, and the horror with which he speaks of it shows that it was indeed the outcome of a revolutionary movement, rather than a mere bargaining for such limited liberties as the charters of the time granted to certain cities and boroughs.[1]

Finally, Count John swore fealty to King Richard, his brother. In turn, the two archbishops, the bishops, the barons, and the citizens of London took oaths of fealty to King Richard and to John, saving their fealty to the king, and swore 'that they would receive John as their lord and king, if the king should die without issue'.

While his fate was thus being decided by his enemies, Longchamp prepared for a siege in the Tower. Although large sums had been spent in repairing that fortress, the chancellor had apparently neglected to lay in provisions for a long siege, a contingency that he would have regarded as extremely remote in the days of his prosperity. Realising that he could not hold out for

[1] Richard of Devizes, pp. 48-9; Diceto, Vol. II, p. 99; *Gesta*, Vol. II, p. 214; J. H. Round: *The Commune of London* (London, 1899), pp. 219-60; Henri Pirenne: 'Northern Towns and Their Commerce', Chap. XV of *The Cambridge Medieval History*, Vol. VI, pp. 518-19.

long, the chancellor sent messengers to find out on what terms he might surrender.

On Wednesday morning four bishops, the venerable Hugh of Lincoln, Richard of London, Godfrey of Winchester, and Hugh of Nonant, came to the Tower to inform him of the decision the council had made. Longchamp was so overcome by the realisation of his utter ruin that he fell to the ground in a faint and had to be revived by cold water thrown in his face.

When he had recovered, he declared that he would neither surrender the castles nor resign his seal of office. The four bishops pointed out that he had no choice in the matter; the decision had already been made.

'If I were to turn over the castles of the realm to anyone except the king,' Longchamp argued, 'I could rightly be accused of treason, and no member of my family has ever been called a traitor.'

'Don't talk to us about your family, but do what must be done', Hugh of Nonant replied. 'Don't put off what you cannot avoid; you're not the first traitor in your family, by any means.'

Longchamp refused to accept the sentence of the council. The bishops left, to report his refusal, and Count John had the Tower more closely invested. In the course of the day the chancellor sent many messengers, with rich gifts and the promise of yet more, to Count John. John had already gained his object; he had control of many of the disputed castles, and he had been recognised as Richard's heir. He was on the verge of leaving the city and letting the negotiations between the council and the chancellor fall through, but Hugh of Nonant and Archbishop Geoffrey persuaded him not to desert them when the end was in sight.

With this last hope dashed, Longchamp, towards the end of an arduous day of negotiations, gave in to the entreaties of his advisors, recognised the hopelessness of his position, and sent his brother Osbert and his chamberlain, Matthew, as hostages for his appearance on the morrow.[1]

Longchamp's downfall was so certain that even while these negotiations were going on, the justiciars, the bishop of London, and the monks of Westminster Abbey set to work to undo one

[1] Gerald of Wales, op. cit., pp. 405-6; Richard of Devizes, pp. 49-51; *Gesta*, Vol. II, pp. 213-14; Diceto, Vol. II, p. 99.

of his most cherished schemes, the advancement of his brother. Walter, the abbot of Westminster, had died on 27 September 1190, and the chancellor had induced the monks to allow his brother, who was a monk at Caen, to take up residence in the abbey, with the promise that they would elect him abbot.

While Longchamp was being reduced to submission, the justiciars and Bishop Richard went to Westminster. In their presence the monks gladly elected their prior, William Postard, as abbot, utterly disregarding the promise they had been forced to make to Longchamp. Bishop Richard led the new abbot to the high altar and seated him in the abbot's chair. On the following Sunday the bishop blessed Abbot William, walked with him in the magnificent procession that was staged at Westminster in his honour, and sat with him at the abbot's table for the great feast that followed.[1]

Early on Thursday morning, 10 October, the bishops and barons and the people of London assembled in an open field outside the walls, to the east of the Tower, and the chancellor came to them to make his submission. The leading men were in the centre of the dense throng, surrounded by the other barons in a circle, with some ten thousand Londoners pressing eagerly around to see the show. Hugh of Nonant, proud, as always, of his reputation as an orator, spoke first and summed up all the charges that had been made against the chancellor at the previous meeting in St. Paul's.

'It does not please us,' he concluded, 'nor is it fitting that you should rule any longer in the kingdom. You will be content with your bishopric and with the three castles that we will allow you and with the shadow of a great name. You will give satisfactory hostages that you will surrender all the remaining castles and that you will not cause any disturbance or stir up any tumults, and then you will be free to go where you will.'

Many others then spoke against the chancellor. The verdict of the assembly was unanimous: he was to be deprived of his offices as chancellor and as chief justiciar and he was to surrender all the castles he had seized after the king had left England. Only the three castles that Richard had given him before his departure, those of Dover, Cambridge, and Hereford, which were so far from each other thay they could not serve as a threat to the peace,

[1] Richard of Devizes, pp. 25, 39, 54; Diceto, Vol. II, pp. 100-1.

were to be left to him, and even those three were to be committed to castellans appointed by the justiciars.

After everyone had had his say, the chancellor attempted to defend himself. He declared that Archbishop Geoffrey had been seized without his knowledge or orders, and he offered to prove his assertion in either a civil or an ecclesiastical court. Concerning the escheats and the marriages of the king's wards, which he was accused of manipulating for his own advantage, he said that he had in every case acted with the advice and consent of the justiciars whom the king had associated with him. Furthermore, he said, he was ready to account to the last farthing for all his expenditures. He would yield to force and give hostages to ensure that he would surrender the castles.

'Finally,' he said, 'let all of you know that I do not lay aside any of the offices that the king entrusted to me. You, being many, have overcome me because you are stronger than I, and I, the king's chancellor and justiciar of the realm, whom you have sentenced contrary to all form of law, bow before superior strength.'

Longchamp then surrendered the keys to the Tower, gave three hostages, his brothers Osbert and Henry and his chamberlain, Matthew, as securities for the surrender of the remaining castles in his possession, and swore that he would not leave the country till the castles had been turned over to the justiciars.[1]

No more striking testimony could be given to the sense of collective responsibility for the good order and government of the kingdom that the barons of England and particularly the justiciars had developed in the last half-century than the orderly way in which they dealt with this crisis. The king was so far away and had left such conflicting instructions that for the time being the barons were on their own and left to their own initiative. William Longchamp, although he was backed by the king's authority, had shown himself unfit to govern, since his every action was devoted to his own aggrandisement rather than to the good of the country. Instead of acting each for himself, as their forebears had done when the royal power under King Stephen was similarly eclipsed, the barons acted with due deliberation, weighed the best interests of the country and what they could make of the king's intentions amidst the welter of contradictory

[1] Richard of Devizes, pp. 51–2; Diceto, Vol. II, p. 100.

orders, and acted as they thought the king would have them do if he had been present.

The functions of the Great Council at this time are difficult to determine with any degree of precision, for few records have been left of its proceedings. Every baron had the obligation to give the king his advice when it was called for, and all important decisions were made by the king in the presence of his council, presumably after the matter had been debated amongst them. That the members of the council were not a mere passive audience to hear the king's decrees is shown, for example, by St. Thomas's successful defiance of the king over the matter of the sheriff's aid in 1163.[1] That they had a high degree of initiative and were accustomed to making balanced judgments on the conduct of affairs is well demonstrated by the competent way in which they handled this crisis. Even more important, they gained a sense of solidarity and the experience of working together on matters of great importance that furnished a pattern for later events. The barons as a body acted independently of the king for the better government of the realm, and the memory of their success on this occasion may well have been with them when they organised their successful resistance to King John.

Although the events of the summer and autumn of 1191 are frequently referred to as the struggle between Count John and William Longchamp, such usage is more convenient than accurate. In so far as we can tell from the surviving records, many of which are highly prejudiced to begin with, the struggle was not so much one between John and Longchamp as it was one between Longchamp on the one side and almost all the leading men of England on the other. John, as the man of highest secular rank in the realm, the king's brother and heir presumptive, would naturally be the figurehead, if nothing more, about which the opposition to Longchamp would gather.

If John had supported Longchamp, as he might well have done if the chancellor had troubled to solicit the count's support instead of working against him, the two together, each in his respective sphere of influence, might have been invincible. The key to the chancellor's downfall, as all the chroniclers agree, was his refusal to work with any of the other chief men of the king-

[1] *Materials for the History of Thomas Becket*, ed. J. C. Robertson and J. B. Sheppard (7 vols., Rolls Series 67, 1875-85), Vol. II, p. 374.

dom and his insistence upon being supreme in every sphere of activity. He had had every opportunity to strengthen himself by an alliance with a number of powerful men in turn, but because such an alliance would have meant a sharing and lessening of his authority he had scorned them all. If he had left the North to the bishop of Durham, as the king had ordered, and been content with governing the rest of the country; if, again as the king had ordered, he had associated the justiciars, with all their experience and knowledge both of the country and of the workings of the government, with him; if he had made the best of the king's arrangements and allied himself with Count John, who held the Southwest and the west Midlands; if he had been willing eventually to relinquish his post as the highest-ranking cleric to Archbishop Geoffrey and to be content with supreme authority in the state: if he had done any of these things and thus bolstered up his position by the support of any one of these powerful men, even at the cost of some part of his almost unlimited authority, he might well have survived his own unpopularity.

As it was, he had, in the jealous defence of his powers, made enemies of many of the great men of the realm and of every class. His persecution of Archbishop Geoffrey was in itself enough to alienate all the clergy and most of the barons; coming as the climax of two years of overbearing arrogance and insatiable rapacity, it furnished the occasion for all his enemies to unite against him.

It is difficult to determine how influential a part Count John played in these events. Although, at the urging of Bishop Hugh of Coventry, he issued the summons to the meeting at Reading, it may be that he was used as an instrument, because of his rank and position, by others. No one bishop, on his own authority, could issue such a summons, and Archbishop Geoffrey, the only cleric in a position to do so, may have felt that since he was newly consecrated and had not yet been installed at York, his brother John was the proper person to avenge Geoffrey's wrongs. On the other hand, there was no one baron of sufficient importance to convene such a council. Many of the most important men had accompanied Richard on the Crusade; of those who remained in England, the earls of Warenne and of Arundel, the oldest and most conservative, sided with Longchamp, for reasons that are not now apparent, and none of the others was in a position to lead the rest. The associate justiciars were logically the ones to summon the meeting, but they seem to have been so cowed by Longchamp that they did not dare, until they were supported by the other barons, to voice their opposition to him.

John was still a young man of around twenty-five. Although he had been his father's favourite son, he had had little practical experience. His expedition to Ireland in 1185, the most important event in his life up to this time, certainly could inspire no confidence in his abilities either military or administrative. When he allied himself with his brother Geoffrey of Brittany and invaded Poitou in 1184 in a hare-brained scheme to take Richard's land away from him, they had been ignominiously routed. John had shown himself to be both foolish and incompetent, and everyone in England knew it. As a figurehead round which the opposition to Longchamp might rally, however, he had the rank and position to lend respectability to the enterprise. His character was apparently too well known for his confederates to advance him to a position of power; the high-sounding title of '*summus rector totius regni*' was a reward that carried little authority. On the other hand, he gained the custody of a number of disputed castles, and, most important of all, he was recognised as his brother's heir. That he behaved with such unusual circumspection may have been due more to the influence of the canny bishop of Coventry, his chief advisor, than to his own wisdom.

One is tempted to see in John's conduct at this time some of the subtlety, cunning, and duplicity that characterised him in later days. It looks almost as though he had set about deliberately to overthrow Longchamp and had accomplished his ends with wisdom and restraint. In view of his conduct during the next few years, when he blindly threw away all the advantages he had gained and resorted to treachery as obvious as it was futile, one should beware of crediting John with more wisdom than he possessed at this time.

Once the summons had been issued, Archbishop Geoffrey played a more active part than did his brother. It is not recorded that John addressed either the meeting at Reading or the one in London, whereas Geoffrey recited his complaints twice at Reading and once at London, and at both assemblies he was the first and leading speaker. Once the meetings had been organised,

Geoffrey's story of the barbarous treatment he had received at Longchamp's hands served as the spark that ignited the resentment of his hearers against the hated chancellor.

The one who benefited the most from the actions of the assembly was Walter of Coutances, archbishop of Rouen, for he succeeded in displacing his rival and taking over his position as chief justiciar. With Longchamp out of the way, it is possible that Archbishop Walter hoped to be elected archbishop of Canterbury, which would greatly increase his power and importance. Since he had the most to gain, one may assume that he would be the most active, at least behind the scenes, in organising the barons against Longchamp. He had the king's letter authorising his participation in the government, which Longchamp had contemptuously rejected, and his main task was to induce the bishops and barons to recognise the authenticity of that letter and the one addressed to William Marshal and to act on those instructions. At both meetings, after the others had declared their grievances against the chancellor, Walter produced the letters, told how Longchamp had ignored them, and left his hearers to determine what course they should take, now that the king's wishes had been clearly made known to them.

Two bishops, finally, played important parts in the proceedings. Hugh of Avalon, the Carthusian bishop of Lincoln, was the most highly respected man in the kingdom, venerated by all classes for his sanctity of life, his devotion to duty, and his fearlessness. That he should have excommunicated William Longchamp as soon as he heard of his treatment of Archbishop Geoffrey shows that the chancellor had forfeited the respect and support of the more responsible members of the episcopate. Bishop Hugh joined the assembly at Reading, not because he wanted to play politics or to meddle with matters that did not concern him, but because his sense of duty and of the responsibilities of his position led him to believe that a crisis had arisen that forced him to do his best for the good of the country. What part he played in the negotiations after the council had assembled we do not know, but we may be sure that his presence alone would set the seal of respectability on the proceedings.

Hugh of Nonant, bishop of Coventry, played a different and less creditable part. He carried the news of Geoffrey's arrest to Count John and urged him to take immediate action. Living up to his reputation as an orator, he translated the king's letters and no doubt commented upon them at the meeting on Saturday, 5 October; he preached at the Mass on the next day, at which the bishops pronounced their sentences of excommunication; he harangued the assembly at St. Paul's on Tuesday, and he took a leading part in the remaining negotiations. He was Count John's leading advisor, and he was probably the brain behind John's plans. His actions seem to have been prompted by a mixture of ambition and of hatred for Longchamp, once his friend and now his detested enemy.

After his public defeat, humiliation, and deposition, Longchamp spent the night in the Tower, and on the following day he went to Bermondsey. On Saturday, 12 October, Gilbert, bishop of Rochester, and Henry of Cornhill, sheriff of Kent, escorted him to Dover, one of the three castles that he was allowed to keep.[1]

On the following Thursday, 17 October, crushed by his disgrace and heedless of the danger to which he exposed his brothers, who were being held as hostages, William Longchamp, contrary to his oath, attempted to leave England. Hugh of Nonant wrote an open letter describing with malicious glee the adventures that befell him. This letter, a masterpiece of sheer spite, was so greatly admired that it was either copied verbatim into the chronicles of the time or paraphrased by the historians.[2] Soon the whole country was rocking with laughter at the ludicrous end of Longchamp's career in England.

William Longchamp, bishop of Ely, papal legate, chancellor and formerly chief justiciar of the realm, was so anxious to get out of the country that he disguised himself as a woman, in a long green gown, with a hood pulled down over his face, and stood on the shore at Dover with a length of cloth, as though for sale, draped over one arm and a staff in his hand, while his servants tried to find a ship in which he might cross the Channel.

As he was thus waiting, a fisherman, wet and cold from the sea, came up and attempted to warm himself by embracing the chancellor. With his left arm about Longchamp's neck, the fisherman attempted certain familiarities with his right hand that

[1] Richard of Devizes, p. 52; Diceto, Vol. II, p. 100.

[2] *Gesta*, Vol. II, pp. 215-20; Howden, Vol. III, pp. 141-7; Newburgh, Vol. I, p. 343; Gervase, Vol. I, pp. 507-8; Diceto, Vol. II, p. 101; Gerald of Wales: *De Vita Galfridi*, pp. 410-12.

revealed the chancellor's sex. When the fisherman tried to summon his mates to admire this marvel of a man masquerading as a woman, Longchamp's servants succeeded in driving him away.

Next came a woman, who fingered the length of linen cloth on his arm and asked the price. Since he knew no English, he was unable to answer. The woman called to one of her friends, and together they pulled back his hood and revealed the face, dark and closely shaven, of a man. The women summoned a mob to help them stone this monster, and a crowd immediately assembled. His servants were unable to rescue him. The mob dragged him through the streets of Dover, spitting on him and stoning him, and held him prisoner in a cellar.

After a week, Count John ordered that he be released. On Tuesday, 29 October, Longchamp took ship to Flanders. Archbishop Walter and the other justiciars promptly seized the temporalities of the bishopric of Ely and deposited the revenue in the Treasury.[1]

Archbishop Geoffrey meanwhile had become something of a national hero. On his triumphal journey to York to take possession at last of his see, he passed through Northampton, where he had gone to school in his youth. The clergy and people went out to meet him, 'and he was received with a most beautiful procession'. When he reached York all the clergy and people turned out to welcome him, and on All Saints' Day, 1 November, he was 'solemnly and magnificently' enthroned in his cathedral.[2]

Once he was duly installed, Geoffrey set to work to reduce his unruly suffragan, Hugh of Le Puiset, bishop of Durham, to submission. At the time when he was protesting against Geoffrey's election, Bishop Hugh had secured from Pope Clement III a writ releasing him from the obligation to make his profession of obedience to his new metropolitan, since he had long ago made such a profession to Archbishop William at the time of his consecration in 1153.

When Clement's successor, Celestine III, had confirmed Geoffrey's election and ordered his consecration, he had cancelled Bishop Hugh's exemption and ordered him to make a profession of canonical obedience to the new archbishop. If Hugh should

[1] Diceto, Vol. II, p. 101; *Gesta*, Vol. II, p. 225.
[2] Gerald of Wales: *De Vita Galfridi*, p. 410.

either refuse or delay to do so, the pope authorised Geoffrey to compel him to obedience by canonical censures. As soon as he received these orders from the pope, Hugh appealed and laid himself, his cathedral, his diocese, and all the churches and clergy of the diocese 'under the protection of the lord pope and the Roman Church', and he renewed his appeal as soon as he learned of Geoffrey's consecration.[1]

Geoffrey had no intention of being fobbed off by such delaying tactics as an appeal against a direct order from the pope. He had the order, the latest document in the series, and he proceeded to act on it. Three times he ordered Bishop Hugh to come to York and make his profession of obedience. When Hugh refused Geoffrey publicly excommunicated him 'with candles burning and bells ringing' in York Minster. Hugh declared that the sentence was void, both because he had been consecrated by the pope himself and because it had been pronounced after he had appealed to Rome. Paying no heed to the sentence, he continued to celebrate Mass and renewed his appeals to Rome.[2]

To show that he meant business, Geoffrey had the altars smashed at which Bishop Hugh had celebrated Mass and the chalices broken with which any other priest had celebrated in the bishop's presence. Count John, who was not one to trouble himself about such matters, spent Christmas with his kinsman at Hugh's manor of Howden. Geoffrey then declared that John and all others who had eaten and drunk with the excommunicated bishop shared his sentence.[3]

While the archbishop of York was thus dealing manfully with his problems, the archbishop of Rouen as chief justiciar took up the matter of electing an archbishop of Canterbury. It will be remembered that although the king had ordered Archbishop Walter to supervise the election and had recommended Archbishop William of Montreale for the post, Longchamp had refused to allow Walter to go to Canterbury. On 10 October, the very day of Longchamp's deposition, Archbishop Walter, with the consent of Count John and of the other justiciars, wrote to Geoffrey, prior of Christ Church at Canterbury, to order him to come to London on 22 October with twelve of 'the more

[1] *Gesta*, Vol. II, p. 209; Howden, Vol. III, pp. 74, 169.
[2] *Gesta*, Vol. II, pp. 225-6.
[3] *Gesta*, Vol. II, p. 235; Howden, Vol. III, pp. 169-70.

discreet monks', armed with letters from the convent authorising them to elect an archbishop.[1]

On the appointed day, Prior Geoffrey and his fellows appeared before the chief justiciar and the assembled bishops. When Archbishop Walter asked him if they were ready to elect the king's nominee, the prior stoutly declared that it would be a disgrace to God and the Church, the king and the realm to elect an unknown foreigner to the highest ecclesiastical position in England. This reply no doubt pleased his audience and especially Archbishop Walter, who had some hopes of being transferred from a poor and unimportant see to the most influential one in Christendom. The monks thereupon went back to Canterbury to wait 'until we shall feel the help of the Lord upon us.'[2]

The monks of Canterbury meanwhile were undergoing pressure from other quarters. Savaric, archdeacon of Northampton, was related both to the Emperor Henry VI and to Reginald, bishop of Bath. He had been sent to the king, while Richard was in Sicily, on some sort of official business, and he had made use of the occasion to secure from the king a letter containing 'his consent, and more than consent' that he should be promoted to whatever bishopric he might be elected to. Savaric sent this letter to his kinsman, Bishop Reginald, and went on to Rome, where he made himself agreeable to such members of the papal court as might be useful to him.[3]

When Savaric learned of the vacancy at Canterbury he conceived a plan for advancing both himself and Bishop Reginald. Since he could hardly hope to be elected archbishop of Canterbury, he formed the scheme of having his cousin Reginald elected archbishop. That would leave the see of Bath vacant, and with the help of Reginald, the king's letter, and such other pressure as he could bring to bear, he could be fairly sure of being elected bishop of Bath.

As a result of Savaric's efforts, both the emperor and the king of France wrote to the monks of Canterbury concerning the approaching election. Henry VI urged them to follow the

[1] *Epistolae Cantuarienses*, p. 348.

[2] Gervase, Vol. I, p. 508.

[3] William Stubbs, introd. to *Epistolae Cantuarienses*, p. lxxxvii, n. 1; Richard of Devizes, p. 29; David Knowles: *The Episcopal Colleagues of Archbishop Thomas Becket* (Cambridge, 1951), pp. 18-22, 159.

advice of his 'beloved kinsman, the archdeacon Savaric, who is most devoted to your church'. Philip II advised them, at the recommendation of his faithful friend Savaric, to elect Reginald, a wise and discreet man whom Philip's father, Louis VII, had loved.[1]

On 9 November the chief justiciar wrote to the monks to inform them that he, the other justiciars, and Count John would come to Canterbury on Monday, 2 December, to supervise the election. At the same time, Richard, bishop of London and dean of the province, wrote to the suffragans of the southern province in the same vein. On 27 November, the Thursday before the election was scheduled, Count John, Archbishop Walter, and the bishops of Bath, Rochester, Hereford, and St. David's arrived in Canterbury. The monks, who claimed to have the exclusive right of electing the archbishop and who jealously fought the bishops' claim to share in the election, were convinced that this group had come in order to catch them unawares and force the bishops' nominee on them.

While the bishops were wrangling over which of them had the highest rank and therefore the deciding voice in the election, since both Richard of London and Godfrey of Winchester, the dean and precentor of the province, respectively, were detained in London on official business, Prior Geoffrey and his monks, who had probably already made their decision, forestalled the bishops by acclaiming Bishop Reginald as their choice. They seized him, dragged him, 'crying, weeping, and protesting', from the chapter house into the cathedral, and seated him on the throne of St. Augustine. The monks chanted the *Te Deum* and then made their profession of obedience to their new archbishop. Walter of Coutances, pale and trembling at the ruin of his hopes, followed them into the cathedral, protested against the election, and announced that he was appealing to Rome against it, and the other bishops joined in his appeal.[2]

Bishop Reginald had been a firm friend of the monks in their differences with Archbishop Baldwin. Although they would no doubt have preferred to elect one of their own members, such an action would have aroused a storm of protest from the bishops,

[1] *Epistolae Cantuarienses*, pp. 350-1.

[2] Gervase, Vol. I, pp. 510-11; Diceto, Vol. II, p. 103; *Gesta*, Vol. II, p. 226; Richard of Devizes, p. 55.

whereas by electing a bishop who was not a monk they forestalled the opposition. Archbishop Walter's appeal was based on his disappointed hopes, and the bishops probably joined in more through resentment at not having even been consulted by the monks than because they disapproved of their choice.

Not content with appealing to Rome, Archbishop Walter summoned Reginald and Prior Geoffrey to London. On 2 December, in the presence of many of the leading men of the realm, he gave them a thorough grilling. Both of them stood firm, however; Reginald declared that he accepted the election, and Geoffrey that the convent stood by their choice. They both appealed to Rome, and Geoffrey and his monks wrote to the pope to defend their actions and to ask him to approve the election and to send the pallium to their new archbishop. Walter of Coutances refused to turn any of the temporalities over to Reginald, but Reginald immediately assumed all the spiritual functions of the archbishop of Canterbury.

He was not long to enjoy them. He went to Bath to arrange his affairs there and to recommend his kinsman Savaric to the good offices of the prior and convent. He gave them the king's letter consenting to Savaric's election, and they duly elected Savaric bishop of Bath. On his way back to Canterbury Reginald fell ill at his manor of Dogmeresfield, in northeastern Hampshire, on Christmas Eve. On Christmas Day, after hearing Mass at dawn and receiving Holy Communion, he became so much worse that his life was despaired of. In his extremity he dictated the following letter:

> Reginald, by the grace of God bishop of Bath and the unworthy archbishop-elect of the most holy church of Canterbury, sends greetings, love, and his blessing to Prior Geoffrey and the convent of Christ Church at Canterbury.
>
> I do not think that God wants me to be your archbishop, but I want and long to be a monk of your fellowship. Bring me the habit as quickly as you can to Dogmeresfield, my lord prior and subprior, with any others you may choose. Farewell, and of your goodness pray for me without ceasing, without ceasing.[1]

Before Prior Geoffrey could reach his archbishop, however, Reginald died on 27 December. Shortly before the end,

[1] *Epistolae Cantuarienses*, p. 355.

Walter, prior of Bath, who had accompanied him on the journey, clothed his beloved bishop in the monk's habit, and Reginald made his profession as a monk of Canterbury.[1]

[1] *Epistolae Cantuarienses*, pp. 354-5; Richard of Devizes, pp. 55-7; Gervase, Vol. I, pp. 511-12; *Gesta*, Vol. II, pp. 226-7.

IV

1192

THE year 1192 opened with a resounding series of excommunications. William Longchamp had of course sent messengers to the pope to complain of the treatment he had received. Celestine III, on 2 December 1191, wrote an open letter to the bishops of England, expressing his horror at the reports he had received of the outrages that Count John 'and certain others' had perpetrated on William Longchamp, bishop of Ely, whom the pope referred to as 'the legate of the apostolic see', as though his office had never lapsed. 'If Count John or anyone else has laid violent hands on the bishop, or seized him, or extorted any oath from him by violence, or held him in captivity, or in any way changed the state of the realm from the tranquillity in which the king had disposed it at his departure', the pope ordered the bishops to assemble and with candles burning and bells ringing to excommunicate publicly the aforesaid count and all his advisors, accomplices, and partisans.

This letter was sent to Longchamp for delivery in England. On the strength of it, Longchamp, styling himself 'by the grace of God bishop of Ely and legate of the apostolic see, and the lord king's chancellor', wrote to 'his venerable brother and dearest friend', Bishop Hugh of Lincoln, ordering him to call together all the bishops and carry out the orders of the pope's mandate. He directed that the excommunication of Count John be put off till Quinquagesima Sunday, 16 February, to give him a chance to repent of his wicked ways. The chancellor then gave a list of those whom the pope had excommunicated and he himself, the pope's legate, had denounced. The roster included Archbishop Walter of Coutances, the bishops of Winchester and Coventry, the four justiciars, Gerard of Camville, John Marshal, and Stephen Ridel, Count John's chancellor.

A special sentence was reserved for the bishop of Coventry,

who had disgraced his office by word and deed, who had faithfully promised Archbishop Baldwin that he would not act as sheriff and yet continued to do so, and who was the manifest promoter and author of all the disruption of the realm, a disturber of the peace, and a public advocate against the royal dignity and well-being. He was to be strictly avoided by all men, so that a sheep so diseased might not henceforth corrupt and soil God's flock.

Neither the saintly Bishop Hugh nor any other of the bishops paid the slightest attention to these sentences of excommunication launched by the pope and his legate.[1]

Hugh of Le Puiset, bishop of Durham, appeared to be flourishing under the excommunication that his archbishop had pronounced, and he showed no signs of repentance. On Candlemas Day, 2 February, Archbishop Geoffrey proclaimed in his cathedral and had the sentence published throughout his diocese that not only was Bishop Hugh excommunicated because he had refused to obey his metropolitan but also that the sentence was extended to all those, both clerk and lay, who ate or drank with him or sold him anything or received him under their roof or had any communication whatever with him. In spite of all this, Bishop Hugh bore himself bravely and merrily and prosecuted his appeal to the pope.[2]

Whilst the clergy were thus amusing themselves, matters of considerable moment were under way in France. King Philip II had deserted the crusade and sailed for home at the beginning of the previous August. He arrived in France in December and began at once to plot against his fellow-crusader Richard with all the hatred of a coward for a brave and fearless man who had publicly shown his contempt for the coward. Although he had sworn, before leaving the Holy Land, that he would not disturb any of Richard's lands and although those lands were under the protection of the holy see whilst Richard was on crusade, Philip nevertheless, shortly after his return, began to plan to invade Normandy, and only the refusal of his nobles to dishonour themselves by such conduct prevented him from launching a direct attack.[3]

[1] *Gesta*, Vol. II, pp. 221-5.
[2] Ibid., Vol. II, p. 237.
[3] Howden, Vol. III, p. 187.

Philip then started to work on Count John, whose faithlessness he well knew. The king of France sent an invitation to John to visit him and held out as bait the hand of his sister Alice and the promise to give John all of Richard's lands on that side of the Channel. The prospect of marrying Alice may not have been especially attractive to John, who was in any case already married, for Richard had been betrothed to Alice for over twenty years and had at last refused her, telling Philip that his sister had been King Henry's mistress and had borne a son by him.[1] The offer of Richard's lands, however, coming from Richard's overlord, was a strong temptation to John, who was not troubled either by any scruples about loyalty to his brother or by any doubts as to Philip's ability to keep his promise.

News of these negotiations, as well as of Philip's suspicious activity in arming and stocking his castles along the Norman border, reached Queen Eleanor, and she crossed over from Normandy to England, landing at Portsmouth on 11 February. She found her youngest son ready to sail from Southampton and exerted every effort to persuade him to abandon his designs. The queen called four successive meetings of the Great Council, at Windsor, Oxford, London, and Winchester, and at last she and the nobles succeeded in wringing a promise from him that he would stay in England, with the threat that if he crossed the Channel they would seize all his lands and castles. John consoled himself by persuading the castellans of Windsor and Wallingford to turn those castles over to him.[2]

With her son's treasonable designs checked for the time being, Queen Eleanor turned her attention to the squabbling clergy. When she had occasion to visit some of her manors within the diocese of Ely, the inhabitants told her of the misery in which they had been placed because of the quarrel between their bishop, William Longchamp, and the chief justiciar. Walter of Coutances had confiscated the revenues of the bishopric of Ely, and William Longchamp in retaliation had laid an interdict on the diocese. No Masses could be celebrated, the bodies of the dead lay unburied in the fields, and the wretched people suffered bitterly because of a quarrel in which they had no part.

Dropping her own affairs, 'for she was very merciful', the

[1] *Gesta*, Vol. II, p. 160.
[2] Richard of Devizes, pp. 58-61; *Gesta*, Vol. II, pp. 236-7.

queen hastened to London and ordered Archbishop Walter to restore his revenues to the bishop of Ely, who was then in Normandy, and to lift the sentence of excommunication that he had had proclaimed throughout the province of Rouen. Longchamp was then persuaded to lift the excommunication he had imposed upon Archbishop Walter and the justiciars and to revoke the sentence of interdict on the diocese of Ely.[1]

The queen then summoned Archbishop Geoffrey and Bishop Hugh of Durham to London in an effort to compose their quarrel. When they appeared before the queen, the chief justiciar, and most of the bishops shortly after Mid-Lent, 15 March, Bishop Hugh magnanimously offered to accept the verdict of the assembly. Archbishop Geoffrey, however, displayed his usual stubbornness and said that he would not submit to arbitration unless Bishop Hugh first came to York Minster and begged for absolution and submitted himself to his archbishop.

Hugh, of course, refused to accept such a condition and countered with the demand that Geoffrey publicly declare in York Minster that the sentences he had laid on Hugh were null and not to be observed. Geoffrey refused, and the quarrel was resumed with all its usual bitterness.

Archbishop Geoffrey had been something of a hero up to this time, but now he displayed an arrogance that cost him many supporters. In addition to his obdurate replies to the queen and the council, he caused his processional cross to be carried before him when he went from the New Temple, where he had taken up residence whilst he was in London, to Westminster to the deliberations of the council. Bishop Richard of London and the other bishops of the southern province declared that he had no right to have his cross carried before him in the province of Canterbury.

Bishop Richard swore that if he continued to do so they would break his cross into bits; indeed, they would already have done so if he had not been the son of King Henry and the brother of King Richard and a newly consecrated archbishop into the bargain. Bishop Richard then suspended the New Temple from all celebration of divine services and the ringing of bells for such time as Archbishop Geoffrey was present there. In marked contrast to his triumphs of the preceding autumn was Geoffrey's

[1] Richard of Devizes, pp. 59-60.

subdued return to York, and he made a special point of not having his cross carried before him as he left London.[1]

Count John's action in taking over the castles of Windsor and Wallingford had not gone unnoticed. At a meeting of the Great Council in London in March, probably the same meeting at which Archbishop Geoffrey and Bishop Hugh had appeared, a discussion was held concerning the means that should be taken to curb John. While the council was sitting, messengers arrived from William Longchamp, who had landed at Dover and was then staying at Dover Castle with Matthew of Clare and his wife Richeut, Longchamp's sister.

The messengers saluted the queen and the great men on Longchamp's behalf and announced that the chancellor, now confirmed as papal legate, had come back to arrange for the return to him of the offices and lands of which he had been deprived, a polite way of saying that he had come back in order to seize power once more.

For all their condemnation of John's presumption, the assembly decided that he had his uses as 'supreme governor of the whole realm'. They therefore sent urgent messages to him at Wallingford, where he was 'laughing at their futile gathering'. After listening to their humble supplications, John graciously went to London and appeared before the council. All their complaints against him were forgotten; the nobles pressed forward to greet him as the one man who could save them from the chancellor.

When they asked him for his advice, John replied: 'This chancellor neither fears the threats nor seeks the friendship of any or all of you, if he can only have my favour. He is to give me £700 within the week, if I will not meddle between you and him. You see that I need money; a word to the wise is enough.'

Although Richard of Devizes treats this matter rather as a joke, it is obvious that the prospect of an alliance between John, with the prestige of his rank and the power of his control over a wide section of the country, and William Longchamp, who still had the favour of the king and the support of the pope, offered a serious threat to the orderly government that had heen instituted during the preceding autumn.

The council gave in to John's blackmail and paid him £500 as the price of his neutrality. The queen, the justiciars, and the

[1] *Gesta*, Vol. II, p. 238.

bishops all wrote to Longchamp to proceed no farther but as he valued his life and limbs to leave England immediately. Without John's support the chancellor could hope to accomplish nothing; he therefore left England on 3 April.[1]

Hugh of Le Puiset, bishop of Durham, was recalled to public service during this spring to act as peace-maker in Normandy. Two cardinal legates during the preceding winter had attempted to enter Normandy in an effort to settle the quarrel between Archbishop Walter of Coutances and William Longchamp, but the constable of Gisors and the seneschal of Normandy, William son of Ralph, forbade them to enter the duchy. No papal legate, they stoutly declared, could enter Normandy without King Richard's permission. The common people supported the seneschal and turned out with sticks and clubs to drive the legates away. The cardinals gave up the idea of visiting Normandy, but they excommunicated the seneschal and the castellan and laid the duchy under interdict. They then took refuge with King Philip in Paris.

Queen Eleanor and the justiciars turned to Bishop Hugh, an experienced diplomat, and asked him to go to induce the cardinals to lift the sentences. To this flattering invitation Hugh replied that he would not leave England till the affairs of his friends in the diocese of York had been straightened out. Henry Marshal, dean of York, Bourchard of Le Puiset, the treasurer, two canons, Hugh Murdac and Adam of Thornover, and Peter of Ros, archdeacon of Carlisle, had been excommunicated by Archbishop Geoffrey, who had confiscated the revenues attached to their offices. Hugh demanded that Geoffrey restore their revenues to them as a condition for his going to Normandy. The justiciars wrote to Geoffrey under the royal seal and ordered him to do so without delay. They also ordered William of Stuteville, one of the itinerant justiciars with large holdings in Yorkshire, either to see to it that Geoffrey obeyed their orders or else to confiscate the temporalities of the see of York.

Archbishop Geoffrey refused to surrender their revenues to the excommunicated men unless they first came barefoot to the cathedral, begged for absolution, and gave security that they would submit to the judgment of the canons of York. All of them except Henry Marshal complied, and the archbishop ab-

[1] Richard of Devizes, pp. 61-3; *Gesta*, Vol. II, pp. 239-40.

solved them, gave them the kiss of peace, led them to their stalls, and restored their revenues to them. Henry Marshal, however, remained obdurate. 'He spoke proudly against his lord the archbishop', who thereupon 'added curse to curse' and ordered that no services were to be celebrated and no bells rung in the city of York as long as Henry remained there.

With his honour thus satisfied, Bishop Hugh went to Paris to see the legates. The cardinals, however, refused to lift the sentence of interdict till the seneschal admitted them to Normandy, and William son of Ralph in turn refused to allow them to enter without King Richard's specific permission. Luckily, Pope Celestine intervened, lifted the sentences, and ordered his legates to keep out of Normandy.[1]

The envoys of both Archbishop Geoffrey and Bishop Hugh had meanwhile been busy at Rome, but Geoffrey, who was in any case hard pressed for money, neglected to send the customary gifts. In the spring of 1192, apparently, Pope Celestine wrote to Bishop Hugh of Lincoln, Bishop Gilbert of Rochester, and Abbot Benedict of Peterborough, ordering them to declare that the sentences Geoffrey had pronounced on Hugh of Le Puiset and others were null. He directed them, furthermore, to find out whether or not Geoffrey had demolished the altars at which Hugh had said Mass and had had the chalices broken that had been used in Masses celebrated in Hugh's presence. If Geoffrey had in fact done these things after Hugh had appealed to the pope, Celestine directed that the bishop of Durham should not make his profession of obedience to the archbishop of York.

The case was heard at Northampton, but on the advice of Bishop Hugh of Lincoln it was adjourned first till 1 September and again till 14 October. By this time everyone concerned had grown tired of the pointless haggling, and the bishop of Lincoln no doubt exercised his persuasiveness on the two disputants. The bishop of Durham, says Gervase of Canterbury, was 'recalled to the obedience of his metropolitan', which probably means that the bishop of Lincoln succeeded in working out a formula that salved the wounded dignity of both sides.[2]

These quarrels seemed even more childish than usual as a great uneasiness began to be felt concerning the king. Richard had

[1] *Gesta*, Vol. II, pp. 246-50; Richard of Devizes, pp. 57-8.

[2] Newburgh, Vol. I, p. 372; *Gesta*, Vol. II, pp. 170-2; Gervase, Vol. I, p. 513.

made a truce with Saladin on 2 September 1192 and had sailed from Acre on 8 October. The English crusaders began arriving home before Christmas and hoped to find their king waiting for them. When they were asked for news of Richard, they replied: 'We do not know, but we saw, at Brindisi in Apulia, the ship in which he had embarked.'[1]

[1] Howden, Vol. III, p. 194.

V

1193

WHILE all sorts of rumours were running through England as to what had happened to King Richard, the Emperor Henry VI, a cold and unscrupulous man, wrote to King Philip of France to inform him, with much satisfaction, that Richard had been captured in attempting to cross Austria and was now being held in prison near Vienna by Leopold, duke of Austria, whom Richard had mortally offended at the siege of Acre.[1]

The emperor did not attempt to conceal his joy; Richard was a prize of almost inestimable value. He was the brother-in-law of Henry the Lion, duke of Saxony and leader of the Welf faction against which the emperor was bitterly fighting; he was the ally of Tancred, king of Sicily, whose kingdom the emperor planned to take, and he was hated by King Philip, whom the emperor hoped to bring to subjection. Richard, in short, was the solution, Henry thought, to all his problems, and the emperor intended to use him to the utmost advantage. The fact that Richard, as a crusader, was under the Church's protection meant nothing to Henry; he had defied more than one pope in the past and laughed at their excommunications.

Philip lost no time in communicating the good news to Count John. John crossed over to Normandy in January and was met by William son of Ralph, the seneschal of Normandy, and many of the leading men of the duchy, who had heard rumours of the king's imprisonment. They begged John to come to a council to be held at Alençon, where they planned to discuss measures for setting the king free.

John replied: 'If you will receive me as your lord and swear fealty to me, I will go with you, and I will defend you before the king of France; if not, I will not go with you.'

[1] Howden, Vol. III, pp. 195-6.

The Normans would have nothing to do with such a treasonable plan, and John went on to Paris to meet Philip. He now accepted the many invitations that Philip had been extending. He became Philip's man, so it was reported in England, and swore fealty to him for Normandy and all King Richard's lands on that side of the Channel and for England as well; he swore that he would marry Alice, whom Richard had discarded, and give Philip Gisors and the Vexin, which Henry II had acquired as Alice's dowry. Philip in turn swore that he would help John with all his strength to take Richard's lands away from him.[1]

The chief justiciar meanwhile had acquired a copy of the emperor's letter to King Philip, and he had heard that Savaric, who had gone to Rome to be consecrated bishop of Bath on 19 September 1192, was then at the court of his kinsman the emperor, treating for Richard's release. He therefore called a meeting of the Great Council at Oxford on Sunday, 28 February, to consider what measures were to be taken.

When the council met they decided to send the abbots of Boxley, in Kent, and Robertsbridge, a Cistercian house in Sussex, to Germany to find out where the king was, for at this time they knew only that he had been captured near Vienna, and to discover whether the emperor might be induced to release him and on what terms. In view of the threatening news of John's activities across the Channel, they ordered that oaths of fealty to the king were to be taken throughout the country, and they took energetic measures to strengthen the defences of the kingdom.[2]

John and his ally were now assembling a fleet at Wissant in order to invade England with a multitude of mercenary soldiers. Some of their messengers in England were captured, and thus their plans became known to Queen Eleanor and the justiciars, who called out the fyrd in the southeast. 'By order of Queen Eleanor, who then ruled England, at Passiontide and Easter and thereafter nobles and common people, knights and peasants flew to arms and guarded the seacoast that looks towards Flanders.'

While his fleet was assembling, John landed secretly in England to raise troops from amongst the Welsh and the Scots. Although he succeeded in hiring a number of Welsh mercenaries, the king of Scots refused to have anything to do with his plans. The

[1] Howden, Vol. III, p. 204.
[2] Ibid., Vol. III, pp. 196-8; Diceto, Vol. II, pp. 105-6; Gervase, Vol. I, p. 514.

wisdom of Richard's treaty with King William in 1189 was now apparent, for William regarded the English king as his friend and would do nothing to harm him.

John installed his troops in the castles of Wallingford and Windsor, which he had seized during the previous year, and then, coming out into the open, went to London to see the justiciars. He demanded that they turn the kingdom over to him and have all the inhabitants swear fealty to him, for King Richard, he said, was dead. When the justiciars indignantly refused, John went to Windsor Castle and prepared for war. His Welsh mercenaries devastated the region between Kingston and Windsor and took all the food they could find to stock their two castles.[1]

While the queen and the justiciars were preparing to subdue John, they were greatly cheered by the results of their careful measures on the southeast coast. England was so formidably defended that the would-be invaders lost heart. Most of them dispersed; the few who attempted to land in England were captured and put in chains.

Eleanor and the justiciars were even more cheered by the return of the two abbots shortly after Easter. They brought the news that not only had they found the king alive and cheerful but also that the emperor had stated his terms for freeing him. The ransom was set at a hundred thousand marks; in addition, since Richard could not violate his treaty with Tancred and join the emperor in his proposed conquest of Sicily, he was to furnish Henry with fifty galleys and two hundred knights for a year.

When they told him of John's treason, Richard remarked: 'My brother John is not the man to seize any land by force, if anyone meets his attack with even the slightest resistance.' He sent for ships and for Alan Trenchmere, the master of the king's galley, and Robert of Thornham, one of Richard's companions on the crusade, arrived in London with some of the king's baggage.[2]

Certain now that the king was alive and would soon return, the justiciars turned with renewed vigour to deal with Count John. The siege of Windsor Castle began, apparently, on 29 March, Easter Monday. The account rendered by Geoffrey son of Peter in the Pipe Roll for this year shows that the besieging

[1] Gervase. Vol. I, p. 515; Howden, Vol. III, pp. 204-5.
[2] Howden, Vol. III, pp. 198, 205-6.

army included 500 foot-soldiers recruited from the Welsh marches, 66 sergeants with hauberks and two horses apiece, and 67 slingers, and William Marshal was in charge of a further 500 foot-soldiers.[1]

Abbot Samson of Bury St. Edmunds appeared at the siege, leading a number of knights under his standard, although his biographer admits that he shone 'rather in council than in prowess'. The Pipe Roll accounts for 'cords and iron and hides and other necessities bought for the two stone-throwers at Windsor, . . . and again for stones and for cords and arrows and siege-engines and shields and sulphur and pitch sent to the aforesaid army'. Three shiploads of stones were sent from Kent to be used in the stone-throwers. The mention of sulphur and pitch is particularly interesting. If they were used to make Greek fire, as no doubt they were, this marks the introduction into England of a method of warfare brought back by some of the crusaders.[2]

While the justiciars and barons were thus occupied in the south, equally energetic measures were being taken in the north. Archbishop Geoffrey, Hugh Bardolf, sheriff of Yorkshire, and William of Stuteville collected an army and fortified Doncaster as a check to John's castle at Tickhill, ten miles to the south. The Pipe Roll shows that 26 knights, 15 sergeants with two horses apiece, and 140 foot-soldiers were stationed there for 40 days, and an engineer built a palisade and brattices, or wooden breastworks, around the town.[3]

Archbishop Geoffrey, remembering the martial exploits of his youth, wanted to go on and lay siege to Tickhill. Both Hugh Bardolf and William of Stuteville, however, were John's men, and hence could not attack him. Geoffrey then withdrew, calling them 'traitors to the king and the realm'. The stout-hearted bishop of Durham, however, had no such scruples, and he closely invested Tickhill.

As the weeks passed and communications were established with King Richard in Germany, the first feelings of elation gave way to a growing uneasiness. No orders arrived from the king for the collection of his ransom; no date was set for his return; no formal treaty had been concluded with the emperor, and Henry

[1] Pipe Roll 5 Richard I, pp. 99, 148.
[2] Jocelin of Brakelond, p. 55; Pipe Roll 5 Richard I, pp. 158, 165.
[3] Pipe Roll 5 Richard I, pp. 57, 73.

VI was known to be in communication with King Philip, Richard's most determined enemy. Philip would of course be willing to give almost anything he had to prevent Richard's release, so that he might proceed with the intended subjugation of Normandy, and, eventually, of all Richard's lands on that side of the Channel. It became apparent that the emperor was skilfully playing Richard against Philip and making them bid against each other, the one for his liberty, the other for any sort of an arrangement that would prevent Richard from returning to his domains till Philip had completed his conquests. Even while the justiciars were deliberating these points. Philip invaded Normandy, took Gisors and Neaufle, and appeared before Rouen.[1]

John made the most of the situation by declaring that his brother would never return, and so plausible were his arguments that many men were won over by them. The justiciars realised that John was still the heir presumptive and that the man whom they were besieging at Windsor might one day be their king. Gervase of Canterbury, who had no love for Walter of Coutances, accuses him of being half-hearted in besieging Windsor because several of his kinsmen were with John's forces in the castle. It may also be that the justiciars lost some of their enthusiasm for punishing John as these considerations began to occupy their minds.[2]

Matters were clarified somewhat by the arrival of Hubert Walter, bishop of Salisbury, directly from the king in Germany. Bishop Hubert had accompanied Archbishop Baldwin to the Holy Land and had been with him when he died there. After Baldwin's death Hubert became the foremost churchman in the crusading army and won respect and admiration by his energetic measures to relieve the sufferings of the common soldiers during the siege of Acre. He had taken a leading part in the negotiations with Saladin that resulted in the truce of September 1192. On his way home, he learned in Sicily that the king had been captured, and he hastened to Richard's side.[3]

The king sent him to England, where he arrived on 20 April with news that was far from reassuring. Richard had not yet had an interview with the emperor; he was being held prisoner at Trifels, in Bavaria, and although he hoped to purchase his free-

[1] Howden, Vol. III, pp. 206–7. [2] Gervase, Vol. I, p. 515.
[3] *Gesta*, Vol. II, pp. 115, 145; *Itinerarium*, pp. 134–5; Newburgh, Vol. I, p. 388.

dom and the sum of 100,000 marks had been set as a tentative ransom, he had as yet had no firm assurance that the emperor would release him. Hubert was certain of one thing: if Richard were to be set free, a huge sum of money would be needed. It was imperative that peace be restored in England and that every effort be made to collect as much money as possible.

Probably on Bishop Hubert's advice, the justiciars, although they were on the point of capturing Windsor, made a truce with Count John to last till the following All Saints' Day, 1 November. Since John was on the point of losing it in any case, he agreed to surrender Windsor Castle, together with his castles at Wallingford and the Peak, to his mother, with the understanding that they would be returned to him if his brother's release was not effected. He was allowed to retain his castles at Nottingham and Tickhill, to the infinite disappointment of Bishop Hugh of Le Puiset, who was on the point of capturing Tickhill, an exploit that would have delighted his heart.[1]

At last came the news from the king that everyone had been waiting for. He wrote on 19 April to inform 'his dearest mother, Eleanor, queen of England, and his justiciars, and all his faithful men in England' that after Bishop Hubert had left, 'our dearest chancellor, William, bishop of Ely', came and arranged for an interview between Richard and the emperor at Hagenau, at which 'a mutual and indissoluble treaty of love' had been agreed upon. The principal provision was that Richard was to be detained till 70,000 marks of the ransom had been paid. The remainder of the letter consisted of exhortations to raise as much money as possible and of directions as to how they were to proceed.

The king asked his justiciars to give an example to the rest of the nation by the generosity and magnificence of their help to him. They were to take all the gold and silver vessels from the churches under a written pledge to return their value when the king was freed. Hostages for the payment of the remainder of the ransom were to be taken from all the barons and assembled under Queen Eleanor's supervision, so that they could be quickly sent to Germany under the care of the chancellor, who was coming to England as soon as he had finished his negotiations in Germany. The money that was collected was also to be en-

[1] Gervase, Vol. I, p. 516; Howden, Vol. III, pp. 207-8.

trusted to Eleanor and those whom she might name. The king asked that he be sent a list of the names of all his nobles, with the contribution of each one noted, 'so that we may know by how much we are beholden to each of them'.

The queen and the justiciars set about devising means for raising the ransom. England, it would seem, had been stripped almost bare by the king before his departure and by William Longchamp afterwards in an effort to raise funds for his master, who had borne most of the costs of the crusade and had paid the wages of the greater part of the army. Now the government were faced by the task of raising a sum almost beyond their calculations. They decreed that both laymen and the clergy, who had hitherto been exempt from taxation, except for the Saladin Tithe of 1188, should pay a fourth of their income for the year, that each knight's fee should be assessed 20 shillings, that the churches should contribute all their gold and silver, as King Richard had directed, and that the Cistercian abbeys and the houses of the order of Gilbert of Sempringham, which by the rules of their orders were not allowed to possess gold or silver, should give their wool-clip for the year.[1]

Collection of the ransom began immediately, and before Michaelmas treasure was being hauled to London from every part of the country. The money was stored in chests in St. Paul's Cathedral under the custody of Hubert Walter, Bishop Richard of London, William, earl of Arundel, Hamelin, earl Warenne, the king's uncle, and Henry son of Ailwin, the mayor of London, and under the seals of Queen Eleanor and the archbishop of Rouen.[2]

The king meanwhile had written to his mother, to the bishops of the southern province, and to the monks of Canterbury, ordering that Hubert Walter be elected archbishop of Canterbury. The bishop of London, as dean of the province, accordingly summoned the bishops and the monks to meet in London on Sunday, 30 May, for the election. The monks, ever jealous of their privilege, elected Hubert on the Saturday before and then sent Prior Geoffrey to London to announce the election to the assembly.

The bishops, equally jealous of their privileges, ignored the

[1] Howden, Vol. III, pp. 208-11; Richard of Devizes, pp. 42-3.

[2] Doris M. Stenton, Introd. to Pipe Roll 5 Richard I, pp. xxi-xxiii.

election made by the monks and proceeded to elect Hubert as their archbishop. Queen Eleanor's tact smoothed over the situation, and the chief justiciar, Archbishop Walter of Coutances, confirmed by the king's authority the election of Hubert Walter to the post to which he himself had twice aspired in vain.[1]

Richard had learned to respect and admire Hubert while they were together on the crusade for his zeal, his efficiency, his concern for the welfare of the army, his skill in negotiating with the Saracens, and above all for his administrative genius. Other bishops far excelled him in learning; others, such as Hugh of Lincoln, far outshone him in the outward signs of holiness; none, however, could approach his knowledge of the common law, his administrative skill, or his genius at leading and governing men. Hubert was not the product of the cloister; he was not a scholar who had passed his life far from the world of men and affairs; he was an immensely practical and experienced man whose whole life had been passed amongst men and who, to judge from his popularity amongst the crusaders, was most at home when dealing with practical problems of supply and organisation.

He was, of course, the product of his upbringing and education. He was not trained as a theologian, and abstract speculation meant nothing to him. He had no pretensions to holiness of life, and his contemporaries considered him proud, avaricious, hungry for power and the trappings of power, unscrupulous, and ostentatious.

Shortly after Hubert's election, William Longchamp returned to England with a golden bull from the Emperor Henry VI announcing his alliance with King Richard and urging the people of England to show their devotion to their king. Longchamp also bore messages from the king, expressed no doubt in less high-flown language, concerning the collection of the ransom.[2]

Even though Longchamp stood higher than ever in the king's favour, he was given a humiliatingly chilly reception in England. After landing at Ipswich and spending the night at Hitcham, he sent word to Abbot Samson that he wanted to hear Mass at St. Edmund's shrine. Since he was still under excommunication as far as Samson knew, the abbot ordered that no services should be celebrated in Longchamp's presence. When the chancellor

[1] Howden, Vol. III, p. 213; Diceto, Vol. II, pp. 107-9; Gervase, Vol. I, pp. 516-19; *Epistolae Cantuarienses*, pp. 363-6.

[2] Howden, Vol. III, p. 211.

entered the abbey church, the priest at the altar stood motionless and silent until the excommunicated man was ushered out of the church.[1]

Because the citizens of London would not tolerate his presence in their city, the queen, the justiciars, and some of the nobles met him at St. Albans, but no-one would give him the customary kiss of greeting. Not until he had assured the assembly that he came, 'not as a justiciar, not as legate, not as chancellor, but as a simple bishop and messenger from the lord king', would they allow him to deliver his messages. The king, he said, had ordered the bishops of Rochester and Chichester, Benedict, abbot of Peterborough, Earl Richard of Clare, Roger Bigod, earl of Norfolk, and a number of others to come to him in Germany. Longchamp also said that the king had ordered him to bring back with him the noblemen's sons who were to serve as hostages for the payment of the ransom. Queen Eleanor refused to entrust her grandson, William of Winchester, the son of Henry the Lion, duke of Saxony, to Longchamp, and the others followed her example.

'We will put our daughters in his care,' Gerald of Wales represents them as saying, 'but never our sons', in reference to Longchamp's evil reputation. Richard quickly recalled his chancellor, perhaps upon representations from his mother.

The king summoned Hugh of Nonant, who had been associated with Count John in some of his questionable activities, to come to him in Germany. Hugh wisely started out with all the money he could lay his hands on, but he was robbed of all he had near Canterbury. Matthew of Clare, Longchamp's brother-in-law and castellan of Dover, was suspected of sheltering the thieves, and he was excommunicated on that account by the bishops of England.[2]

Every effort was being made, meanwhile, to raise the money for the king's ransom. The bishops apparently were charged with the duty of collecting the tax from the lower clergy or at least of making sure that they paid their share. Archbishop Geoffrey of York demanded of his canons that they, like the rest of the clergy, contribute a fourth of their incomes to the fund. The canons not only refused; they accused their archbishop of

[1] Jocelin of Brakelond, p. 53.
[2] Howden, Vol. III, pp. 211-12; Gerald of Wales: *De Vita Galfridi*, pp. 415-17.

trying to destroy the freedom of the Church by consenting to this levy.

Geoffrey had already got himself into another quarrel with his chapter over the appointment of a new dean. King Richard had nominated the dean of York, Henry Marshal, as bishop of Exeter to succeed John the Chanter, who had died on 1 June 1191. Geoffrey claimed the right to name the new dean and bestowed the office on his brother on his mother's side, Peter, archdeacon of Lincoln. Peter, however, was in Paris at the time, and the king sent urgent messages to Geoffrey asking him to appoint John of Béthune, the brother of one of Richard's best friends.

Geoffrey, on the other hand, wanted as dean a man whom he could rely on to take his side in the apparently endless squabbles with the chapter, and he feared that unless his appointee was installed immediately the king would fill the vacancy. He therefore gave the office to the one whom he considered the most trustworthy and faithful of all his clerks, Master Simon of Apulia, a learned canonist who had pleaded Geoffrey's cause at Rome. Shortly after this, however, when Peter returned to England, the archbishop tried to undo the appointment by saying that he had merely given the office to Master Simon to hold in trust for Peter, and he ordered Simon to surrender the office to him.

At this point the chapter intervened, claimed that they had the right to elect the dean, and chose Master Simon. Geoffrey refused to acknowledge their right to elect, quashed all previous appointments, and gave the office to Master Philip of Poitiers, one of the king's favourite clerks and companions, whom Richard had named archdeacon of Canterbury and whom he now seems to have recommended instead of John of Béthune as dean of York as well.

What with Geoffrey's attempts to make the canons contribute to the king's ransom and the dispute over who was to be dean, relations between the archbishop of York and his unruly chapter were now worse than ever. Master Simon went to the king to protest against the way he had been treated, and at the same time Geoffrey sent messengers whose instructions were to go first to the king and explain the situation and then to Rome and appeal to the pope on Geoffrey's behalf. When Richard learned what was afoot, he strictly forbade either side to appeal to Rome. As he had done when Cardinal John of Anagnani had attempted to settle the dispute at Canterbury, the king declared that he was quite capable of handling these matters himself and that he would tolerate no interference from Rome. Although he stood high in the Church's favour because of his character as a crusader, Richard nevertheless, like his father, exercised a close supervision over appeals to Rome and especially distrusted papal legates.

Richard sent one of Geoffrey's messengers back to him with an order to come to him immediately, so that the king might hear the whole story and make his decision known to his brother. As Geoffrey was on the point of leaving for Germany, he was faced by the most extreme actions that his canons had yet taken in the stormy course of their various quarrels. To protest against Geoffrey's insistence on their contributing their share of the ransom and against his actions concerning the appointment of a dean, the canons of York suspended the cathedral from the celebration of all divine services and silenced the bells, to the great distress of the people of York. The canons stripped the altars, locked up the archbishop's stall in the choir, and barred the door by which he entered the cathedral. To deal with this fresh rebellion on the part of his contumacious canons, Geoffrey turned back to York and ordered them to resume the services. They refused, and the cathedral remained empty and silent.[1]

Early in July the justiciars learned that Richard had had another interview with the emperor, beginning on 25 June, at Worms. King Philip's frantic attempts to induce the emperor either to keep Richard captive indefinitely or to turn him over to Philip led the emperor to place an even higher valuation on him. After four days of bargaining the emperor agreed to a fresh set of terms. He raised the ransom to 150,000 marks, of which 50,000 were in lieu of the help Richard had promised him in his proposed expedition against King Tancred of Sicily.

The emperor agreed to release Richard when two-thirds of the money had been brought to Germany at Richard's risk, and hostages, as before, were to be given for the payment of the remainder. Richard's niece, Eleanor of Brittany, was to be betrothed to the son of Duke Leopold of Austria, Richard's captor. Finally, Richard agreed to turn over to the emperor Isaac Comnenos, self-styled emperor of Cyprus, and his daughter, whom Richard had captured on his outward voyage.

[1] Howden, Vol. III, pp. 221-3, 225.

When he learned of this treaty King Philip concluded that Richard would soon be set free. He sent word immediately to Count John to be on his guard, 'for the devil is already loose'. John did not dare to face his brother, whose arrival in England he concluded to be imminent. He quickly crossed the Channel and joined King Philip.[1]

In the earlier days of his captivity Richard had been kept in close confinement and under strict guard, but when the treaty with the emperor was concluded he was allowed considerable freedom. He had his falcons sent to him from England, and the Pipe Roll records the purchase of 'scarlet cloth and green cloth and hauberks and capes of doeskin and of lamb's wool and three silver cups bought and sent to Germany, £44 11s. 2d., by the king's brief and by view of Robert of Thornham and other law-worthy men of the city of London'.[2]

The justiciars meanwhile were making every effort to collect as much money as possible as quickly as possible, for upon the speedy payment of the ransom depended the king's return to England. No records survive either of the exact means by which the money was raised or of the amount collected. It is not improbable that the levy of a fourth of each man's income was assessed by juries of sworn neighbours, much as the Saladin Tithe had been assessed in 1188. The money did not pass through the Exchequer and hence no mention of the sums collected is found in the Pipe Rolls. The justiciars had only the vaguest idea of how much the various assessments would bring in, for they had no precedents, beyond that of the Saladin Tithe, to guide them. William of Newburgh says that since the first levy failed to raise enough money, a second and then a third were imposed. He states that the failure was due to the dishonesty of the collectors, which may well be true, for it was almost impossible to set up a system of auditing their accounts, similar to that used by the barons of the Exchequer, when no-one knew how much money they were to account for in the first place.[3]

There was a great outcry, of course, at the harshness with which the collectors went about their work, and the loudest pro-

[1] Howden, Vol. III, pp. 214-17.

[2] Ralph of Coggeshall, p. 58; Newburgh, Vol. I, p. 398; Pipe Roll 5 Richard I, pp. 2, 14, 158.

[3] Newburgh, Vol. I, pp. 399-400; Gervase, Vol. I, p. 519.

tests came from the clergy. Abbot Samson dared the Exchequer officials to take any of the gold and silver that encrusted St. Edmund's shrine, reminding them that 'the fury of St. Edmund can reach those who are absent and far away; much more will it strike those who are present and desire to strip his shirt from off him'.[1]

Before the end of the summer some of the emperor's agents had arrived in England to take an instalment of the ransom back with them. Late in the autumn, apparently, they returned to Germany with 'the greater part of the ransom', which probably means that by this time the major instalment of 100,000 marks had been collected. At any rate, enough was paid that the king summoned his mother and the archbishop of Rouen to meet him at Speyer, where they celebrated Christmas together, and the emperor, on 20 December, set 17 January as the date for Richard's liberation.

Richard probably used the absence of the archbishop of Rouen from England as a pretext for appointing Archbishop Hubert Walter to succeed him as chief justiciar. Richard could hardly have had any serious complaints against Walter of Coutances, for he had filled his difficult position capably if not brilliantly, keeping order at a time when Count John sorely troubled the peace of the realm and the patience of the justiciars with his various plottings and treasons. Certainly Walter had shown zeal and efficiency in collecting the money for the ransom so speedily. Hubert Walter, however, was in every way a greater man, and Richard, probably from the time he had observed his outstanding abilities in the Holy Land, had determined to advance him to the highest secular post in the realm.[2]

[1] Jocelin of Brakelond, p. 97.
[2] Howden, Vol. III, pp. 226-7.

VI

1194

ARCHBISHOP Geoffrey of York at last reached the end of his patience in dealing with his canons. Since they refused to conduct any services in the cathedral, the archbishop, after consulting men learned in the canon law in order to make sure of his rights, came to York on New Year's Day, 1194, and installed clerks in the silent minster to perform the functions that the canons would not discharge. Four canons then went to the king, in Germany, and laid their complaints before him. Since Richard was already angry with Geoffrey because he had neglected to obey his summons to come to Germany, the king gave the canons leave to carry their complaints to the pope, in the hope that he would add spiritual punishments to the measures that Richard contemplated taking against his brother. Geoffrey, too, sent envoys to Rome to present his side of the dispute.

When he heard their arguments concerning the right to appoint the dean of York, Pope Celestine declined, on the ground of insufficient knowledge of the situation, to pronounce as to whether the archbishop had the right to appoint or the chapter the right to elect the dean. Putting that question aside for later consideration, the pope, overriding the claims of both parties, conferred the office on Simon of Apulia, one of the four canons there present.

Since Simon had been the canons' choice, they saw his appointment as a victory for their side and seized the opportunity to press their accusations against the archbishop. He was a violent despoiler, they said, of the possessions both of the archbishopric and of other clerks; he rode roughshod over the rights of the Church; he sold ecclesiastical benefices; he forbade appeals to Rome (always the most telling accusation at the papal court); he paid no heed to the privileges of the Roman pontiff; he was a disgrace to the office of bishop; and he was addicted to hawking, hunting, and other knightly pursuits. The pope took the matter under advisement.[1]

In Germany, meanwhile, Richard, his mother, and his friends were waiting impatiently for the date of his release. Although the emperor had promised that he would release the king on 17 January 1194, he began to regret his decision when King Philip and Count John, spurred to action by the imminence of the king's liberation, made him a variety of proposals that appealed greatly to his avarice. Philip offered 50,000 marks and John 30,000 if the emperor would agree to prolong Richard's captivity till the following Michaelmas, by which time the pair may have hoped to make themselves masters of Richard's lands. If those terms did not suit Henry, they promised him £1,000 a month as long as he kept Richard in prison. Finally, Philip offered 100,000 marks and John 50,000, which would come to the sum that Henry had set as Richard's ransom, if the emperor would either deliver Richard over to them or agree to hold him for a full year. These offers were so tempting that the emperor postponed the date of Richard's release till 2 February in order to give himself time to think them over.[2]

John and Philip were so certain of the success of their appeal to the emperor's cupidity that John sent Adam of St. Edmund, a clerk who enjoyed his confidence, to England with letters to the keepers of his castles, ordering them to lay in arms and supplies and put the castles in a state of defence. John evidently planned, in case the emperor accepted his offers, to use his castles as bases for bringing the whole country into subjection to him; in case Richard were set free, John intended to resist him to the best of his ability.

When he arrived in London, Adam, who seems to have been as foolish as his master, had dinner with Archbishop Hubert Walter and boasted loudly of Count John's favourable prospects and of his close friendship with the king of France. Philip, he said, had already given John the castles of Driencourt and Arques and would have given him many more if John had only had faithful men to whom he could entrust them. Adam in his simplicity thus revealed the greatest weakness of John's position, apart from his blundering stupidity: the fact that he had been contemptuously rejected by the Normans when he had tried to claim their

[1] Howden, Vol. III, pp. 229-30. [2] Ibid., Vol. III, p. 229.

allegiance. Even when Richard had attempted, during the previous December, to win back John's fidelity and had ordered the Normans to turn over to John the castles that belonged to him, they had refused to obey, so great were their dislike and contempt for the count of Mortain.

Out of respect for the archbishop's table, at which he had been a guest, Adam was allowed to leave unmolested. When he reached his lodgings, however, the mayor of London seized him and all of Count John's letters, of which he was the bearer, and turned them over to the archbishop. On the following day Hubert Walter summoned all the bishops, earls, and barons who were then in London and showed them John's letters to his castellans.

When they learned of John's treasonable designs, 'by common counsel of the realm' they decreed that he should be deprived of all his lands in England and that his castles should be besieged. He was deprived of the Honour of Lancaster, which was put under the archbishop's brother, Theobald, as sheriff. Theobald was both corrupt and unpopular, but no-one dared complain against him till a new king was on the throne. He contrived to acquire the wardship of a number of heiresses, and in the autumn of this year he brought suit against one of them for having married without his permission. It was probably at this time, also, that Hugh of Nonant, bishop of Coventry and John's chief advisor, was deprived of his manors.[1]

Immediately after this decision Archbishop Hubert Walter, Bishops Hugh of Lincoln, Richard of London, Gilbert of Rochester, Godfrey of Winchester, Henry of Worcester, William of Hereford, Henry Marshal, bishop-elect of Exeter, and many abbots and other members of the clergy assembled in St. Catherine's Chapel at Westminster and solemnly pronounced a sentence of excommunication upon Count John and all his supporters and advisors as disturbers of 'the king's peace and of his realm of England'.

The hated William Longchamp had been one of the first to join King Richard in Germany and now stood higher than ever in his favour. To guard themselves against a repetition of their previous troubles, the clergy now 'appealed to the lord pope

[1] Howden, Vol. III, pp. 227-8; Jolliffe: *Angevin Kingship*, pp. 65-8; *Rotuli Curiae Regis*, Vol. I, p. 10; Pipe Roll 6 Richard I, p. 44.

against William, bishop of Ely, lest he should exercise his office of legate in England in the future'. All the bishops put their seals to this document and sent their messengers to show it to the king, so that he might know how they felt about his chancellor, before taking it on to the pope.[1]

On the second date appointed for Richard's release, 2 February, the king, accompanied by Queen Eleanor, Archbishop Walter of Coutances, Bishop William Longchamp, and Savaric, bishop of Bath, met the emperor and his court at Mainz. Henry showed himself more than a little inclined to accept the offers of Philip and John and keep Richard in captivity still longer, with the object of collecting both a monthly subsidy from them as long as they were willing to pay it and the ransom from Richard when Henry should at last set him free. In the presence of the messengers sent by Philip and John, amongst whom was Robert of Nonant, the brother of the bishop of Coventry, the emperor showed Richard the letters from the treacherous pair and informed him that he was considering accepting their offer.

Both Richard and the leading men of the empire protested so violently against this repudiation of his promise that Henry at last agreed to abide by his original undertaking and set Richard free. More effective than these appeals to his sense of honour was probably the sober reflection that for all their fine promises Philip and John had precious little money between them and that the great sums they had promised were contingent upon their taking over Richard's lands and collecting the money there.

After two days of negotiations, the emperor released King Richard on 4 February, but he kept as hostages for the payment of the remainder of the ransom Archbishop Walter, Bishop Savaric, and the sons of Richard's noblemen who had been sent to Germany for that purpose. Richard asked Robert of Nonant to act as a hostage, but Robert refused, declaring that he was Count John's man. Richard had him seized and held prisoner, and he also sent a letter to Bishop Hugh, who was hiding in France, ordering him to come and stand his trial in the king's court as a traitor. Richard then began a leisurely trip back to England by way of Cologne and Antwerp, where he stopped to make alliances with the German princes and the leading men of the Low Countries.

[1] Howden, Vol. III, pp. 236-7.

Richard landed at Sandwich on Sunday, 13 March, and went to Canterbury, where the monks met him with a procession and led him to the cathedral. The king gave thanks at the shrine of St. Thomas for his safe return. On the next day, as he drew near Rochester, he met Archbishop Hubert Walter, who was hurrying to meet him. Richard dismounted and knelt before the archbishop, the companion of his crusading days, and Hubert likewise knelt before his king. They rose to their feet and embraced with tears. Then they went on to London.[1]

The city was 'crowned' in Richard's honour; the streets were decorated, houses were hung with tapestries and gay banners, and throngs of rejoicing citizens crowded to catch a glimpse of their king, almost a legendary figure by now, as returning crusaders brought back tales of his lion-like courage, his daring exploits, and his single-minded devotion to the cause. The king was led in procession to St. Paul's Cathedral, where he was welcomed by all the clergy of the city.[2]

The Germans in Richard's train were amazed at the wealth and prosperity of London, which they had imagined would have been reduced to the utmost poverty by the payment of the king's ransom. They declared that if the emperor had known the true extent of the wealth of Richard's realm he would not have released him for such a trifling sum as 100,000 marks seemed to be.[3]

After staying only one day at Westminster, the king went to Bury St. Edmunds to pray at the shrine of the English saint for whom he seems to have had the greatest devotion, the martyred king of East Anglia. Then he set out for Nottingham.[4]

Immediately after the meeting of the Great Council on 10 February, Archbishop Hubert Walter had directed that vigorous steps be taken to seize John's castles. Elaborate preparations were made. Stone-throwers and 'many machines' were brought to Nottingham from Leicester; 22 carpenters and 20 slingers came from Northampton; Urric the Engineer and Elias the Carpenter came from London to supervise the technical operations; and a stone-thrower and a mangonel were sent from Windsor Castle. A supply of 49 chains, 4,000 arrows, shields, bolts, and Greek fire was sent from London to Marlborough; Winchester Castle con-

[1] Howden, Vol. III, pp. 231-5; Gervase, Vol. I, p. 524.
[2] Diceto, Vol. II, p. 114. [3] Newburgh, Vol. I, p. 406.
[4] Ralph of Coggeshall, p. 63.

tributed a stone-thrower, a mangonel, 30 chains, 20 shields, 12 ladders, and pitch and sulphur; and a stone-thrower and a mangonel were sent from Reading.[1]

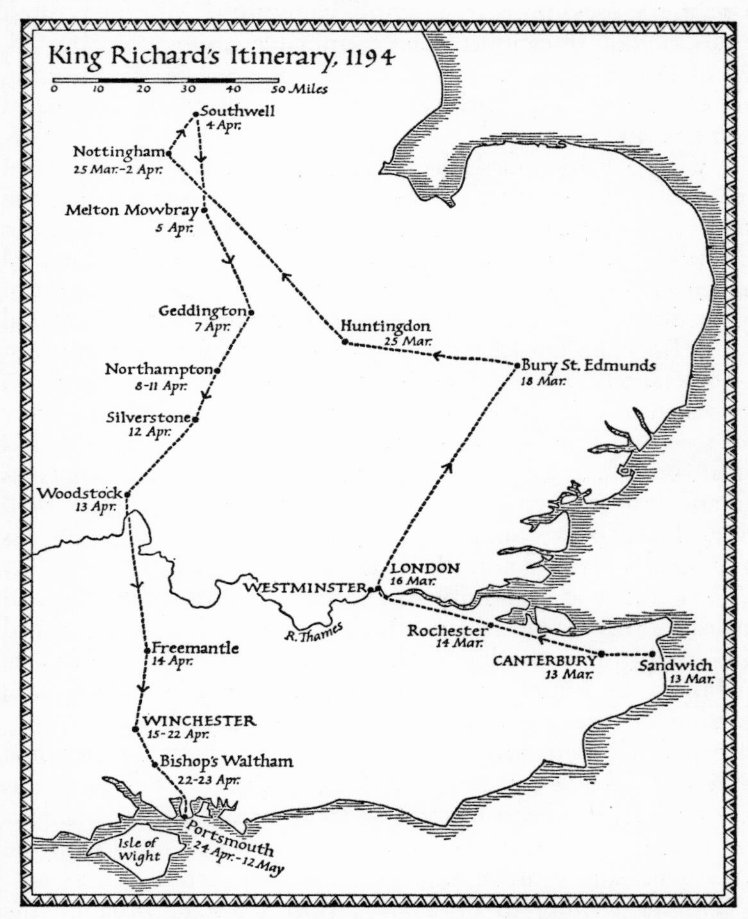

The archbishop himself led an army to Marlborough, where John's adherents surrendered within a few days, and then to Lancaster, where he had similar success. The constable of St. Michael's Mount, in Cornwall, died of fright when he learned that King Richard was on his way back to England.

John's two chief castles, those of Tickhill and Nottingham,

[1] Pipe Roll 6 Richard I, pp. 43, 68, 175-6, 212, 251.

were not so easily taken. Bishop Hugh of Durham collected a large army from Yorkshire and Northumberland and laid siege to Tickhill. He had been forced to abandon the siege of that castle in the previous year, and now he returned with the greatest joy to the task of capturing this formidable stronghold. David, earl of Huntingdon, the brother of the king of Scots, Rannulf, earl of Chester, and Earl William Ferrers meanwhile besieged Nottingham.

When Richard landed, these two castles were still holding out after more than a month's siege. When they learned that the king was in England, the garrison of Tickhill, with Bishop Hugh's permission, sent two knights to find out if the king had indeed returned and to offer to surrender to him if he would promise not to put them to death. They satisfied themselves that Richard was in England, but he refused to accept anything except an unconditional surrender. They returned and told Robert Delamere, the castellan, and the other members of the garrison what they had seen and heard. Robert asked Bishop Hugh's advice, and when the bishop on his own authority promised them safety in life and limb if they would surrender they did so. How well Tickhill was provisioned is shown by the fact that the surplus stocks that were sold after the surrender brought in £145 17s.[1]

The garrison at Nottingham continued to resist stubbornly and made no effort to communicate with the king. Richard marched to Nottingham, collecting an army as he went, and arrived there on Friday, 25 March, 'with such a multitude of men and such blowing of trumpets and horns' that the garrison were greatly disturbed. They refused to believe, however, that the king had come and deluded themselves with the belief that the show was put on by the besiegers in order to trick them. Richard had his tent pitched so close to the castle walls that the archers on the battlements shot some of his men at his very feet.

Without waiting to draw up proper plans or organise the attack, Richard in an access of rage put on his armour and led an assault on the castle to such good effect that he captured the outer works, burned some of the gates, and shot a knight with his own hand. After this warning that he was in earnest, Richard had siege engines built after the latest model, and he also had gallows erected in plain view of the castle, on which he hanged some of

[1] Howden, Vol. III, pp. 237-8; Pipe Roll 6 Richard I, p. 87.

John's men who had been captured in the assault. On this day Archbishop Hubert Walter joined the king.

On Sunday, the 27th, the gallant bishop of Durham arrived from Tickhill, bringing with him the prisoners he had taken there. When Richard heard of the bishop's approach he went to meet him. The king and his kinsman dismounted when they met and embraced each other warmly.

While the king and his friends were at dinner, two knights from the besieged garrison, sent by their fellows, came to see if the king was truly present. When they had satisfied themselves that the king was indeed there, they went back and reported to the castellans, Ralph Murdac and William of Wenneval, what they had seen. Their account of the king's presence and of his preparations to take the castle so impressed the garrison that William of Wenneval, Roger of Muntbegun, and twelve others came to Richard, surrendered to him, and threw themselves on his mercy.

The surrender of these men and the persuasions of Archbishop Hubert Walter convinced the remainder of the garrison that it was folly for them to try to hold out against the greatest warrior of the time. The entire garrison marched out of the castle and surrendered to the king on Monday, 28 March.

With the yielding of Nottingham, the last of John's castles to hold out, all resistance collapsed. The leaders had been John's particular friends, who thought that they stood to gain more by their support of the count than by loyalty to the king, and they succeeded in attracting to themselves some of those restless and rebellious spirits who were enemies of established order under any form. That they received little or no popular support is shown by the ease with which the king forced them to surrender.

Richard had, at some time after his landing, summoned a meeting of the Great Council, and he now fittingly decided to hold it at Nottingham, in the very centre of John's country and of the rebellion. While the members were assembling he spent Tuesday, 29 March, in viewing Sherwood Forest, which he had never seen before and in which he took great delight.

The council opened on Wednesday in Nottingham Castle, where hasty repairs had been made. Queen Eleanor was present and Archbishop Hubert Walter sat at the king's right and Archbishop Geoffrey at his left. Six earls and seven bishops were present, including Hugh of Durham, flushed with his success at Tickhill, and William Longchamp of Ely, who had returned to England in his master's company and under his protection.[1]

The principal business of the council, Richard lost no time in informing them, was to devise means of raising money. As Ralph of Coggeshall points out, the king urgently needed money for two reasons: to pay the remainder of his ransom and thus redeem the hostages whom he had left with the emperor, and to raise an army to repel Philip's attacks on Normandy, where the French king had already captured a number of castles and had even appeared before the walls of Rouen.[2]

Richard was disappointed with his English subjects, who had been slow, as he thought, in paying his ransom, and he was determined to grind every penny possible out of them. They had sat at home in peace and safety whilst he and his gallant crusaders, amongst whom there had been precious few Englishmen, had gone to the furthermost ends of the world, endured untold privations, been racked by hunger and disease, and had fought with reckless courage against a foe that greatly outnumbered them, all in defence of the highest and noblest ideal, so the crusaders thought, that men had ever known.

Richard came back from his crusade a different man, changed not only by the passage of more than four years of strenuous toil, of reckless daring, of sickness and exposure to a lethal climate, of disappointment and disillusionment as one by one his fellow crusaders perished or, worse still, turned craven and fled back home, and of humiliation as he, a crusader and a king, lay shackled in prison. On the day when Richard covered his face lest his eyes behold the Holy City he had been unable to win back from the Saracens and when he declined to visit Jerusalem under a safe-conduct from Saladin, refusing 'to enjoy as a privilege from the pagans what he could not have as a gift from God',[3] something broke in Richard's heart.

He had started on his crusade full of hope and confidence; he came back disillusioned and bitter, and the knowledge that he had done more than any other man could have done was scant comfort to him. Then he had been inspired by hope; now he was

[1] Howden, Vol. III, pp. 238-41; Pipe Roll 6 Richard I, p. 80.
[2] Ralph of Coggeshall, p. 63; Howden, Vol. III, p. 207.
[3] Richard of Devizes, p. 84.

filled with hatred. Just as his zeal for the crusade had earlier been his driving force, now all his actions were inspired by his hatred for Philip of France.

Two men of similar rank and station could hardly be more different than were Richard and Philip. Richard was impulsive, rash, open-hearted, recklessly brave, hot-blooded, imaginative, and a poet; Philip was cold, sly, cautious, cowardly, and scheming. By his desertion in the summer of 1191, Philip, Richard was convinced, had contributed more than anyone else to the failure of the Third Crusade. That alone would have been enough to bring down on Philip Richard's hatred and scorn. But Philip had done far more than merely desert a fellow crusader when his hopes were highest; he had sneaked back to France, encouraged John in his rebellion and treachery, tried to induce the emperor to keep Richard in captivity or to sell him like a slave to the king of France, and, to crown it all, had taken advantage of Richard's absence to try to steal Normandy from him. The best measure of the depth of Richard's hatred for Philip is found in his confession, on his deathbed in 1199, that he had not dared to receive Holy Communion for almost seven years 'because in his heart he bore a mortal hatred for the king of France'.[1]

With a heart thus hardened Richard faced his barons at Nottingham and made his demands. He was lean and toughened by privation and imprisonment; his barons were fat and soft. He proposed now to melt some of the fat off them. Just as he had at the beginning of his reign, he put up offices for sale. The fact that many of these offices had been bought and paid for in 1189 meant nothing to Richard in 1194. Those who had bought offices, the king reminded them, had had ample opportunity to recover their expenses and more besides.[2]

All the sheriffs except seven—those of Cumberland, Cambridgeshire and Huntingdonshire, Herefordshire, Kent, Shropshire, Wiltshire, and Westmorland—were turned out of office and their posts given to the highest bidders. Some payments no doubt were made on the spot and thus did not enter the records. The Pipe Roll shows, however, that almost every sheriff paid in order to keep the county at the old farm, promised an increase on the

[1] Ralph of Coggeshall, p. 96. As we shall see, however, Richard received Holy Communion at Winchester on 17 April 1194.

[2] Newburgh, Vol. II, pp. 415-16.

old farm, or offered a gift to the king. In Lincolnshire, for instance, Gerard of Camville, who would have been relieved of his position in any case, was replaced by Simon of Kyme, who paid £100 as an increment for the half-year beginning at Easter and 20 marks as a gift and promised a further 20 marks. In Staffordshire, Hugh of Nonant, deep in the king's disfavour and hiding in France, was replaced by Hugh of Chacombe, who offered 100 marks 'to have the county at the old farm for as long as the king pleases'.[1]

With the return of William Longchamp, his brothers were restored to office. Osbert became sheriff of Norfolk and Suffolk in place of Robert son of Robert and paid 50 marks as a 'new increment' for half a year. Henry, who had been imprisoned at Bristol when his brother fled the country, replaced William Beauchamp as sheriff of Worcestershire and paid an increment of 30 marks for the half-year.[2] William Longchamp bid 1,500 marks down and 100 marks a year thenceforth as an increment from each of the counties if he might be named sheriff of Yorkshire, Lincolnshire, and Northamptonshire. Archbishop Geoffrey, however, outbid him with an offer of 3,000 marks and a yearly increment of 100 marks for Yorkshire alone. Although Geoffrey still owed £1,533 6s. 6d. and made no effort to reduce his debt, the king accepted his offer. 'And thus he became the king's servant and put himself into his power.'[3]

On the second day of the council, 31 March, the king laid before the meeting his accusations against Count John and Bishop Hugh of Nonant. John, Richard declared, in violation of his oath of fealty, had seized his castles, laid waste his lands on both sides of the Channel, and entered into an alliance with his worst enemy, the king of France, against him. Richard charged that Bishop Hugh, whom he considered John's chief advisor, had deserted his king and gone over to the king of France and to Count John, whom he was helping with his not inconsiderable talents to plot harm to Richard.

The council decided that the two should be cited to appear before it within forty days. If they did not come to stand their trial, Count John should be judged to have forfeited the right to

[1] Pipe Roll 6 Richard I, pp. 103, 39.
[2] Pipe Roll 6 Richard I, pp. 47, 127; Gerald of Wales: *De Vita Galfridi*, p. 407.
[3] Pipe Roll 6 Richard I, p. 154; Howden, Vol. III, p. 241.

the succession, since he had already been deprived of all his lands, and Bishop Hugh, to employ a distinction made popular by William the Conqueror, should have judgment pronounced on him by the bishops concerning those matters in which he had acted as a bishop and by the lay judges concerning his conduct as one of the king's sheriffs. It was probably at this time that many of John's followers were deprived of their lands and heavily amerced, and even his wife, Isabel, had to pay £200 to keep her dowry lands and marriage portion.[1]

On the third day of the council Richard brought up the subject of taxation. Still outstanding were many unpaid assessments to raise the king's ransom, and demands for the payment of these arrears were sent out by the Exchequer officials. To raise money for the defence of Normandy and to supply the leaders for his army, which would of course be made up largely of mercenaries, the king demanded that a third of the knight-service of England, something under 2,000 knights, cross over to Normandy with him. It is not likely that Richard expected 2,000 knights to report for service, but the demand furnished him with a basis for exacting money in lieu of service.[2]

In his efforts to raise money by every means possible, Richard turned to the oldest of all land-taxes, the Danegeld as it was formerly known, or hidage, as it is called in the Pipe Rolls of this period, or carucage, as contemporary writers refer to it. In its simplest form it was a tax of two shillings on every hide of ploughland or carucate of cultivated land, although lands belonging to the Church and those making up the royal demesne, as well as those belonging to certain favoured individuals, had hitherto been exempt. It had last been levied in 1162. Richard now ordered that a hidage of two shillings be collected from all land, whether it belonged to laymen or to the Church.[3]

The tax was assessed according to the figures in Domesday Book.[4] Since 1086 these figures had of course become obsolete, for much more land had been brought under the plough to keep pace with the growth in population. In Lincolnshire, for example, 'the men of Kesteven and Holland owe 100 marks that

[1] Howden, Vol. III, pp. 241-2; Pipe Roll 6 Richard I, pp. 193-4.

[2] Pipe Roll 6 Richard I, p. 176; Howden, Vol. III, p. 242.

[3] Howden, Vol. III, p. 242; Newburgh, Vol. II, p. 416.

[4] F. W. Maitland: Introd. to *Three Rolls of the King's Court in the Reign of King Richard the First, A.D. 1194-1195*, Pipe Roll Society, No. 14 (1891), pp. xxiv-xxv.

they may be at such service of the carucates and hidage as they used to be in the times of the lord king's ancestors, namely, so as to defend 5 carucates of Kesteven and Holland as against 2 carucates of Lindsey'.[1]

Lady Stenton has pointed out that the Domesday assessment in Lindsey was so much lower than the amount of land under the plough that the men of Kesteven and Holland, where the figures approached more closely to actual conditions, were allowed to pay the same tax on five carucates that the men of Lindsey paid on two.[2] We now find them offering to pay 100 marks in order to be assessed at the old rate, based on Domesday, rather than on the acreage under cultivation.

Only fragmentary records of the collection of this tax are preserved in the Pipe Rolls. By Michaelmas 1194 Worcestershire had paid in full its assessment of £99 12s.; Somerset, assessed at £293 18s. 2d., had paid all but £11 5s. 2d.; and Dorset, assessed at £241 3s. 9d., had paid all but £3 10s. 11d.[3] These three are the only counties whose contributions are recorded for this year.

At the Easter session in 1195 a number of small sums were paid in. William Marshal paid 4s. as hidage from his estates in Sussex; Berkshire paid £3 7d.; the Honour of Wallingford £1; Yorkshire, £20 15s. 7d.; and William of Ste. Mere-Église paid £1 from the escheated lands in Oxfordshire.[4]

By Michaelmas 1195 the sheriff of Cumberland had offered £20 'as the fine that he made with the justiciars for the hidage in Cumberland that was exacted throughout England as an aid for the king's ransom', but he paid nothing. The men of Kesteven and Holland, on the other hand, paid £45 on the 100 marks that they had promised in 1194.[5]

The obvious explanation for the fragmentary character of these returns is that since the hidage was collected for the king's ransom it was not accounted for in the ordinary way by the sheriffs but, like the other sums collected for the ransom, was paid directly into the special treasury set up for that purpose. These few instances cited found their way into the Pipe Roll, one surmises, by accident; certainly they cannot represent the whole of the sums collected. In 1196 nothing whatever was entered in the Pipe Roll.

[1] Pipe Roll 6 Richard I, p. 118. [2] Introd. to Pipe Roll 6 Richard I, p. xxiv.
[3] Pipe Roll 6 Richard I, pp. 130-1, 193-4.
[4] Pipe Roll 7 Richard I, pp. 261-2. [5] Ibid., pp. 214, 160.

By taxing all the land under cultivation and requiring military service from a portion of his tenants-in-chief and scutages from the rest, Richard demanded a contribution from every landholder in the kingdom, both clerk and lay, with one exception. The Cistercians, who probably were now as numerous and who held as much land as the black monks, had been established in England only since the first quarter of the century and had thus not been included in the system under which the abbeys of black monks were considered as tenants-in-chief of the Crown and were assessed knight service on that basis. Furthermore, they specialised in sheep-farming and kept little land under the plough. Thus they were liable neither for knight service nor for carucage.

Richard got round this difficulty by the same device that had been used to collect the money for his ransom: he ordered that they contribute their wool-clip for the year. Assuming that they had given up their clip in the preceding year (and the Pipe Roll of that year shows the costs of hauling wool from various places in Yorkshire, where the greatest Cistercian houses were, to Holme in Norfolk and of hiring ships to carry it to Germany),[1] this would mean that they would be forced to sacrifice the major part of their income for two years in succession. When the monks protested that the king was laying a heavier burden on them than on any other of his subjects, Richard allowed them to purchase their exemption. William of Newburgh, however, says that the king, after praising the loyalty and generosity of the Cistercian abbots in fulsome terms, told them that he was pledging their wool as security, to be redeemed in the following October, for his necessary expenses.[2]

The cities and towns, too, were forced to contribute in a variety of ways. The citizens of Lincoln, for instance, paid 500 marks 'to have such confirmation by the lord king of their liberties as the burgesses of Northampton have'. The citizens of York offered 200 marks 'as a gift for their joy at the lord king's return from Germany', while those of London were assessed 1,500 marks 'as their gift for the king's goodwill and to keep their liberties and as their aid for the lord king's ransom'.[3]

On the last day of the council, 2 April, the king heard a number

[1] Pipe Roll 5 Richard I, pp. 44, 69.
[2] Howden, Vol. III, p. 242; Newburgh, Vol. II, pp. 416-17.
[3] Pipe Roll 6 Richard I, pp. 118, 163, 182.

of complaints against the archbishop of York. Many people, both clerk and lay, accused him of trying to exact money from them unjustly. Since these complaints probably referred to Geoffrey's effort to make the clergy of Yorkshire contribute to the king's ransom, which the canons, at least, had steadfastly refused to do, it is hardly surprising that Geoffrey did not even deign to answer his accusers and that the king dismissed the charges against him.

The charges that were then brought against Gerard of Camville, the constable of Lincoln, were much more serious. At the chancellor's instigation, as it was said, Gerard was accused of harbouring thieves and robbers who sallied forth from Lincoln Castle to rob merchants on their way to the great fair at Stamford. Furthermore, it was charged, he was guilty of contempt for the king's majesty, since he refused to appear before the king's justiciars when they summoned him or to turn the alleged robbers over to them. To all their summonses Gerard merely replied that he was Count John's man and would stand his trial in John's court. Finally, he was accused of being hand in glove with Count John and others of the king's enemies and of having helped them seize the castles of Nottingham and Tickhill.

Gerard denied all these charges, and both sides gave pledges that they would defend their right. The outcome of the trial, if it was ever held, is not recorded, but by Michaelmas of this year Gerard owed 2,000 marks 'to have the lord king's goodwill and to have his lands', and his wife, Nicholaa, owed 300 marks 'to marry her daughter where she will, except to the king's enemies'.[1]

The last subject for discussion was the possible diminution or impairment of his kingly state that Richard might have undergone as a result of his capture, imprisonment, and humiliation at the hands of the emperor. It was probably also known in England that Richard had surrendered the kingdom to the emperor and had given him his cap as a symbol of investiture. The emperor had immediately given England back to Richard, to be held of the emperor as his feudal superior, and had invested Richard with a golden cross. Richard had then promised to pay a yearly tribute of £5,000 sterling.[2]

[1] Howden, Vol. III, pp. 242-3; Pipe Roll 6 Richard I, pp. 118-19.

[2] Howden, Vol. III, pp. 202-3; Ralph of Coggeshall, p. 64; Gervase, Vol. I, p. 524, Vol. II, p. 407.

The barons decided that Richard should be crowned again, to remove any possible doubt as to his being, in his own right, truly king of England. They may have had in mind the precedent set by King Stephen, who either had himself crowned again or else wore his crown in a ceremony of special solemnity at Canterbury at Christmas 1141, after he had been released from his captivity by the Empress Matilda. Although he was in a fever of haste to go back to the Continent and defend his lands against Philip's depredations, Richard reluctantly[1] agreed to go through with the ceremony. He announced that he would be crowned again at Winchester on 17 April, and he ordered all those who had been captured in the various castles that had held out against him and his officials to present themselves before him at Winchester on the day following his coronation. He then went to Clipstone to meet William, king of Scots, and stayed there on the following day, Palm Sunday, so that all the ceremonies of the great festival might be properly observed.[2]

Richard, we are told in his obituary notice, took a great pleasure and interest in ecclesiastical ceremonies and provided rich and splendid vestments for the clerks of his chapel, which, of course, like all the rest of the royal household, travelled with him wherever he went. Ralph, abbot of Coggeshall, tells us that 'by gifts and requests he stimulated his clerks, chanting in loud, clear voices, to sing in a more festive manner, and walking here and there amidst the choir he inspired them, by voice and hand, to sing more loudly'.[3] 'By voice and hand' ('voce ac manu') is an ambiguous expression. Does it mean that Richard sang loudly, beating time with his hand to lead the choir, or does it perhaps mean that the king urged the singers to louder and lustier efforts and administered an occasional buffet where it would do the most good?

The two kings and their attendants went to Southwell on Monday, 4 April, and to Melton Mowbray on the following day. Richard was in such a benevolent mood that King William thought it an opportune time to raise the question of the border counties of Northumberland, Cumberland, and Westmorland, which the Scottish kings had claimed intermittently but never with any success. To William's request that Richard grant him

[1] 'Licet aliquantulum renitens', Ralph of Coggeshall, p. 64.
[2] Howden, Vol. III, p. 243.
[3] Ralph of Coggeshall, p. 97.

those counties 'by right of his predecessors' Richard gave an evasive answer, unwilling to offend a faithful friend and ally, and said that so important a matter would have to be discussed with his barons.

Continuing their progress, the kings were entertained on Wednesday by Peter, the chief forester of Rutland, and reached Geddington on Thursday, where they remained to celebrate the solemnities of Good Friday. They arrived at Northampton on Saturday. After observing Easter with all possible pomp, Richard conferred with the members of his council on Monday concerning the Scottish king's claim. Their decision, of course, was that it could not be allowed, particularly in these perilous times when Richard's enemies in France were threatening him. To soften the refusal, however, an elaborate charter was drawn up in the presence of Queen Eleanor, Archbishop Hubert Walter, Bishop Hugh of Durham, Bishop Jocelin of Glasgow, and many other notables, both English and Scottish, to provide for the honours to be shown to the king of Scots whenever he was summoned to the English court.

On Tuesday, 12 April, King Richard left Northampton and reached Silverstone on his way south. Archbishop Hubert Walter and Bishop Hugh of Durham went on to Brackley, where Hugh had maintained a hospice for the last thirty years. While the bishop's servants were cooking dinner, King William's servants arrived on the scene, claimed the hospice for their master, and attempted unsuccessfully to throw the bishop's servants out. The Scots then bought provisions in the market and set up their kitchen in another part of the hospice.

When Bishop Hugh arrived all this was reported to him. The bishop, who had royal blood in his veins, refused to give up his hospice to the king of Scots. He ordered the tables to be set up and dinner to be served. While he was at table Archbishop Hubert arrived. Knowing that King William was already in a touchy temper after Richard's refusal to give him the northern counties, the archbishop advised Hugh to give up his hospice as a friendly gesture to the king of Scots and offered to share his lodgings with the bishop.

Before the matter could be settled, King William, who had been hunting in the forest, learned of the bishop's inhospitable attitude. He fell into a rage, ordered that the dinner that had been prepared for him be distributed to the poor, and went to Silverstone to complain to King Richard of the bishop's insolence.

Bishop Hugh, by this act of arrogance, lost all the goodwill he had gained by his capture of Tickhill and his other exertions on the king's behalf. Richard in a fury marked him down for punishment at the first opportunity.

The king reached Woodstock on 13 April and Freemantle on the next day and arrived in Winchester on the 15th. When Bishop Godfrey of Lucy came to welcome him, the king took away from him Winchester Castle, the two manors that Godfrey had bought and paid for in 1189, and the greater part of his inheritance. There is no evidence that Godfrey had done anything to deserve such harsh treatment. He had played an honourable part in effecting peace between John and Longchamp in 1191 and had actively opposed John's subsequent treachery, being one of the bishops to pronounce the sentence of excommunication upon him in February 1194. He had, however, incurred the enmity of Longchamp when the latter was deposed, and it was no doubt through the influence of Longchamp, who was all-powerful with the king, that he was now disgraced.[1]

After dinner on Saturday Richard left Winchester Castle and went to St. Swithun's Priory, where he 'had himself bathed' and spent the night. On Low Sunday, 17 April, the ceremony of the king's coronation took place. Two archbishops, Hubert Walter of Canterbury and John of Dublin, and eleven bishops, those of Durham, Lincoln, London, Rochester, Ely, Chichester, Exeter, Hereford, Worcester, St. Davids, and Bangor, were present. Archbishop Hubert with the other bishops and the monks of St. Swithun's went in procession to the king's chamber in the monastery, where the regalia were laid out on a fair cloth. The king was clothed in his royal robes, and the archbishop placed in his left hand the golden verge tipped with the likeness of an eagle and in his right the regal sceptre. Then Hubert placed the golden crown on the king's head.

The procession went from the king's chamber into the cathedral, with clerks, monks, abbots, bishops, and archbishops in due order, all singing, let us hope, loudly and joyfully enough to please the king. Next came four barons carrying lighted candles and then William, king of Scots, with Hamelin, earl of Warenne,

[1] Howden, Vol. III, pp. 243-6; Pipe Roll 6 Richard I, pp. 7, 10.

on his right and Rannulf, earl of Chester, on his left, all three carrying swords in golden scabbards. King Richard, wearing his crown and carrying the verge and the sceptre, with his chancellor, William Longchamp, bishop of Ely, on his right and Richard, bishop of London, on his left, walked under a silken canopy supported on the points of four lances carried by Roger Bigod, earl of Norfolk, William of Fors, count of Aumale, William Longsword, the king's bastard half-brother, earl of Salisbury, and William, earl of Ferrers.

Earls, barons, knights, and a vast multitude of people brought up the rear of the procession, filling every space in the cathedral. When they arrived before the high altar, Richard knelt, and the archbishop recited the customary prayers, beginning 'O Lord, save the king'. Richard was escorted to his throne, on the epistle side, by the archbishop of Canterbury and the bishop of London. The archbishop, wearing his pallium, celebrated Mass, in the course of which he recited the collect for the king after the collect of the day, and three clerks sang the antiphon 'Christus vincit', which was customarily sung in the king's presence on great festivals. At the offertory Richard made his offering with the same ceremonies as were used at his coronation, and he received Holy Communion.

Queen Eleanor and her maids sat on the gospel side, facing her son. Berengaria, queen of England, was not there. After leaving the Holy Land at about the same time that Richard did, but not in his company, she went to Rome and stayed there for half a year, and then to Poitiers, where she presumably was at this time. John, of course, was still in France with his ally, King Philip. Archbishop Geoffrey had been warned by Richard on the day before not to attempt to have his cross carried before him in the procession, since they were in the province of Canterbury. Geoffrey, rather than relinquish a show of authority to which he stubbornly clung, absented himself from the ceremony. So, too, did the hapless Bishop Godfrey, now in disgrace with the king through Longchamp's machinations, although the pageant was enacted in his cathedral.[1]

Although contemporary writers refer to this ceremony as a coronation, it is clear that it was not the coronation service proper, such as was observed in September 1189, that took place, for the

[1] Howden, Vol. III, pp. 228, 246-8; Gervase, Vol. I, pp. 524-7.

anointing and hallowing of the king by the archbishop of Canterbury partook of a quasi-sacramental character and could not be repeated, any more than the consecration of a bishop, on which the rite was closely modelled, could be repeated. This was, instead, a revival of the old ceremonial crown-wearing of the English kings, which had been last observed by Henry II at Worcester in 1158, so long ago that the details of the ceremony had been forgotten and information had to be obtained from Canterbury, where records had been kept of King Stephen's crown-wearing in 1141.[1]

That Gervase of Canterbury, who, as sacristan, probably supplied the information, should have been reminded of Stephen's crown-wearing is significant, for that ceremony was observed partly in order to clear Stephen from the taint of having been imprisoned by the Empress Matilda and declared deposed by a council at Winchester in 1141. Gervase evidently thought that there was a likeness between the cases of Richard, newly returned from captivity, and of Stephen, recently released from prison by the empress.

Most significant of all, the elaborate pageantry of the king's showing himself crowned and in all his majesty before his people, surrounded by the bishops and barons of the realm, indicates how strongly the sacred character of the kingship was still felt. The king was king by the grace of God; his reign began with his anointing and crowning by the Church; and the coronation rite was thought to imprint a character somewhat similar to that imparted by the consecration of a bishop. The divinity that 'doth hedge a king' was still a very real one, and the king's person was regarded with an awe that Richard's crown-wearing would naturally increase in the minds of the spectators. This awe was not something that the king attempted to impose upon his subjects; it had existed from the earliest times and was regarded as a natural adjunct of kingship, as is shown by the fact, reported by Ralph of Coggeshall, that it was the Great Council that insisted upon the crown-wearing ceremony, to which Richard, impatient to repel Philip's encroachments upon his territories, consented reluctantly.[2]

After the ceremonies in the cathedral had been completed, the

[1] J. H. Round: *Geoffrey de Mandeville* (London, 1892), p. 138.
[2] Ralph of Coggeshall, p. 64.

procession escorted the king back to his chamber, where he took off the heavy crown and robes of state and exchanged them for lighter and more comfortable ones. The bishops, earls, and barons then went with the king to the monks' refectory for a banquet almost as sumptuous as the one served at the coronation in 1189. After some dispute between the citizens of London and those of Winchester, the men of London, by which the chronicler no doubt means the leading citizens, paid 200 marks for the privilege of serving in the pantry, and the men of Winchester had to be content with serving in the kitchen. After the feast the king returned to Winchester Castle, which he had taken away from Bishop Godfrey.

Bishop Hugh of Durham, as we have seen, had incurred the king's ill will because of his discourteous behaviour to the king of Scots. On Thursday, 19 April, the bishop, 'of his own free will, without any compulsion', surrendered to the king the county of Northumberland, for which he had promised 2,000 marks, still unpaid four years later.[1]

The king of Scots immediately renewed his request and offered Richard 15,000 marks for the county 'and its appurtenances', advancing the claim that his father, Henry, earl of Huntingdon, had held it as a gift from King Henry II and that his brother, King Malcolm, had then held it in peace for five years. Richard asked the members of his council for their advice in this matter and then told William that he might have the county, but without the castles, for 15,000 marks. This was not at all what the king of Scots was bargaining for, since the possession of the county without its castles would be an empty honour, and William declined the offer.

On the following day, Wednesday the 20th, Richard dealt with the prisoners who had been captured at Nottingham, Tickhill, and elsewhere and had been brought to Winchester for judgment. The king allowed the less important ones to be freed on condition that they find sureties for 100 marks each that they would come when they were summoned and stand their trials. The richer ones, however, did not get off so lightly; Richard ordered that they be put in prison and held for ransom, and one may be sure that the king fixed the figures high enough to bring in a substantial sum. The Pipe Roll shows the expenditure of

[1] Howden, Vol. III, pp. 248-9; Pipe Roll 6 Richard I, p. 134.

29s. 9d. for fetters and chains with which to hold the prisoners at Winchester. So many estates were confiscated or fell into the king's hands that instead of being farmed out in the usual way to the highest bidder they were placed under the supervision of two escheators, William of Ste. Mère-Église for the south and William Bardulf for the north, and the profits were paid directly into the Exchequer.[1]

King William, with dogged persistency, renewed his request, on Thursday, for Northumbria, complete with castles, and again Richard refused. He held out the hope, however, that when he returned to England from settling affairs in Normandy he would be inclined to give a more favourable answer. 'Grieving and perplexed' by Richard's repeated refusals, King William set out for Scotland on 22 April.

Richard meanwhile was receiving more and more alarming reports of the condition of his lands across the Channel. He left Winchester on 22 April and set out for Portsmouth, reaching Bishop's Walton that night. On the following day Archbishop Geoffrey arrived at his brother's court with his cross carried before him, although he was not in his own province. Archbishop Hubert complained to the king of his brother's arrogant conduct, but Richard, who had no taste for petty ecclesiastical quarrels when his own rights, or what he considered his rights, were not being infringed upon, brusquely told the two archbishops that it was no concern of his where they had their crosses carried and ordered them to refer the matter to the pope. Geoffrey was still in his brother's good graces, as is apparent from the fact that Richard gave back to him Baugé and Langes in Anjou, of which he had deprived Geoffrey in an earlier fit of displeasure.

The king had of course heard all the unsavoury details of the quarrel between his brother and Bishop William Longchamp, with Geoffrey complaining of the way in which Longchamp had treated him and Longchamp in turn telling of the ignominious fashion in which he had been driven from England. On 24 April, accordingly, the king, on hearing Geoffrey's complaints anew, forced them to agree to 'a final peace and concord', and Bishop William Longchamp swore an oath, supported by a hundred priests as oath-helpers, 'that he had neither ordered nor willed that the archbishop of York be seized'. With this matter

[1] Howden, Vol. III, p. 249; Pipe Roll 6 Richard I, pp. 213, 1–27.

settled, Richard, Queen Eleanor, and their attendants went on to Portsmouth, where over £100 had been spent in making the king's houses ready for the party.[1]

Richard's army meanwhile had been assembling at the port. In addition to the third part of the feudal tenants who had been summoned and who had not offered a fine in order to escape military service, the king's agents had been recruiting mercenaries, chiefly in the Welsh marches, and assembling ships to ferry the army and its provisions across the Channel. While the ships were being loaded, Richard went hunting at Stanstead. During his absence the mercenary soldiers at Portsmouth began fighting amongst themselves, and the king had to return in order to establish order.

When all was ready, such a storm arose that the fleet could not sail. Richard became more and more impatient at the delay. Although the storm had not abated, on Monday, 2 May, he ordered that all the men and horses go aboard. Against the advice of his sailors, he put out to sea in his 'long ship' in the teeth of the gale. After being tossed about all that day and the following night, he turned back to Portsmouth on the 3rd. The storm continued for over a week.

As soon as the wind had blown itself out, on Thursday, 12 May, King Richard, Queen Eleanor, the English knights, and the army of mercenaries set sail in a fleet of a hundred vessels and landed at Barfleur. Richard was never to see England again, nor did Eleanor return during her son's lifetime; she spent the remainder of Richard's reign in retirement at Fontevraud.[2]

Bishop Hugh of Durham, it will be remembered, had given up the county of Northumberland 'of his own free will, without any compulsion'. After the king had left the country, however, the bishop began to regret his surrender and sent a messenger to the king to offer him 2,000 marks if he might have the county back again. It is not stated whether this sum was to be in addition to the 2,000 marks that he still owed for the county or whether he merely undertook to pay the amount he had originally promised.

Hugh Bardolf, meanwhile, one of the justiciars, whom the king had appointed sheriff of Northumberland when Hugh re-

[1] Howden, Vol. III, pp. 250-1; Pipe Roll 6 Richard I, pp. 6, 7, 10.

[2] Howden, Vol. III, p. 251; H. G. Richardson: 'The Letters and Charters of Eleanor of Aquitaine', p. 205.

linquished the county, demanded that the bishop turn it over, together with the castles of Newcastle-upon-Tyne and Bamborough, to him as the rightful custodian. When Bishop Hugh's messenger returned, he bore a letter from the king that expressed an unflattering distrust of the bishop's offer and of his readiness or ability to pay. Richard ordered Hugh Bardolf to turn over the county and the castles to the bishop, but only if the bishop could give trustworthy pledges that he would pay the promised sum.

Hugh Bardolf, who had neither the county nor the securities, proposed to Bishop Hugh that the bishop turn the county over to him, as he had promised at Winchester in April. Once he had formal possession of the county, Hugh Bardolf said, he would return it to the bishop, as the king had ordered, provided of course that Bishop Hugh found the stipulated pledges that he would pay the 2,000 marks.

'There is no point', Bishop Hugh replied, loftily ignoring the matter of the 2,000 marks, 'in my giving the county and the castles to you, merely so that you can give them back to me. I have them already, and I will hold on to them.'

Hugh Bardolf reported all this to the king, who in a blazing fury ordered that the bishop should be deprived immediately of the castles and the county, that he should nevertheless still pay the promised 2,000 marks, and that he should in addition give up the manor of Sadberge, which he had bought from the king in 1189.

Archbishop Geoffrey had enjoyed the king's protection as long as his brother was in England. Once Richard had left, however, Geoffrey's enemies had the upper hand, for the king had entrusted supreme authority to Archbishop Hubert Walter, who had been dean of York at the time of Geoffrey's election and the leader of the protest against it. The canons of York renewed their complaints against their archbishop, to which the king had previously paid no attention, before the chief justiciar, who lent a more attentive ear to them. Hubert sent a commission made up of Roger Bigod, earl of Norfolk, William of Warenne, William of Stuteville, Hugh Bardolf, William Briwerre, Geoffrey Haket, and William son of Richard, to York to conduct a hearing on the charges. They ordered that the archbishop's men, who had seized the property of the recalcitrant canons when they refused to contribute to the king's ransom, should be imprisoned on charges of robbery. Although his servants had acted at Geoffrey's orders, the justiciars would not allow him to stand surety for them.

The justiciars then summoned the archbishop, who was at his manor of Ripon, to appear before them, but Geoffrey would not recognise their competence to judge between him and his chapter and refused to come. They punished him by confiscating all his estates except Ripon and installed William of Stuteville and Geoffrey Haket as custodians both of the archbishop's property and of the county of York.

As a crowning insult they re-installed the contumacious canons whom Geoffrey had driven out of their stalls because they refused both to celebrate divine services and to contribute to the king's ransom. Although Geoffrey had been stubborn and high-handed, the canons, by refusing to perform their duties, had placed themselves so clearly in the wrong that the justiciars' actions could have proceeded only from Hubert Walter's instructions to them to humiliate Geoffrey in every way possible. Leaving aside the question of the justice of these actions, the lay justiciars could not possibly have had the authority to institute the canons of a cathedral in defiance of their archbishop, even though they were acting at the orders of Hubert Walter, who was not one to observe the legal niceties of a situation and did not always take the trouble to make it clear whether he was acting as archbishop or as chief justiciar.[1]

The latter part of Howden's story is thrown into doubt because it apparently does not agree with the entries in the Pipe Roll for this year. As Lady Stenton points out in her introduction to the Pipe Roll, 'If this story were true the two custodians whom Howden named should only have accounted at most for a month's revenues of the lands of the archbishopric of York at Michaelmas 1194. . . . The two custodians do not jointly account for the whole of Geoffrey's lands, nor do they account for the whole of the lands of the archbishopric.' Geoffrey Haket accounts for two manors for half a year and William of Stuteville for Ripon for half a year and for the archbishopric of York for a whole year, which they probably would not have done if the archbishop had been deprived of his property in late August or early September, the apparent date of these happenings. Further-

[1] Howden. Vol. III, pp. 260-2.

more, Geoffrey continued to act as sheriff of Yorkshire, with Roger of Batvent as his deputy.[1]

There is the possibility, on the other hand, that the dispossession was made retroactive to the date when Geoffrey had last collected the revenues. If he had collected the income from his manors of Sherburn, Othey, and Ripon at Easter and had postponed the accounting for the other manors till a year's audit could be held at Michaelmas, the custodians of the confiscated estates could have collected all the outstanding revenues at Michaelmas 1194 and thus accounted for a half or a whole year, as the case might be, even though they had been in possession for a shorter time. King Richard and his officials were concerned much more with collecting as much money as possible than with observing scrupulous fairness in their proceedings.

Roger of Howden is particularly well informed and reliable concerning events in Yorkshire, and one hesitates to discard his testimony concerning the dispossession of Geoffrey, since it is corroborated by Gervase of Canterbury, who says:

> In the month of August the archbishop of Canterbury, at the royal order [*ex mandato regio*; Howden says *auctoritate regia*], confiscated the archbishopric of York. The king demanded from the aforesaid archbishop, his brother, a thousand marks of silver and more than that, it was rumoured. Although he crossed over and sent messengers to Rome, he could neither be reconciled with his brother, the king, nor regain his archbishopric. For these and other reasons the justiciars called itinerant at the order of the archbishop of Canterbury were sent throughout England in the month of September to deal with the affairs of the realm.[2]

After sustaining this crushing blow from the lay authorities in August, a month later Geoffrey suffered a heavy defeat at the hands of his clerical enemies. Hamo, the precentor of York, Geoffrey of Muschamp, archdeacon of Cleveland, and Master William Testard, archdeacon of Nottingham, arrived in York from Rome, where they had gone with Simon of Apulia and others from the chapter to lay their accusations against Geoffrey before the pope. They bore a variety of letters from Celestine III, which they apparently divulged at intervals as they thought the occasion warranted.

[1] Pipe Roll 6 Richard I, pp. xxviii-xxix, 145; Pipe Roll 7 Richard I, p. 81.
[2] Gervase, Vol. I, p. 528.

One set of letters absolved the canons from the excommunication that Geoffrey had laid on them, lifted the sentence of interdict that he had placed on the churches belonging to them, and ordered that their possessions, sequestrated by Geoffrey, be restored to them. Bishop Hugh of Le Puiset, to whom the publication of these orders was entrusted, celebrated Mass in York Minster on Michaelmas Day and announced to the congregation that their archbishop's sentences had been nullified by the pope.

Geoffrey immediately appealed to Rome and then crossed over to Normandy to lay his troubles before the king. Richard, on 3 November, wrote to the justiciars to inform them that Geoffrey had made his peace with him and had offered satisfactory assurances for 2,000 marks of his debt, in view of which the king ordered that Geoffrey's estates be restored to him.

Geoffrey of Muschamp had formerly been one of the archbishop's friends and owed his position as archdeacon of Cleveland to him. Now that the archdeacon had turned against him, Archbishop Geoffrey confessed to his brother that at the time of their father's death he had fraudently affixed the Great Seal, of which he had possession as chancellor, to the letters appointing Geoffrey of Muschamp archdeacon of Cleveland and William of Stigandby and Master Erard canons of York.

Richard, no doubt at Geoffrey's prompting, ordered that the three clerics be deprived of their benefices and compelled to refund the incomes they had received from them. Although Roger of Howden gives the text of Richard's letter, dated at Mamers in Maine on 3 November 1194, Geoffrey of Muschamp was still archdeacon of Cleveland in June 1195 and the two canons apparently continued to enjoy their benefices. The Pipe Roll for 1195 records that they owe £100 'to have the lord king's favour and their rents in peace', which may explain why the writ was not obeyed.[1]

Archbishop Geoffrey did not return to England during the remainder of his brother's reign and thus passes from these pages, although the unseemly doings at York, where dissension raged almost unchecked, will occasionally be noted.

Geoffrey's quarrel with his chapter has been described at perhaps inordinate length because it is an excellent illustration both

[1] Howden, Vol. III, pp. 272-4, 294; Pipe Roll 7 Richard I, p. 91.

of some of the defects of the Church in England at the time and of some of the evils that accompanied the extension and consolidation of the papal power that had been going on for the past century or so. Although the increased centralisation of the Church's government was in many respects salutary and indeed necessary, it was nevertheless accompanied by some evils, as may be seen from Geoffrey's case.

Many of Geoffrey's troubles arose from his character and temperament. He was impatient and hot-tempered, and, having lived and worked for many years in close association with his father, he was unable to accommodate himself to another sphere, in which he was not backed up by the royal authority. Another personal element was introduced by the chapter of York, who seem to have been as quarrelsome and stubborn a group of men as could be found anywhere in England and who were bitterly opposed to Geoffrey's nomination in the first place. The fundamental difficulty, however, lay in Geoffrey's unsuitability for the episcopal office. He had once before declined to be consecrated bishop; he had neither the character nor the training that would fit him for such an office, and he accepted it in the end only as a last resort, when his brother's accession forced him to find another niche for himself.

Beyond the personal elements, Geoffrey's sorry career illustrates some of the evils that were prevalent in the Church in England at the time. In spite of the fiction of free election by the chapters, bishops were in almost every case nominated by the king; only in the poorer and more obscure sees were chapters allowed to elect whom they chose as their bishops. In making his choice the king was rarely guided by the criteria of learning and holiness of life, although here there were some outstanding exceptions, most notably in Henry II's choice of Hugh of Avalon as bishop of Lincoln. Ordinarily, however, the king used the office to reward the faithful clerks of his household who had earned his gratitude and favour by their administrative abilities, by their service on diplomatic missions, and by their performance at the Exchequer and in the courts.

To such men the king gave the office as a reward for their services and expected those services to continue. In many cases the bishop's services as a royal official continued to make the first claim on his time and energy, with his diocese coming a poor second. Hubert Walter, as we shall see, was first and foremost chief justiciar of England and only incidentally archbishop of Canterbury, and it was as chief justiciar that he made his mark on his times, rather than as archbishop. In fairness, however, one must admit that there is little evidence that he neglected his more obvious duties as archbishop; the wonder is that he found the time to do as much as he did.

The result of this system of selection was that bishops were usually good administrators, if nothing more, and all too often they were nothing more. They spent more time at the king's court or in his service than in their dioceses, and the dioceses inevitably suffered. Most of the bishops were well versed in law, which had its unfortunate aspect, for this learning made them both legalistic in an unfavourable sense and unduly litigious. Knowing legal procedure as well as they did, they fought with the utmost tenacity for every right, real or imagined, and spent much time and money in pursuing every quarrel through all the ramifications the courts allowed.

The chroniclers of the time record these unseemly quarrels with minute attention, but none of them mentions what the people thought of these doings or how the Church, in the persons of its lowliest members, must have suffered either from their neglect at the hands of their shepherds or from the unedifying spectacles that these quarrels provided. What, for instance, could the people of York have thought as they watched the scenes of discords and of violence that were played out before their eyes by the very men whose chief aim in life should have been the welfare of the souls entrusted to them? How could they have respected the spiritual authority of these men as they watched them hurling excommunications right and left and prohibiting divine services in order to punish their foes?

The writers of the time boast that there was no heresy in England, as there was, for instance, in the south of France with the Albigensians, but one suspects that sheer indifference, which is almost as bad as heresy, must have been rife. As Chaucer expresses it in much stronger language, a flock is no better than its shepherd. What, then, could have been the state of religion in Yorkshire or in the diocese of Ely or of Coventry?

Even if the bishops had been all that they should have been, the growing centralisation of power in the hands of the papal curia had so weakened their authority that it could often be flouted with impunity. A certain degree of centralisation had no doubt become necessary if the Church were not to lapse into anarchy, and no-one could deny that the great reforms instituted by Gregory VII and his successors gave new life to the Church at a critical time in its history. But as the popes asserted and made effective their claim to be the universal ordinary—to have direct authority, that is, over every Christian—the authority of the bishops was weakened in two ways: by the growing frequency of appeals to Rome and by the granting of exemptions.

Appeals from the sentence of a bishop or other ecclesiastical superior to the judgment of the pope assured that individuals would not be oppressed by unjust rulers and that a fairly uniform code of law should exist through the Church. On the other hand, appeals to Rome meant that almost indefinite delay could be obtained if either party to a suit were rich or persistent enough. Appeals were costly affairs, involving journeys to Rome and, so the writers of the time assert, rich gifts to the members of the papal curia, so that often the winner was the man with the longest purse.

Appeals were judged by men who often knew of the circumstances of the case only as much as the interested parties chose to tell them. Most serious of all, they weakened the authority of the bishops, against whose every decision there could be an appeal to Rome, thus forcing the bishops to spend a great deal of time and money in defending their actions. Even if the pope came down on the bishop's side, the ultimate acquiescence of his opponent might come many years after the original decision.

The popes realised the dangers of frustratory appeals and tried to curb the worst of them by appointing delegates to hear and decide cases on the spot, with no appeals allowed against their decisions. They often undid the good effect such a procedure might have, however, by entertaining appeals against a decision even when it had been stated in the judges' commission that no appeal would be allowed, and thus the evil continued. The case of Archbishop Geoffrey and his canons shows how the organisation and administration of a diocese might be disrupted for years on end by the use of frustratory appeals.

The second factor in weakening the bishops' authority was the pope's practice of granting exemptions from that authority to certain groups, usually monasteries, within a diocese and of making those groups answerable only to the pope or his legates, thus bypassing the authority of the bishop. Although this protected a monastery from the arbitrary action of an ill-disposed bishop, on the other hand it meant that almost every diocese had areas where the bishop's authority did not extend. While bishops normally had little interest in the internal affairs of monasteries unless they formed their cathedral chapters, they were gravely concerned when the monasteries had possession of parish churches, to which the monks attempted to extend their exemptions, and many conflicts arose from this source.

Added to Archbishop Geoffrey's difficulties with his chapter was his capricious treatment at the hands of his brother and of his brother's chief justiciar. Archbishop Hubert Walter's treatment of Geoffrey was grossly unfair. Bishop Stubbs calls it 'one of the most arbitrary and high-handed proceedings of Hubert's ministry; and hardly anything, either on moral, legal, or constitutional grounds, can be said in excuse for it'.[1] There is the possibility, however, that Archbishop Hubert may have been acting, not wholly on his own initiative, but on the king's instructions, for the only consistent feature of Richard's treatment of Geoffrey was his effort to wring money from him and to subject him to humiliating alternations of favour and of disgrace, culminating always in the exaction of more money.

Affairs at York were by now in such a tangled state that it would have defied a legal genius to straighten them out. Archbishop Hubert, who was above all a practical man, may have acted as he did in an attempt to restore some sort of order, which Geoffrey was apparently unable to do, and at least to put the cathedral chapter on a working basis again.

Now that he was left in almost complete charge of the country whilst the king was in Normandy, Hubert Walter set to work with a will. His genius as an administrator appears in its most favourable light in this summer of 1194, when he sent the itinerant justiciars about the country to restore order and to catch up with the arrears in the courts. In the troubled times before Hubert's accession the legal system had continued to function, but it did so rather fitfully without the driving force of a strong man behind it, and the large area under Count John's jurisdiction had

[1] Preface to Howden, Vol. IV, p. lxii.

been exempt from the justiciars' visitations. Those who were involved in the massacre of the Jews in 1190 had not all been properly punished; the property of the Jews who had been slain had not been fully accounted for; the king's rights over escheats and wardships had been disregarded; and those who had sided with Count John had not been fully brought to account. Finally, the king's sale of offices and Longchamp's favouritism had put into positions of authority men who abused that authority, and such abuses had to be enquired into and corrected.

The articles of the eyre of 1194[1] form the most important legal document of Richard's reign. Drawn up by Hubert Walter, the greatest legal expert in England, to guide the itinerant justiciars in their work, they form a logical continuation of the great measures of the reign of Henry II.

The preface provides for the setting up of juries of presentment, the forerunners of the later grand juries. The regular use of the jury of presentment was one of the most important contributions of Henry II to the development of English law. The sworn inquest had been used in England even before the Norman Conquest,[2] but it was Henry II who gave it formal recognition as a permanent and regular part of legal procedure and greatly extended its functions.

In Chapter VI of the Constitutions of Clarendon, in 1164, Henry tried prematurely to introduce the jury of presentment into the proceedings of the courts christian.[3] The procedure he proposed was simple. The sheriff was to nominate twelve lawful men, that is, men of good reputation, of the neighbourhood, who would be presumed to know the facts of the matters under investigation, and have them swear in the bishop's presence to give truthful answers to the questions they were to be asked. The bishop would then question them as to those offences against morals that lay within the jurisdiction of the courts christian. Thus, 'if the offenders are of such condition that no-one wants or dares to accuse them', they might nevertheless be brought to justice by the bishop, acting on the information given him by the jurors.

[1] Howden, Vol. III, pp. 262-7.

[2] See Naomi D. Hurnard: 'The Jury of Presentment and the Assize of Clarendon', *English Historical Review*, LVI (July 1941), pp. 374-410.

[3] *Materials for the History of Thomas Becket*, Vol. V, p. 75.

This procedure was intended both to protect laymen from denunciation by the unsupported word of archdeacons and rural deans, who had a bad reputation for abusing their powers,[1] and to ensure that great and powerful men did not escape unpunished. The quarrel between Henry and St. Thomas and the pope and the rejection of the Constitutions by both St. Thomas and the pope, however, prevented this provision from being put into effect.

Two years later, in 1166, Henry introduced the regular use of the jury of presentment into the civil courts by the provisions of Chapter I of the Assize of Clarendon. Without specifying how they were to be selected, although presumably they would be nominated by the sheriff, this chapter provides that a jury made up of twelve law-worthy men of the hundred and four law-worthy men of each township were to be put under oath to speak the truth. The justiciars and the sheriff were then to ask 'if there is any man who is charged or is publicly known as a robber or a murderer or a thief, or anyone who was a harbourer of robbers or murderers or thieves, since the lord king became king'.[2]

The Assize of Northampton, in 1176, repeated the provisions of the Assize of Clarendon, but Chapter I was somewhat more specific as to the composition of the jury of presentment. Twelve knights from the hundred were to be chosen, again presumably by the sheriff, but if no knights were present their places might be taken by twelve 'free and law-worthy men.' They were to be joined by four men, of unspecified condition, from each township of the hundred in turn, and this jury of sixteen was to be interrogated by the justiciars. In addition to the crimes of robbery, murder, and theft, the Assize of Northampton added those of forgery, arson, and treason to the list of offences the justiciars were to enquire into.[3]

Although the Assize of Clarendon had provided that the juries were to be questioned by the justiciars and the sheriff, the Assize of Northampton mentioned only the justiciars. Between the two assizes came the great Inquest of Sheriffs in 1170, through which so many cases of malfeasance and corruption were uncovered that Henry deprived almost all the sheriffs of their

[1] See, e.g., William son of Stephen, in *Materials*, Vol. III, pp. 44-5.

[2] *Gesta*, Vol. II, p. cxlvii.

[3] *Gesta*, Vol. I, p. 108. See also Richardson and Sayles: *The Governance of Medieval England*, pp. 438-49.

offices and instituted new ones. Because of the opportunities for peculation inherent in their office, the sheriffs were one of the weakest links of the whole administrative system, and Henry tried various expedients both to appoint men whom he could trust and to reduce their powers.

The office was a highly profitable one, as may be seen from the large sums that were offered for it. As the resident fiscal officer of the Crown in the county, the sheriff's principal function was to collect the farm of the manors in the royal demesne and the profits of the courts and transmit the money to the Exchequer. The farm of the county, which had been fixed long before this time, was usually far below the amount actually brought in. By Richard's time, in a period of rising prices and some increase in agricultural efficiency, the gap had become particularly apparent, and Richard, as we have seen, attempted to narrow it, both by selling the office at a high price and by exacting an increment on the fixed farm.

In the earlier part of Henry's reign the sheriffs had been mostly local magnates with strong local ties and interests and hence incapable, in many cases, of administering impartial justice. Ralph of Diceto tells of the various expedients Henry employed, using first one class of men and then another, in an endeavour to find sheriffs who were both reliable and honest in collecting and transmitting the money due from the county and impartial in trying the cases that came before them in the county court.[1]

Since such men were hard to find and apt, when found, to be corrupted by the opportunities the office presented, Henry gradually reduced the judicial functions of the sheriffs and transferred their powers to his justiciars, a small group of men who travelled over the country to hear cases and who were directly under the king's eye and presumably free of local ties and bias.

The Assize of Northampton thus marks the first formal step in depriving the sheriffs of some of their judicial functions by making the juries of accusation answerable only to the justiciars, although it is assumed that the sheriff selected the jurors in the first place.

The Great Assize, which Henry instituted in 1179, provided that a tenant whose right to the land he was occupying was challenged might have the question settled by a jury of knights

[1] Diceto, Vol. I, p. 434.

rather than by the old-fashioned duel with his challenger. The members of this jury, instead of being selected by the sheriff, were removed from his direct nomination, which would indicate that Henry's distrust of his sheriffs had not lessened. According to the writ for establishing the jury for the Great Assize, the sheriff was directed to summon four law-worthy knights, who would then elect, under oath, twelve law-worthy knights. These twelve, constituting the jury, would then be put on oath and questioned by the justiciars concerning the ownership of the land in dispute.[1]

The instructions for the conduct of the eyre of 1194 begin with the method of organising the juries of presentment, and it is significant that Hubert Walter, the author of these instructions, should carry on the principles developed by Henry II and thoroughly familiar to Hubert Walter through his legal experience in the circle of his uncle, Rannulf Glanville. Hubert provided that the selection of the jury should be removed one step further still from direct nomination by the sheriff. The instructions of 1194 direct that four knights are to be elected from each county, who will on their oath select two law-worthy knights from each hundred or wapentake. These two, in turn, are to elect ten knights or, if there are not enough knights, law-worthy and free men, from the hundred or wapentake, to join with the two in constituting a jury of twelve, who will on oath answer to the itinerant justiciars concerning the matters set forth in the body of the instructions.

The difficulty in interpreting this provision lies in the meaning to be given to 'elect' (*eligere*). Bishop Stubbs believed that the four knights of the shire 'were elected by the county court'.[2] One may object, however, that if they were to be so elected, it seems pointless to arrange such an elaborate procedure as to elect four knights, who are in turn to elect two knights, who are then to elect ten knights. With the precedents of the earlier assizes to guide him, it seems strange that Hubert Walter should deliberately introduce one more step into the process unless he wanted thereby to introduce some sort of a safeguard. Judging from

[1] Glanvill: *De Legibus et Consuetudinibus Regni Angliae*, ed. George E. Woodbine (New Haven, 1932), p. 66; Doris M. Stenton: *English Justice between the Norman Conquest and the Great Charter, 1066-1215* (Philadelphia, 1964), p. 49.

[2] Preface to Howden, Vol. IV, pp. xcvii-xcix.

the earlier difficulties with the sheriffs, one would suppose that he wanted to make sure that the members of the jury were as far removed as possible from the sheriff's influence. On the other hand, the sheriff could not well be bypassed completely, for he was the one officer responsible for the whole county and he would know which knights were available for jury-duty and would be well informed on conditions in their neighbourhoods.

If the knights, in other words, were to be chosen by direct election by the county court, it would be much simpler to provide for the election of the jurymen as such rather than for the complicated procedure set forth.

It seems more likely that 'elect' is used here in the sense of 'select' and that the sheriff nominated the initial four knights. In any case, one must beware of reading into the twelfth century the democratic procedures of the nineteenth and twentieth centuries, in which a numerical majority of votes constitutes an election. Votes were weighted in the twelfth century, as we may see from accounts of episcopal and monastic elections, with the votes of the older and wiser members of a community, the 'seniores et saniores', counting for more than those of the younger ones. In most cases, a unanimous verdict was expected, although no doubt a great deal of wrangling and jockeying often preceded the decision. In the same way, one may doubt that the decision of the county court would be reached by a mere show of hands. The sheriff and other magnates of the county had ample means of making their choices known and of securing agreement on them.

In any case, whether the initial four knights who set the machinery in motion were selected by the sheriff or elected under his eye by the county court, it seems clear that Hubert Walter introduced the safeguards contained in this provision in order to remove the jury of accusation from undue influence by the sheriff.

Once selected, the members of the jury are to be put on their oath to tell the truth and then are to answer a searching set of questions contained in the body of the instructions. The questions reveal the mind of a trained and highly efficient administrator who was taking over the government of the country after a period of disorder and uncertainty and who was determined to obtain the clearest possible picture of the state of the country and of its administration and particularly of the diminutions of its rights and revenues that the Crown might have suffered under the succession of incompetent or corrupt officials.

The first two chapters are concerned with the pleas of the Crown, both old and new, and with all pending pleas. The pleas of the Crown embraced those offences over which jurisdiction was reserved to the royal courts or the king's justiciars: robbery, murder, and theft, as specified by Chapter I of the Assize of Clarendon; forgery, arson, and treason, as added by Chapter I of the Assize of Northampton; and the harbouring of men guilty of these offences. Hubert Walter's object was to clear up the arrears of cases that had accumulated during the last few years, both of the pleas of the Crown properly speaking and of all cases that had come before the royal justiciars through an appeal from a lower court or by means of a writ specially issued to bring a case into the royal courts, such as a writ of novel disseisin, of mort d'ancestor, and the like, which had the effect of removing the case from the court of the lord of whom the disputed land was held into the king's court.

A number of scattered chapters direct that enquiry be made specifically concerning malefactors and those who harboured or helped them (Chap. VII), forgers (Chap. VIII), usurers who had died and their chattels, which would be forfeited to the Crown (Chap. XV), and those who sold wine and other commodities by false measures (Chap. XVI). A further attempt to catch up on the arrears of justice may be seen in the enquiry to be directed into the hearings of the Great Assize concerning the ownership of land worth a hundred shillings or less (Chap. XVIII), and into the defaults of those who failed either to pay their amercements or to prosecute an appeal once they had begun it (Chap. XIX).

Chapters III to VI direct that a careful enquiry be made into all escheats, presentations of churches, wardships, and marriages belonging to the Crown, so that none of the rights and, of course, none of the income rightly due the Crown may be diminished. These were valuable rights. Escheats were the estates of those who had fled the realm or had forfeited their lands for some offence. Presentations to churches were the Crown's principal means of providing for those members of the clergy who coped with the ever-increasing paper-work, if one may call it such, that a centralised administration entailed. If a tenant-in-chief died and his heir was under twenty-one, the heir became a ward of the Crown and the income from his estates, apart from what was required for his maintenance, accrued to the Exchequer. The marriages of heiresses whose fathers had died and who were therefore wards of the Crown and the marriages of widows of tenants-in-chief were a considerable source of revenue, for the hapless women were often auctioned off to the highest bidder or, in the case of widows who had had their fill of married life, were forced to pay heavily for the privilege of not being compelled to marry again.

Some of the most important provisions of this document are those dealing with the Jews. It has already been mentioned that the massacres of the Jews in the first year of the reign were regarded with the utmost seriousness by the king and his advisors because they were a flagrant breach of the king's peace, because the Jews were under the king's special protection, and because in the ensuing disorders the records of debts owing to them, which should have escheated to the Crown, were destroyed, thus depriving the Exchequer of a considerable sum of money.

Hubert Walter, who of course knew of the handsome sums that were still accruing from the debts owed to the deceased Aaron of Lincoln, now being collected by the Exchequer, realised to what extent the Crown had been defrauded, and in Chapters IX and XXIV he took steps both to recover what could be salvaged from the previous uprisings and to make sure that the financial dealings of all the Jews in the kingdom should henceforth be closely watched by responsible agents. These provisions give us our most detailed knowledge of the extent to which the financial affairs of Jewish money-lenders were supervised by the Crown.[1]

The chief justiciar directed that in the forthcoming eyre searching questions should be put concerning those who had taken part in the massacre, with the order that those who had not yet paid a fine for their offences should be seized and not released till they had done so. An investigation is also to be made 'concerning the bonds of the Jews who had been killed, and their chattels, and lands, and debts, and charters, and who had them, and who owed them how much, and what pledges they had, and who holds them, and how much they are worth, and who has the income

[1] H. G. Richardson: *The English Jewry under Angevin Kings*, pp. 118-20.

from them'. All these possessions of every sort are to be seized for the Crown.

In order to place the Jews and their financial dealings under the direct supervision of the Exchequer, Hubert Walter directed in Chapter XXIV that 'all debts, pledges, lands, houses, revenues, and possessions' of the Jews should be registered under pain of confiscation if any deceit were discovered. The registers are to be kept in six or seven of the principal cities, under the supervision of two law-worthy Christians, two law-worthy Jews, and two scribes, under the general direction of William of Ste. Mère-Église, who was one of the two Crown escheators, and William of Chimillé.

Every financial transaction is to be recorded in two copies, of which one, sealed by the borrower, is to be kept by the Jewish lender and the other to be deposited in a chest with three locks, to which the two Christians had one key, the two Jews the second, and the two Williams the third. Each of them is also to seal the chest with his seal. As a further safeguard, all charters of indebtedness are to be transcribed onto a roll to be kept by the two supervisors, and every change is to be noted on the roll. A record is to be kept of all payments made on loans, again in three copies, one for the Christians, one for the Jews, and one for the custodians.

Every loan, every payment, and every change in the terms of a loan must be made before the members of the commission and entered on the rolls. The wages of the two scribes who were charged with drawing up the bonds and of the custodian of the rolls are to be met by a tax of 3d. on each charter, to be paid half by the borrower and half by the lender, of which a penny went to each of the two clerks and to the custodian of the rolls.[1]

Arrears of the aid for the king's ransom were still being collected, but it is evident that much was still owing.[2] In an effort to speed the collection, Hubert Walter directed, in Chapter X, that the jury be questioned concerning the aid, to find out 'who had promised how much, and how much he had paid, and how much he was behind' in his payments. Enquiry is also to be made con-

[1] See Alice G. Cramer: 'The Origins and Functions of the Jewish Exchequer', *Speculum*, XVI (April 1941), 226-9; Austin Lane Poole: *From Domesday Book to Magna Carta* (Oxford, 1951), pp. 422-3.

[2] Doris M. Stenton, Introd. to Pipe Roll 7 Richard I, pp. xv-xvii.

cerning the chattels of those who had taken the Cross but had died before setting out for the Holy Land (Chap. XVII). One may infer from this that the king was considered to have inherited these chattels in order to help pay the expenses of the crusade and of his ransom.

We have noted that on 1 April 1194 King Richard had ordered that a tax of 2s. be collected from each carucate. This would be collected from all landholders, but it would not of course affect the cities and towns, whose prosperity and importance were increasing greatly throughout this period. In order to make the cities and towns pay their share, Hubert Walter directed, in Chapter XXII, that they pay a tallage, an arbitrary sum usually assessed by the itinerant justiciars according to the size and wealth of the town and according to the precedents of previous gifts, as these contributions were usually known, since a tallage implied that those on whom it was levied were of servile status.[1]

To make sure not only that the dispossession of Count John was complete but also that all his lands and revenues were properly accounted for and that all those who had supported him in his rebellion were duly punished, Chapters XI to XIV directed that the justiciars find out which of John's supporters had made a fine with the king and which had not, so that fines may be both collected from those who have made their peace with the king and imposed on those who have not yet done so; that the justiciars enquire as to the chattels of Count John and his supporters, to make sure that they have escheated to the Crown; and that they find out how much John's sheriffs and bailiffs had received in those counties over which he formerly had control. A sweeping enquiry is to be made into all the lands, lordships, wardships, escheats, and gifts that had formerly made up his principality, and everything is to be seized except those few possessions that Richard had expressly allowed John to retain when he made his submission. All debts and fines that were owing to John are to be collected for the Crown.

The provision that had the most lasting effect was Chapter XX: 'Furthermore, in each county let there be elected three knights and one clerk as custodians of the pleas of the Crown', thereby introducing the office of coroner. Although their office is described broadly as that of keeping the pleas of the Crown,

[1] A. L. Poole, op. cit., pp. 418-19.

in practice their functions were limited to those of viewing the bodies of those who had died by violence or in suspicious circumstances, examining the witnesses, recording their testimony (hence the clerk, to serve as scribe), and presenting it before the justiciars; of appraising the value of the instrument in case of death by misadventure (if a man was gored by a bull, for example, the value of the bull was to be given to the poor as a deodand); and of claiming wrecks and treasure-trove for the Crown.[1]

Some of these functions had formerly been performed by the serjeant of the hundred.[2] In 1191, for example, in Lincolnshire, Thomas of Wainfleet was amerced half a mark for having buried a dead man 'without his having been viewed by the serjeant', and Jocelin of Humberstone was amerced the same amount for the same offence.[3] This function was now taken over by the coroners, who were 'almost certainly' elected 'in the presence of the eyre justices' in the autumn of 1194.[4] The office was onerous and unpaid and could hardly have been a popular one.

The knights as a body had a great many judicial and administrative duties laid on them by the Crown, and almost all these duties had neither salary nor perquisites attached. As the obligation of serving in the king's army in person became of diminishing importance in the twelfth century, with the substitution in many cases of the payment of scutage in lieu of military service, the unpaid civil and administrative duties of the knights as a class were greatly increased.[5]

Although no writer of the time refers to the matter, one wonders if either the king or the knights thought of these duties as a fulfilment, on the same level as military service, of their obligations to the king. Fundamentally, all landholders held their land as a gift from the king, and their military service, in the cases of those who held by knight-service, which was by far the most common form of tenure, was their due return for that gift. Even though the gift had been made in many cases to an ancestor more than a century earlier, each landholder must still have been keenly aware of the nature of his tenure, both because of the gifts

[1] A. L. Poole, op. cit., pp. 390-1.

[2] H. G. Richardson and G. O. Sayles, op. cit., pp. 187-8.

[3] Pipe Roll 3 Richard I, pp. 12-13.

[4] R. F. Hunnisett: *The Medieval Coroner* (Cambridge, 1961), p. 151.

[5] Austin Lane Poole: *Obligations of Society in the XII and XIII Centuries* (Oxford, 1946), pp. 53-6.

of land with which the king still rewarded his friends and the forfeitures by which he punished his enemies, and because of the reliefs, wardships, and other incidences that kept his dependence upon the Crown clearly before his eyes.

The king obviously considered that he had the right to exact these unpaid services from his subjects, and the subjects never questioned his right. The unpaid knights were not members of the professional civil service, so to speak; their duties were laid upon them because of their position. One may assume that they performed the services as a part of the payment due for their lands and positions; at any rate, the knights of the twelfth century played their part in making unpaid service to the Crown one of the enduring traditions of their class.

Hubert Walter's distrust of the sheriffs is shown by his instructions, in Chapter XXI, that no sheriff may sit as a justiciar in his own county or in any county of which he had been sheriff since the beginning of the reign, for he would have formed local ties that would make it difficult for him to act impartially. Sheriffs were frequently employed as justiciars because the number of men trained in law and administration was limited, but this provision ensured at least a certain amount of impartiality in their proceedings.

Hubert had proposed, soon after his appointment as chief justiciar, to conduct a searching enquiry into 'the exactions and extortions [*tenseriis*, protection-money, which ominously recalls the evil days of King Stephen][1] of all the lord king's bailiffs, both justiciars and sheriffs, and constables and foresters and their servants' since the beginning of the reign, along the lines of the Inquest of Sheriffs of 1170, but in Chapter XXV he announces that the enquiry is postponed. In the first place, the justiciars would have their hands full in conducting the eyre along the lines laid down for them, and in the second place, many of the misdeeds had been tacitly condoned by the king when he had put the offices up for sale to the highest bidder, with the implication that the purchasers were free to wring as much money from their offices as possible.

As a good administrator Hubert Walter was no doubt horrified by many of the practices that had prevailed since the beginning of the reign, but as a practical man of affairs he realised that it

[1] See *The Peterborough Chronicle*, ed. Cecily Clark (Oxford, 1958), p. 56.

would be difficult to bring some of the worst offenders to book. This chapter gave warning, however, that such 'exactions and extortions' were to cease, and the threat of conducting the inquest at some time in the future would make men think twice before indulging in such conduct.

The longest and most detailed section of the document is Chapter XXIII, dealing with the valuation and restocking of lands that were in the king's hands either as escheats or in wardship. Richard had farmed many of these out to the highest bidder, and, as might be expected, the farmers had been concerned only with getting the greatest possible return from the land, with no thought either of maintaining the estates in good heart or in turning back any of their income into maintaining or increasing their value. The worst of them had felled timber and sold stock with no thought of the future.

In no other part of this document does Hubert reveal himself so clearly as a hard-headed, practical man of affairs as in his instructions for preventing such practices in the future and for making sure that the estates are put into a prosperous condition. The process of appraising and restocking the estates in ward or escheat is a cumbersome one, but it is designed to have the task done by the men best qualified for it. The itinerant justiciars are to be accompanied for this purpose by William of Ste. Mère-Église and William of Chimillé, the royal escheators who had general supervision over the estates, and three of the permanent justiciars, Geoffrey son of Peter, William Briwerre, and Hugh Bardolf. The sheriff of each county, meanwhile, is to summon all the knights of the county, whose names, we learn from this document, were kept on a roll, to appear before the justiciars at a stated time and place. The knights are then to swear that they will appraise and restore the estates to the king's best interest, without hatred, favour, or kindness to anyone.

Having been sworn, the knights are then to elect twelve of their number or, if there are not enough knights, enough free and law-worthy men to make up the panel, from each part of the country through which the justiciars are to pass. The members of this jury, having taken the same oath as the whole group of knights, are then to choose free and law-worthy men from the estates in question, who would be in the best position to know the true state of the lands under investigation.

With the help of these local experts, the judges are to appraise the estates, not at the conventional figure of 20s. the ploughland but according to the real worth of the land, whether good or poor. The livestock are to be listed. Cattle and horses are to be valued at 4s. each, fine-woolled sheep at 10d., coarse-woolled sheep at 6d., and sows and pigs at 12d. Once appraised, the estates are to be restocked according to the judgment of the local men as to the amount of stock they can best carry.

The purpose of the minute provisions of this chapter is to make sure that the estates are kept in good condition, that the farmers at the expiration of their leases return them to the Crown with their value increased rather than diminished, and that all escheats and wardships are properly accounted for and in the king's hands.

These instructions were circulated amongst the sheriffs in the summer of 1194, so that they might make ready for the coming of the justiciars. 'In September 1194 justices itinerant visited every English shire except Buckingham and Bedford.' The country was divided into seven circuits, and a total of forty-one justiciars was employed.[1]

Archbishop Hubert Walter heard some cases in East Anglia and the neighbouring counties, although he would of course be too busy to give much time to this work. Three bishops, Gilbert of Rochester, who had been serving regularly as a justiciar for a number of years, William of Hereford, and Richard of London, the treasurer, and three abbots, the redoubtable Samson of Bury St. Edmonds, Robert of Malmesbury, and the abbot of Hyde, as well as Richard Barre, archdeacon of Ely, served as justiciars. Three of the most experienced administrators in the kingdom, Geoffrey son of Peter, Hugh Bardolf, and William Briwerre, who were permanent members of the Curia Regis, also served, as did the escheator, William of Ste. Mère-Église, who no doubt paid particular attention to the escheats and the lands in wardship.

Of the forty-one justiciars, two had served as sheriff at one time or another since the beginning of the reign, twelve as justiciars, and eight in both capacities. Ralph of Arden, Rannulf Glanville's son-in-law, who had shared in Rannulf's disgrace at the beginning of the reign, was restored to favour by Archbishop Hubert and served as a justiciar in Lancashire, North-

[1] Doris M. Stenton: Introd. to Pipe Roll 7 Richard I, pp. xviii-xxii.

amptonshire, and Wiltshire. He still owed £367 16s. 8d. 'for his fine and for having the king's goodwill'.[1]

Since this eyre was made shortly before Michaelmas 1194, the close of the Exchequer year, its results appear in the Pipe Roll for 1195, where one can find ample evidence of the justiciars' activities. Amercements were imposed for all manner of offences, and their number shows how sadly the courts had fallen in arrears. In the counties formerly under John's control heavy amercements were laid on his supporters. The accounts for Lincolnshire show that the investigation into the massacre of the Jews and the punishment of those concerned were being continued and extended.

The men of three counties that had formerly belonged to John found it prudent to offer gifts to the king 'so that they might be treated mildly'. Lancashire offered 20 marks, Cornwall £20, and Devon 100 marks. Three northern counties where the law had never been scrupulously obeyed followed their example, although on a smaller scale. Cumberland offered 10 marks, Westmorland 12 marks, and Northumberland 30 marks.[2]

Gervase of Canterbury tells how the justices visited Canterbury:

> In the month of December the justiciars called 'itinerant', who had been sent throughout England by the archbishop of Canterbury, were at Canterbury. And there, by order of the king's ministers, those criminals who were under the jurisdiction of the royal crown were cleansed or perished by the judgment of water; those, however, who were under the archbishop's jurisdiction were saved in the archbishop's pit at Westgate. Likewise, those who were under the jurisdiction of the prior and convent were saved in the same pit, with the ministers of the prior and convent presiding.
>
> There a certain Elfgar of Hollingbourne, who had been seized under the Assize of Clarendon for having stolen pitchforks and for other thefts, wherefore he was held through the common oath of the hundred of Aihorn and four neighbouring villages, pledged himself to the judgment of water in the monks' court, went to the water in their pit, and was cleansed. There, too, William Hart, who had been seized for thefts and for having broken into houses by the common oath of Feleberge and four neighbouring villages, was cleansed.

[1] Pipe Rolls 7 Richard I, pp. 150, 103, 140; 6 Richard I, p. 32.
[2] Pipe Roll 7 Richard I, pp. 150, 134, 130, 215, 148, 26.

Gervase concludes his account by boasting that this 'dignity', as he calls their right to try and punish their tenants, had been confirmed, along with many other liberties, to the monks of Canterbury 'by kings both ancient and modern by charters with seals attached'.[1]

The results of the eyre that Gervase describes do not show up in the Pipe Rolls till 1197. Under the heading 'Amercements by Oger son of Oger and Geoffrey of Sunderness and their companions', whom Gervase names as the justiciars who visited Canterbury in 1195, is a list of eighteen or nineteen fugitives from justice. In seven cases the men of the tithing to which the fugitive had belonged are fined collectively half a mark (6s. 8d.). The sheriff of Kent accounts for the fugitives' chattels, which were sold and brought in sums ranging from 4d. in the case of Absalon the Clerk to 19s. in the case of Alewi the Merchant. At the end of the list is the note: 'The sum of these debts is £11 10s. 2d., which was not paid because the archbishop claims that these debts belong to his liberty because they are his men's.'[2]

A number of points in Gervase's account are noteworthy. Three courts with three separate jurisdictions, that held by the justiciars to hear the pleas of the Crown in general and those held by the archbishop's officials and by the prior and monks of Christ Church to hear accusations against those men over whom they had been given jurisdiction as a special privilege by the Crown, were held at Canterbury at the same time. The coming of the justiciars was apparently the occasion for the holding of the other courts. Although the independent jurisdictions of the archbishop and the convent are emphasised by Gervase, the justiciars may have exercised some sort of supervision over the conduct of the two independent courts or at least suggested to the responsible officials that they hold their courts at the same time. The reason for this is obvious: Elfgar of Hollingbourne, for instance, who had been seized for theft under the provisions of the Assize of Clarendon and at the accusation of responsible men of his hundred and of the four neighbouring villages, would in all probability be brought first before the justiciars. There he would plead, or the officers of the convent would claim, that he was under their jurisdiction, and, that fact once established, he would be turned over to them for trial.

[1] Gervase, Vol. I, pp. 530-1.

[2] Pipe Roll 9 Richard I, p. 32.

In all three courts and apparently in all the cases before them, only one method of proof was used, the ordeal by water, as prescribed by Chapter II of the Assize of Clarendon. This ordeal, like the other primitive forms of proof, postulated a direct intervention by God to establish the guilt or innocence of the accused man. It could be conducted only in the presence of a priest, who blessed the 'pit' of water and adjured it to receive the accused if he was innocent and to reject him if he was guilty. The accused, firmly trussed, was then thrown into the water. If the water received him, that is, if he sank, he was proved innocent; if he floated he was guilty.

Admirable though the procedures, reforms, and innovations were that Henry II introduced into the English law, they applied largely to cases dealing with the disputed ownership of land. In criminal cases such as those involving theft, murder, and the like, the ancient and irrational ordeals were still used to establish guilt or innocence, even though improved methods, such as juries of inquest, were employed to bring the accused to trial.

That the ordeal by water was almost a religious rite rather than a judicial procedure is shown by the terms that Gervase of Canterbury uses in this passage. The accused whose innocence is established by the ordeal is said to 'cleansed' (*mundatus*) or 'saved' (*salvatus*). Although the irrationality of such a procedure must have been apparent to the more intelligent lawyers of the time, it was not the lawyers but the Church that finally forbade the use of the ordeal. Canon XVIII of the Fourth Lateran Council, in 1215, prohibited the blessing of ordeals 'of hot or cold water or burning iron'.[1]

To conclude this discussion of the eyre of 1194 and to illustrate some of the points dealt with above, it may be of interest to quote the report of a case heard by the itinerant justiciars in Wiltshire in 1194:

> A certain man by the name of Reginald was killed at Langford and Walerand and Philip were accused and imprisoned at Salisbury because of this. And Englishry was presented at the due time on the part of both his father and his mother . . . but they do not know who killed him. But the jury say that Walerand killed him and Philip was in his company. And afterwards the beadle of the hundred and many others came to Reginald who was killed and asked him

[1] *Conciliorum Oecumenicorum Decreta*, p. 197.

who wounded him. And he said that Walerand wounded him and swore before them that if he might live he would prove this on Walerand, but he did not say anything about Philip. And concerning this matter the jury say and think that Walerand killed him, but they have no suspicions of Philip except for the fact that when the beadle came to Walerand's hospice to arrest him, when Philip saw that death was upon Reginald he fled to a monastery with Walerand and was there with him and refused to come out when the beadle ordered him to. And Walerand and Philip came before the justiciars and denied Reginald's death against all men as the lord king's court might decide.

Verdict: Let Philip be kept in custody until it is known what will happen to Walerand, who must cleanse himself by water of this accusation.

Tournaments, the chief sport of the knights across the Channel, had never been allowed in England, except during the reign of King Stephen, who had been too weak to prevent them. Neither Henry I nor his grandson had tolerated them, for the gathering of a large number of knights, armed and attired for war, might have served to cloak the beginnings of a rebellion, a possibility that was always present under the stern rule of those two kings. Richard, however, had grown up in the traditions of Aquitaine, where warfare either of the nobles amongst themselves or of the nobles against the ducal authority was taken almost for granted. Richard, too, was a fighting man, unlike either of the two Henrys, and he prized the knightly virtues above mere obedience and good order.

That the knights of England, taken as a whole, were lacking in a martial spirit was brought home to Richard both by their far from enthusiastic response to the Third Crusade and by their reluctance to support him in the defence of his continental lands against the relentless pressure exercised by King Philip. Richard had found the French knights to be more capable and experienced warriors than the English were, and he took steps to give his English subjects a chance both to obtain some practice in fighting and to contribute to his treasury at the same time.

In a letter dated 22 August 1194, Richard gave his permission for tournaments to be held in England. Five areas were desig-

[1] *Rolls of the King's Court in the Reign of King Richard the First*, ed. F. W. Maitland, pp. 100–1.

nated in which these exercises might be held, and licences to participate were to be sold at prices that varied according to rank: an earl was to pay 20 marks, a baron 10, a knight who owned land 4, and a landless knight 2 marks. Archbishop Hubert appointed his brother Theobald, who was also serving as sheriff of the Honour of Lancaster, as collector of the fees.

Richard evidently had no high opinion of those who would take part in these affairs, for he ordered that the participants, on their way to and from the tournaments, were to pay for their food and drink and whatever else was necessary, rather than to prey off the countryside. Before taking part they were to pay the appropriate fees and take an oath that they would keep the king's peace in all matters and that they would respect his forests and his markets. Those who tried to avoid paying the fees were severely punished. Robert of Mortimer, for instance, was deprived of his lands in Norfolk because he took part in a tournament without a licence.[1]

Experienced or self-confident knights might regard the fees as a good investment, for although the risks were high the rewards to the skilled or lucky might be even higher. Tournaments differed from real warfare only in that the fighting, in which no holds were barred, began and ended at an hour agreed upon in advance. As in warfare, the object was to capture a rich opponent and hold him, his armour, and his horse for ransom.

That the rewards could be high is shown by the fact that William Marshal, a younger son and a landless knight, could support himself in gentlemanly style by the proceeds of his prowess on the tournament field, until, when he was over forty years old, the king rewarded him with the hand of the heiress of Striguil. His biographer records that in his heyday he captured 103 knights in less than a year.[2]

Death or serious injury, on the other hand, might be the lot of the luckless or unskilled. Because 'death to men and peril to their souls frequently result from them', the Church, in the Second and Third Lateran Councils, in 1139 and 1179, had forbidden tournaments under pain of denial of Christian burial to whose who lost their lives in them. Pope Celestine III, in a

[1] Howden, Vol. III, p. 268; Newburgh, Vol. II, pp. 422-3; Diceto, Vol. II, pp. lxxx-lxxxi, 120-1; *Rotuli Curiac Regis*, Vol. I, p. 87.

[2] *Histoire de Guillaume le Maréchal*, lines 3414-24.

letter to the archbishops and bishops of England, in January 1193, had repeated the condemnation and given the admonition that those who wanted to participate in such exercises 'should go to that land [the Holy Land] where they can manfully and to their salvation show off their strength both of body and of soul'. The Church also regarded the ransoms that the winners extorted as unlawful gains, and confessors attempted to enforce restitution of them as a condition for absolution.[1]

In spite of this prohibition, the young English knights joined in the sport with great enthusiasm. Jocelin of Brakelond tells how eighty young knights gathered between Thetford and Bury St. Edmunds and engaged in a match, in defiance of Abbot Samson's orders, and then came to Bury to find lodgings for the night. The abbot, upon their promising not to leave without his permission, entertained them at dinner.

'After dinner, when the abbot retired to his chamber, they all arose and began to dance and sing, sending into the town for wine, drinking and afterwards yelling, robbing the abbot and the convent of their sleep.' They kept this up till evening, in spite of the abbot's orders to cease their rowdiness, and then 'broke down the gates of the town and forced their way out'. Abbot Samson, who was not a man to be trifled with, excommunicated the whole lot of them, on the advice of Archbishop Hubert Walter.[2]

[1] *Concilium Oecumenicorum Decreta*, pp. 176, 197; *Foedera*, ed. T. Rymer, Vol. I, pt. 1, p. 56; *Histoire de Guillaume le Maréchal*, lines 18476-8

[2] Jocelin of Brakelond: *Chronicle*, pp. 55-6.

VII

1195

ALTHOUGH Archbishop Geoffrey had left England, his enemies continued to press their accusations against him. On 15 January 1195 Bishop Hugh of Lincoln, Master Winemer, archdeacon of Northampton, and Hugh, prior of the Cluniac house at Pontefract, arrived in York with orders from the pope to investigate the charges against the archbishop. Geoffrey's enemies, who included eleven Premonstratensian abbots, of an order greatly indebted to Hubert Walter,[1] accused him of being addicted to hunting, hawking, and other knightly pursuits; of neglecting his spiritual duties as bishop; of cursing and excommunicating both clerks and abbots; of destroying the liberties of the Church; of making a mockery of appeals to Rome and of imprisoning those who dared to appeal from his decisions; of robbing the canons of York of their honours and benefices; of breaking into churches with armed bands and ejecting the ministers by violence; and of other misdeeds too numerous to mention.

Bishop Hugh and his colleagues opened the hearing in York Minster, and all of Geoffrey's enemies, who seem to have included most of the higher clergy of the diocese, flocked in to press their charges. The friends of the archbishop, and they were not many, protested on behalf of the absent Geoffrey that the whole proceeding was illegal, since the archbishop had already appealed to Rome and was even then on his way to the supreme pontiff.

The delegates collected evidence and then wisely referred the whole matter to Rome, giving the archbishop four and a half months in which to answer the charges in person before the pope. Geoffrey failed to appear in Rome at the appointed time, 'both because the king had forbidden him and because of the corruption

[1] Stubbs, Preface to Howden, Vol. IV, p. lxiii, n. 1.

of the air at Rome at that season'. The pope then postponed the hearing till the following 18 November.[1]

Master Simon of Apulia, meanwhile, had met with great success in Rome. The pope had confirmed him as dean of York and invested him with a golden ring. On his way back to England he had wisely stopped to see the king and secure his confirmation of the appointment. He had to pay a stiff price for it. The Pipe Roll for this year shows that he owed £666 13s. 4d. as a 'gift', of which he had paid £486 13s. 4d. by Michaelmas.[2]

Simon reached York on Quinquagesima Sunday, 12 February, and a great crowd of clergy and lay people went out to meet him and escort him to the minster. Amongst the crowd were four of Archbishop Geoffrey's supporters, who forbade him to enter the cathedral as dean till the pope had settled the controversy as to who had the right to appoint the dean. They then announced a solemn appeal to Rome, which in theory should have brought matters to a halt.

Confident in the approval of both pope and king, Master Simon refused to listen to these objections, whereupon Geoffrey's supporters laid violent hands on him and tried to prevent him by force from entering the city. At this outrage to his person Simon excommunicated Geoffrey's friends and continued on his way in triumph. The canons received him with a solemn procession and instituted him as dean of York.[3]

Bishop Hugh of Durham, meanwhile, had been renewing his attempts to regain the county of Northumberland. The king at last replied to his repeated offers. If the bishop would go to London, bringing with him the money he had offered, Richard would give him a prize even richer than Northumberland; he would make him an associate justiciar with the archbishop of Canterbury, thus restoring him to the position he had briefly occupied at the beginning of the reign.

Filled with joy at this prospect, Bishop Hugh set out for London. He spent Shrove Tuesday at his manor of Crake, some fifteen miles north of York, where, according to William of Newburgh, he ate so much at the Shrove Tuesday feast that he became ill, and no amount of vomiting would relieve him. Newburgh may have made this diagnosis for its moral value, for

[1] Howden, Vol. III, pp. 230–1; Vol. IV, p. lxv.
[2] Pipe Roll 7 Richard I, pp. 92–3. [3] Howden, Vol. III, pp. 230, 283–4.

according to Roger of Howden the bishop was well enough to be in York on Ash Wednesday, 15 February, where he confirmed the sentence of excommunication that Simon of Apulia had laid on his attackers.

From York he continued on his way to London, and it was not till he reached Doncaster, fifteen miles to the south, that he fell ill, according to Roger of Howden. At any rate, his illness became so serious at Doncaster that, too ill to ride, he had himself carried by barge down the River Don to its junction with the Humber and thence a few miles to his manor of Howden.

His illness became so much worse that it was apparent to all his friends that the bishop had not long to live. He clung stubbornly to the hope of recovery, but at last his friends persuaded him to make his will. In his seventieth year, Hugh of Le Puiset died on 3 March 1195, having been bishop of Durham for forty-three years. 'He was a man most prudent in managing worldly affairs and, although he had not much learning, extremely eloquent. He was most avid for money and highly skilled in acquiring it', says William of Newburgh. Ambitious, worldly, and avaricious though he may have been, Hugh had been the greatest figure in the north of England for half a century, ruling his diocese and his county palatinate with great ability and success. Surely much may be forgiven the man who built the glorious Galilee of his cathedral. Hugh's body was taken back to Durham and buried in the monks' chapterhouse.[1]

His death proved to be a windfall for the Treasury. Even before the bishop's body had been brought back to Durham, Hugh Bardolf, sheriff of Northumberland and Westmorland and royal escheator for the North, took the keys of Durham Castle from Walter of Farlington, one of the bishop's knights who had charge of the castle. The bishop's will was set aside and all his property was confiscated. This was certainly done at the order of Hubert Walter, acting, on the king's behalf, on the precedent set by Henry II in 1181 in the case of Roger of Pont l'Évêque, archbishop of York, who had waited till his deathbed to make his will.[2] The king was across the Channel, and word of Bishop Hugh's death could hardly have reached him in time for his orders to be brought back to England and carried out with the swiftness

[1] Howden, Vol. III, pp. 284-5; Newburgh, Vol. II, pp. 436-41.
[2] *Gesta*, Vol. I, p. 283.

with which Hugh Bardolf acted. Roger of Howden records, too, that Henry of Farlington, another of the bishop's knights, turned Norham Castle over to Hugh 'at the order of the king's justiciar'.[1] This was another instance in which his position as chief justiciar overrode Hubert Walter's duties as archbishop of Canterbury, for it was surely to the Church's best interests that the wills of the clergy, even though made on their deathbeds, should be respected and that the lands of bishoprics should be protected against the sort of spoliation that was carried out in Durham.

The Exchequer accounts show that £3,050 was promptly brought to London, at a cost of £31 16s. 1d. for carriage. This sum probably represents the ready cash in the bishop's coffers at the time of his death, which would no doubt have been distributed amongst the poor and for various pious causes, for the good of the bishop's soul, if his will had been observed. The bishop had 'a great ship', which was repaired at a cost of £12 15s. 1½d. and sent to London with Robert of Stockton as captain and a crew of thirty-two sailors. Hugh Bardolf had custody of the lands of the bishopric from the second Sunday of Lent till Easter, and during those four weeks he accounted for £301 13s. 4d. as the income for that brief period.

At Easter Gilbert son of Reinfrey and Richard Briwerre were made custodians of the bishopric and held it for three-quarters of a year. During that time the amounts they collected are almost beyond belief. The income from the manors came to £1,528 7s. 3½d. gross. In partial payment of 'the debt that Hugh, bishop of Durham, owed the king according to the king's roll', £41 1s. 8d. was collected, and £173 6s. 8d. realised from the sale of last year's wool accumulated at Stockton was applied to the same purpose. The bishop's manors were tallaged, and £305 8d. was collected from them. An aid was levied on the churches that brought in £52 9s. 4d. The clergy made fines to the total of £897 17s. 4d. paid by Michaelmas, and it is interesting to note that Bishop Hugh's son Bourchard, treasurer of York, was assessed 200 marks, of which he paid 90. A scutage amounting to £45 3s. 2d. was collected from the knights of the bishopric. Henry of Le Puiset, the bishop's eldest son, was assessed 2 marks, but he had paid nothing by Michaelmas.

[1] Howden, Vol. III, p. 285.

The entry that is hardest to understand is that pertaining to 'the fines of Bishop Hugh's servants', which realised £391 9d. William of Newburgh implies that the bishop's servants attempted to conceal some of his goods from the king's officials, perhaps with the intention of applying them to the pious purposes that the bishop had directed in his will, or perhaps for their own benefit. The king's officials, however, exacted a more comprehensive accounting from them, and the fines were probably laid on them as punishment for their attempted evasion.[1] Fines were also collected from 'the men of the bishopric for their lands', to the sum of £316 12s. 8d.

At the time of his death Bishop Hugh had no less than ten baronies in his hands: those of Giles Hansard, Robert of Amundeville, Robert son of Meldred, and Henry of Broch, and those of Alden, Hewort, Trimdon, Hardwick, and Sigeston in Yorkshire and Halton in Northumberland. From the baronies the escheators accounted for £326 18s. 10d., of which £104 16s. 4d. was paid into the Treasury and the remainder disbursed on necessary expenses. £30 was realised from the sale of lead and £174 4d. from the profits of the mines of Northumberland and of the exchange. It should be noted that all these sums, unless it is stated otherwise, are the amounts paid into the Exchequer and represent ready cash; the collection of the entire revenue for this brief period required many years.[2]

With Archbishop Geoffrey abroad and Bishop Hugh dead, Bishop John of Whithorn was the only bishop left in the province of York. He accordingly came to York in Holy Week in order to consecrate the chrism and bless the holy oils on Maundy Thursday, but Dean Simon of Apulia and some of the chapter would not allow him to enter the cathedral.

The bishop then went to Southwell, where he was well received and allowed to perform the ceremony. He gave the chrism and oil to the archbishop's officials to distribute amongst the churches of the province. Geoffrey of Muschamp, archdeacon of Cleveland, to show his contempt both for the bishop and for the decencies of Christian behaviour, poured the chrism

[1] See Margaret Howell, *Regalian Right in Medieval England* (London, 1962), pp. 45-7.

[2] Chancellor's Roll 8 Richard I, pp. 18, 253-61. The Pipe Roll for this year is missing; the deficiency is supplied by the Chancellor's Roll, which is identical for all practical purposes. See Richard son of Nigel: *Dialogus de Scaccario*, pp. 17-19.

and oil on a dungheap. The other canons of the cathedral refused to accept the chrism and oil from Bishop John and applied to Bishop Hugh of Lincoln for a supply, but the archbishop's brother Peter, archdeacon of Lincoln, forbade the bishop to give them any and entered an appeal to the pope.[1]

Archbishop Geoffrey, it will be remembered, had bought his way back into the king's favour in November 1194. In the spring of 1195, however, he rashly reproached Richard for his sinful way of life. Richard was touchy on this subject, and there is no reason to believe that Geoffrey, whose conduct had never been noteworthy for its tactfulness, was especially tactful on this occasion. Richard was so exasperated that he ordered that his brother be deprived once more of the lands of the archbishopric. The Pipe Roll accordingly shows Master Thomas of Hurstbourne accounting 'for the manors of the archbishop of York for half a year'. Although Roger of Howden says that Richard also deprived Geoffrey of his post as sheriff of Yorkshire, the same Pipe Roll shows that Geoffrey, acting through his deputy, Roger of Batvent, served as sheriff throughout the financial year.[2]

At about the same time, apparently, Hugh of Nonant, bishop of Coventry, succeeded in buying his way back into the king's favour by a gift of 5,000 marks. His brother Robert, however, who had refused to serve as a hostage for Richard's ransom on the ground that he was Count John's man, was kept in prison at Dover under the watchful eye of Longchamp's sister Richeut till King Richard's death.[3]

Count John, too, made his peace with his brother. Richard half-contemptuously blamed John's treasonable behaviour on his evil counsellors and restored him to favour but not to his position of power and affluence. Although Roger of Howden says that Richard gave him back the county of Mortain, the honour of Eye, and the earldom of Gloucester, with all their appurtenances except the castles, the Pipe Rolls show that John held the honour of Eye only from Easter 1196 to Easter 1197. For the remainder of the time it was farmed by Robert de Lisle, acting as deputy for William Longchamp, bishop of Ely.[4]

[1] Howden, Vol. III, pp. 286–7.

[2] Pipe Roll 7 Richard I, pp. 29, 80; Howden, Vol. III, p. 287.

[3] Howden, Vol. III, pp. 233, 287.

[4] *Histoire de Guillaume le Maréchal*, lines 10368–428; Chancellor's Roll 8 Richard I, p. 121; Pipe Roll 9 Richard I, p. 234.

In Gloucestershire John received throughout the remainder of the reign the third penny, the usual perquisite of an earl, consisting originally of a third of the proceeds from the amercements levied in the court of the county from which the earl took his title. In John's case the third penny consisted of a fixed sum of £20 annually. Richard also settled on him an income of £8,000 in Angevin money (£2,000 sterling), which, even assuming that it was paid regularly, would not appear in the accounts of the English Exchequer.[1]

Pope Celestine III, on 18 March, at King Richard's request, appointed Archbishop Hubert Walter his legate in England and sent letters to all the leading clergy of the country to inform them of the appointment and to order them to show the new legate 'due reverence and honour and humbly to receive and obey his salutary admonitions and orders'.

The news of his appointment would probably have reached the archbishop around the middle of May. His first act as legate was to send two clerks, Peter, prior of the Benedictine house of Binham in Norfolk, and Master Gervase, with letters to the dean and chapter of York and Archbishop Geoffrey's officials, announcing his intention of visiting York and warning them that he would excommunicate anyone who refused to receive him with due reverence and honour, a wise precaution in view of the contumacious attitude that the chapter of York customarily displayed towards any authority other than their own.

Both the canons and Geoffrey's officials replied that they would receive him as legate of the apostolic see but not as archbishop of Canterbury, who, they asserted, had no authority in the province of York, or as primate of England, a title they refused to concede to the archbishop of Canterbury.

Hubert Walter accordingly entered York on Sunday, 11 June, as papal legate and chief justiciar, two titles that gave him all the authority he needed. The clergy and people welcomed him with a solemn procession and escorted him to the cathedral with the reverence and honour that he had insisted upon. Bishop Stubbs describes Hubert Walter's visit as an act of 'ostentatious contempt' for Archbishop Geoffrey, but surely, as Lady Stenton points outs, 'In York, if anywhere, the archbishop's presence was needed'. The archbishop of York was out of the country, his

[1] Pipe Roll 7 Richard I, p. 174; Howden, Vol. III, p. 286.

authority openly defied; the see of Durham was vacant; the only remaining bishop in the province had been treated with studied contempt; and the dean and chapter of York were triumphant in their insolence and insubordination.[1]

The lay judges who had accompanied Hubert Walter held 'assizes of all the pleas of the king's crown, and of novel disseisin, and of mort d'ancestor' on the following day, 12 June, while the archbishop and his clerks presided over the court christian, which dealt with those offences over which the Church had legal jurisdiction.

On Tuesday, 13 June, the archbishop went to St. Mary's Abbey and heard in the chapter-house the complaints of the monks against their abbot, who was so weak and sickly that he was unable to rule his monastery. Although Abbot Robert protested violently and, of course, appealed to the pope, Hubert Walter deposed him. William Longchamp's brother Robert, prior of Ely, was later elected abbot of St. Mary's on 17 March 1197. This was probably that same brother, 'a monk of Caen', who was promised the post of abbot of Westminster and then cast out when William Longchamp fell from power. William may have consoled him with the office of prior of his cathedral monastery of Ely till he could find a better place for him.[2]

During the course of this year Hubert Walter as legate visited a number of monasteries and reformed what he found amiss. He deposed Robert, the abbot of Thorney, who was accused of despoiling the abbey and wasting its goods, and kept him in prison in chains at Gloucester for a year and a half, in spite of the abbot's appeals to Rome. When Bishop Henry of Worcester died in October 1195, Hubert as chief justiciar seized the lands of the bishopric for the benefit of the Exchequer and as papal legate took drastic steps to enforce discipline in the cathedral monastery, which was rent by dissensions and quarrels. He scattered the ringleaders amongst various other monasteries and sent two monks from Canterbury to restore order and to overhaul the administration of the monastic estates.[3]

[1] Howden, Vol. III, pp. 290–3, and Vol. IV, p. lxvii; Doris M. Stenton, Introd. to Pipe Roll 7 Richard I, p. xxvii.

[2] Howden, Vol. III, p. 294; Diceto, Vol. II, pp. 151–2; Richard of Devizes, pp. 39, 54–5.

[3] Gervase, Vol. I, p. 530: Howden, Vol. III, p. 299; David Knowles: *The Monastic Order in England*, pp. 651–2.

After his energetic measures at St. Mary's, Hubert Walter held a legatine council in York Minster on Wednesday and Thursday, 14 and 15 June, at which the canons of the cathedral, the abbots and priors of the religious houses, and the secular clergy of the diocese of York were present. This was one of six councils held in England during the twelfth century at which legatine canons were promulgated; the last previous one had been held in 1151.[1]

After a number of chapters providing for the proper celebration of the Mass and the administration of the sacraments, Archbishop Hubert decreed that churches be kept in good repair and furnished with fitting ornaments. One may presume that a number of parsons had allowed their churches to become dilapidated from the fact that the legate set a date one year from the beginning of his legation, by which time the repairs were to be effected; if the repairs had not been made by that date the income of the church was to be forfeited to the legate, who would then provide for the repairs and pay for them with the sequestered monies.

The articles dealing with the dress and morals of the clergy are particularly interesting because they give us some idea of the conditions prevailing in the northern province at this time. The clergy were to wear the tonsure under pain of deprivation of their benefices, and priests were to dress in clothing suitable to their order, eschewing the use of gaudy and elaborate cloaks.

Monks, canons regular, and nuns were not to go on pilgrimages or travel about the country without 'certain and reasonable cause'. In no case were they to travel alone, and nuns were forbidden to leave their convents unless they were accompanied by their abbess or prioress. Priests were not to frequent taverns or to take part in public ale-drinkings.

Finally, the legate took up the most difficult problem that faced the Church in connexion with the morals of the clergy, that of enforcing clerical celibacy. The Church had by this time succeeded in enforcing its prohibitions against the marriage of the clergy and the ordination of men already married.[2] It had not, however, been able to prevent priests from keeping concubines.

[1] C. R. Cheney: 'Legislation of the Medieval English Church', Part I, *English Historical Review*, L (April 1935), p. 195.

[2] See C. N. L. Brooke: 'Gregorian Reform in Action: Clerical Marriage in England, 1050-1200', *Cambridge Historical Journal*, XII (1956); reprinted in *Change in Medieval Society*, ed. Sylvia L. Thrupp (New York, 1964), pp. 49-71.

Gerald of Wales, a caustic critic of his fellow clergymen, affirms that almost all the parish priests of England followed 'the damnable and detestable custom' of keeping a woman as 'a companion in public, a housekeeper for his hearth, and a concubine for his bed', and he paints a dismal picture of the priest who keeps 'a concubine in his house to suffocate and make a mockery of all virtue in him and to keep his miserable house crammed full of babies and cradles, midwives and nurses'.[1] Gerald was no doubt exaggerating grossly, but the repeated decrees of synods and councils against clerical incontinence indicate that his allegations had some basis in fact. The archbishop now decreed that priests were not to keep concubines (*focarias*, hearth-companions) in their houses or, in an effort to evade this prohibition, to install them in other houses and visit them there, under penalty of suspension from their offices and benefices.[2]

While the council was sitting, Master Peter of Dinan claimed the archdeaconry of the West Riding, to which Archbishop Geoffrey had presented him in the previous autumn before leaving England. Dean Simon of Apulia and the chapter protested, however, on the ground that Geoffrey had failed to act within the six months laid down by the Third Lateran Council in Canon VIII[3] and that the presentation had therefore reverted to them. Geoffrey's officials, Master Gerard and Master Honorius, who were watching after their master's interests while he was out of the country, appealed against such an interpretation and renewed the appeal to the pope that Geoffrey had made before leaving England.

Although the terms of Hubert Walter's appointment expressly stated that no appeals would be allowed against his decisions and actions, he deferred to Gerard and Honorius and allowed their appeal to stand. The controversy hinged, apparently, on the date of Geoffrey's presentation, which in turn depended on the date of the death of Ralph, the previous archdeacon, who is said merely to have died on his way back from Rome. Hubert Walter may well have wanted to delay matters both until these elements could be straightened out and until the pope could be consulted as to

[1] Gerald of Wales: *Gemma Ecclesiastica*, ed. J. S. Brewer, *Opera*, Vol. II, p. 277, and *Speculum Ecclesiae*, ed. J. S. Brewer, *Opera*, Vol. IV, p. 170.

[2] Howden, Vol. III, pp. 294-7.

[3] *Concilium Oecumenicorum Decreta*, p. 191.

whether or not the provisions of the Lateran Council applied in this case.[1]

Hubert Walter in the course of this year made his second great contribution to the development of English law. He directed that all men fifteen years old and over should appear before knights 'assigned for this purpose' and swear 'that they will keep the lord king's peace and that they will be neither outlaws nor robbers nor thieves nor receivers of such'. They were also to swear that they would pursue malefactors with full hue and cry and when they caught them turn them over to the knights (presumably the ones before whom they took the oath), who would in turn hand them over to the sheriff to guard and keep till the next eyre. If anyone failed to follow the hue and cry or abandoned the pursuit of the criminals without permission from the bailiffs or the leaders of the pursuit, he was to be treated in the same way as the captured malefactor.[2]

By directing that this oath be taken before knights 'assigned for this purpose' (one must assume that they were appointed by the sheriff, since he kept a nominal roll of all the knights in the county), Hubert Walter instituted the office that grew into that of justice of the peace.[3] The duties of the first justices of the peace, to call them by their later name, as defined by this document, were to administer the oath to keep the peace to the men of their neighbourhood, to receive captured criminals, and to turn them over to the sheriff to hold for trial. From the beginning, however, it is obvious that their powers were greater than those mentioned in the instructions. Roger of Howden says:

> In order to carry out these instructions, chosen and faithful men were sent through every county in England, who on the oath of faithful men of the neighbourhoods seized many men and shut them up in the king's prisons. Many, however, warned of this in advance and having guilty consciences, fled, leaving their houses and possessions behind.[4]

This makes it clear that the justices of the peace had some of the functions of the itinerant justiciars, in that they could hear

[1] Howden, Vol. III, pp. 273, 297-8.
[2] Howden, Vol. III, pp. 299-300.
[3] Charles Austin Beard: *The Office of Justice of the Peace in England in Its Origin and Development* (New York, 1904), pp. 17-18.
[4] Howden, Vol. III, p. 300.

accusations against malefactors and imprison them till the next eyre. In other words, they had power to arrest on reasonable accusation and to hold for trial, but not to try; that function could be exercised only by a regularly constituted court.

Simple though these instructions were, they had an enormous effect, as may be seen both from the greatly increased work of the itinerant justiciars in the next eyre and from the large number of fugitives who fled the country (Scotland for men in the north and Ireland for those in the west were favourite places of refuge) rather than take the oath, as is recorded in the Pipe Rolls for this and the following year.

In Warwickshire and Leicestershire, for instance, no less than seventeen men abandoned what few possessions they had, to a total value of £9 13s. 5d., and fled the country. Six others also fled, leaving nothing behind, with the result that the members of the tithing to which they had belonged were amerced half a mark in each case.[1]

In view of the greatly increased number of criminals who were apprehended, tried, and amerced by the itinerant justiciars at this time, it is difficult to determine how much of the increase is to be attributed to the use of the juries of accusation by the justiciars in the eyre of the preceding year and how much may be ascribed to the activities of the justices of the peace. That they did play an important part in helping to keep the peace and in apprehending criminals is obvious from the fact that their office has continued from 1195 to the present day and that their powers were greatly increased as time went on.

While Hubert Walter was thus busy keeping order in England and governing the country with an efficiency worthy of the great days of Henry II, his royal master called on him for still more men and still more money with which to pursue his operations against King Philip. Fighting had broken out anew in July of this year. Hubert Walter sent 1,300 foot soldiers, 55 mounted soldiers, and 3 'master knights', who were probably in command of the group, across the Channel, and the Pipe Roll records many shipments of treasure.[2]

The chief justiciar levied a scutage for 'the second army of Normandy' late in the summer, apparently, for only a few re-

[1] Pipe Roll 7 Richard I, pp. 197-8.
[2] Howden, Vol. III, p. 301; Pipe Roll 7 Richard I, pp. 204-5.

ferences to it, to be commented on later, are noted in the Pipe Roll compiled at Michaelmas 1195,[1] usually in this form:

> Reginald of Balun renders account of 10 marks so that he may not cross over in the second army of Normandy and that he may be quit of his scutage of one knight's fee.[2]

One of the chief sources of revenue was a tallage or 'gift' that Hubert Walter and the itinerant justiciars had levied during the course of the eyre of 1194 and that was collected, not without difficulty, during this and subsequent years. Worcester was assessed 80 marks and paid the whole sum by Michaelmas 1195; York, assessed at 300 marks, paid 100 marks, but Scarborough and Doncaster, assessed at £100 and 50 marks, respectively, paid nothing. Northampton, assessed at 300 marks, and Oxford, assessed at £100, also paid nothing. Gloucester, on the other hand, paid the whole of its tallage, £100. Winchester, assessed at 100 marks, paid £30, but Southampton, assessed at 40 marks, paid nothing. Carlisle paid nothing on its assessment of £50, but, as an illustration of how even small villages did not escape the justiciars' attentions, in Cumberland Scotby paid 30s., Dalston 40s., Penrith 4 marks, Salkeld 2 marks, Langwathby 20s., and Stanwix 10s.[3] The citizens of London, however, paid not a penny of the 1,500 marks that they had been assessed 'as their gift to keep the lord king's goodwill and their liberties and as their aid for the lord king's ransom'.[4]

The Exchequer received two notable windfalls in the course of this year. Robert of Lacy, the last male of his immediate line, had died in 1193. In 1195 Roger, the constable of Chester, as Robert's first cousin twice removed and apparently his nearest heir, compounded with the king for Robert's great honour of Pontefract. He offered £2,000 'for all the lands and castles that had belonged to Robert of Lacy of the honour of Pontefract Castle, which the lord king kept in his hand, without the town'. This was no mere empty promise; Roger, who henceforth called himself 'of Lacy', paid £1,913 before Michaelmas 1195, and the remaining £87 was forgiven him in consideration of the income

[1] Pipe Roll 7 Richard I, pp. 22, 110, 166, 216, 242.
[2] Ibid., p. 110.
[3] Ibid., pp. 12, 91, 105, 146, 182, 211, 215.
[4] Pipe Roll 6 Richard I, p. 182; 7 Richard I, p. 118.

the Crown had received whilst the lands were in the king's hand.[1]

This payment was the customary feudal relief that the heir paid upon taking possession of his lands; the only unusual features were its size and the promptness with which it was paid. The second large sum collected from an individual during this year was of a more exceptional nature. Gerald of Wales records that Robert Bloet, bishop of Lincoln from 1094 to 1123, gave King Henry I a mantle of imported sable, black with white markings, lined with the finest cloth and valued at either £100 or 100 marks, and bound his successors to do likewise. Bishop Alexander (1123-48) continued the custom, and his successor, Robert of Chesney (1148-66), is said to have given the king a mantle 'several times'.

Henry II left the see of Lincoln vacant from 1166 to 1173, when his bastard son Geoffrey, then around twenty years old, was elected. Geoffrey declined to be consecrated and at last resigned in 1182. Walter of Coutances was elected bishop of Lincoln in May 1183 and was translated to Rouen in November 1184. Thus when Hugh of Avalon was elected in 1186 the see for all practical purposes had been without a bishop for twenty years.

When King Richard was casting about for means of raising money to meet his unprecedented and continuous expenditures for the defence of his continental domains, certain unnamed 'evil persons' told him about the custom of the yearly gift, now far in arrears, of a mantle by the bishop of Lincoln. The most likely person to have made this suggestion was Hubert Walter, on whom the king's demands fell the most heavily and who would probably know of this ancient custom. The archbishop of Canterbury, furthermore, seems to have had little love for the bishop of Lincoln, who had several times openly rebuked him for neglecting his spiritual duties as archbishop in order to fulfil his secular duties as chief justiciar.

The king now demanded from Bishop Hugh a sizable sum of money as arrears for this newly discovered tribute. Although the revenues of the bishopric of Lincoln amounted to almost £1,500 a year,[2] Bishop Hugh spent the money as fast as he received it, not on vain ostentation but on worthy objects. He

[1] Pipe Roll 7 Richard I, p. 98.
[2] Margaret Howell, op. cit., p. 223.

maintained the state proper to his position; he was generous to the members of his household; and he contributed substantially to the cost of rebuilding his cathedral, which had been shattered by the great earthquake of 1185. Finally, his purse was always open to anyone in need, and his alms were so generous that he was often obliged to borrow money.

The king was so insistent in his demands that at last Bishop Hugh was forced to compound with him for the arrears and at the same time to purchase exception from the tribute henceforth for himself and his successors. He saw no way to raise the money except by retiring to the Charterhouse at Witham, which he had left with the greatest reluctance to become bishop and to which he returned with the greatest joy for a month's retreat every year, and staying there, meanwhile turning over all the revenues of his see to the Exchequer, till the debt should be paid. The clergy of the diocese, however, in an unprecedented expression of their love for their bishop, would not hear of such a plan and raised the money by voluntary contributions amongst themselves.

Richard's charter of release, dated at Le Mans on 23 July 1194, in ascribing his action to 'the love of God and of Blessed Mary ever virgin, His mother, and for our salvation and that of our ancestors and successors', does not tell the whole truth, for the Pipe Roll for 1195 records that Bishop Hugh paid 2,000 marks to be quit of the claim forever.[1]

The canons of York meanwhile were complaining to Bishop Hugh that no measures had been taken against Archbishop Geoffrey, who had failed to present himself before the pope as he had been ordered to do. They now demanded that Hugh, as judge delegate, suspend Geoffrey from his office. Hugh replied that he would be hanged before he would pronounce such a sentence upon Geoffrey. The archbishop certainly has appeared in no attractive light in the course of this narrative, but that his difficulties arose as much from the obstinacy and contumacy of his canons as from any faults of his own is apparent from the fact that Bishop Hugh, a fearless, incorruptible, and just man, who knew many of the facts of the case that are now lost to us, sided

[1] Gerald of Wales: *Vita Sancti Remigii*, ed. James F. Dimock, *Opera*, Vol. VII, pp. 33-41; *Magna Vita S. Hugonis Episcopi Lincolniensis*, ed. James F. Dimock (Rolls Series 37, 1864), pp. 183-7, 246; Howden, Vol. III, p. 303; *The Registrum Antiquissimum of the Cathedral Church of Lincoln*, ed. C. W. Foster (Lincoln, 1931), Vol. I, p. 123; Pipe Roll 7 Richard I, p. 195.

with Geoffrey. Hugh had been Geoffrey's friend and supporter during his difficulties with Longchamp, and the highest praise that can be accorded the unfortunate archbishop is that Bishop Hugh regarded him as a friend.

When Bishop Hugh refused to act, the canons sent messengers to Rome both to press their charges against Geoffrey and to complain that Hugh and the other judges were failing to obey the pope's instructions. By failing to appear before the pope on 18 November 1195, Geoffrey lost his suit by default. On 23 December Pope Celestine suspended him 'from the use of the pallium, and the execution of the episcopal office, and from all administrative functions both spiritual and temporal, and from receiving any benefices'.

The administration of the diocese of York was committed to the dean, Simon of Apulia, whose triumph was now complete. Geoffrey's officials, whom he had left in charge of his interests, were deposed, and the estates of the archbishopric were again forfeited to the Crown. Master Thomas of Hurstbourne accounted for £400 8s. 3d. as the income from the manors for half a year, from Easter till Michaelmas 1196. Geoffrey was allowed, however, to retain his position as sheriff of Yorkshire, acting through his deputy, Roger of Batvent.[1]

Hubert Walter took the unusual step, for an archbishop of Canterbury, of keeping his Christmas at York and of celebrating the Mass of the Nativity in York Minster, perhaps in order to remind the self-willed canons that as papal legate he was keeping them under his eye. Hubert had a number of affairs to attend to in the north. William, king of Scots, and King Richard had been corresponding for some time concerning a marriage between William's only daughter, Margaret, and Richard's favourite nephew, Otto, the son of his eldest sister Matilda and Henry the Lion, Duke of Saxony.

William as yet had no son, and when he became gravely ill earlier in the year he proposed to marry Margaret to Otto and make the young man his heir. His barons opposed the project vehemently, and William postponed it for the time being. King Richard, who had a great affection for Otto, a young man after his own heart, was not content to drop the matter, and in Decem-

[1] Howden, Vol. III, pp. 282, 305-6, 308-17; Chancellor's Roll 8 Richard I, pp. 164, 188.

ber he sent Hubert Walter to sound King William again. In the course of the negotiations William agreed to give Otto Lothian as well as the hand of his daughter, and Richard for his part promised to give his nephew Northumberland and Westmorland. At this point, however, it was learned that Queen Ermengard was pregnant, and King William refused to conclude the agreement in the hope that his queen would bear him a son.[1]

The archbishop was also charged with the duty of supervising the election of a successor to Bishop Hugh of Durham. On 29 December Bertram, prior of Durham, met Hubert Walter at Alverton, 'and there in the archbishop's presence he elected Master Philip, a clerk and familiar friend of Richard, king of England, as bishop of Durham'; in other words, on behalf of the monks who formed the chapter at Durham he agreed to accept the king's nominee as their bishop.

Philip had served Richard in Poitou, accompanied him on the crusade, and been one of the few who went with him on his journey through Austria. The king had tried to provide for him in 1193, when he induced Archbishop Geoffrey to name him dean of York, but the determined opposition of the canons brought that scheme to naught. Although Richard followed his father's usual practice of using vacant bishoprics to reward his friends, he departed from his father's practice by filling vacancies with unusual speed. Hard pressed for money though he was, Richard scorned to fill his coffers by leaving bishoprics vacant for long periods and pocketing the revenues.[2]

[1] Howden, Vol. III, pp. 298-9, 308.

[2] Howden, Vol. III, pp. 222, 308; Ralph of Coggeshall, p. 54.

VIII
1196

ALTHOUGH King Richard and his chief justiciar were laying heavier taxes on England than had ever been known before, the amounts collected were disappointingly small, in the king's estimation. Almost every resource known to the chief justiciar and the Exchequer officials was being exploited. In addition to the levies for paying the king's ransom, gifts and tallages were being exacted from the cities, towns, and the royal demesne; sheriffs were forced to pay for their offices either by outright purchase, by increments on the old farm, or by gifts to keep in the king's good graces; John's adherents were heavily amerced and their lands confiscated; scutages were levied in 1189-90, 1194, 1195, and 1196; the judicial eyres, particularly the great one of 1194, were relied upon to bring in sizable amercements; escheated estates were made to yield the greatest possible returns; and large reliefs were exacted from heirs to the greater baronies.

The sheriffs and their officers had always had a bad name for peculation, and the temptations of their position were great, largely because no effective system of auditing their receipts could be devised. The fact that the office was openly bought and sold shows that it was regarded as an opportunity to make money on a large scale. Robert, the abbot of St. Stephen's at Caen, a man 'poorly educated but extremely clever and eloquent in worldly affairs', told King Richard that half his revenues were being embezzled by his officials in England. The king therefore sent him, accompanied by Philip of Poitiers, bishop-elect of Durham, to England to conduct a searching enquiry into the operations of the Exchequer and the conduct of the sheriffs, who were summoned to appear in London to give an account of themselves.

The abbot, when he arrived in London, had dinner with Archbishop Hubert Walter on Passion Sunday. He was taken ill at table and died five days later, on 11 April. 'Those who feared his coming did not mourn his going', says William of Newburgh.[1]

Philip of Poitiers remained in England. Although he did not attempt to carry out the mission alone, he at any rate served as an official of the Exchequer. In company with Hugh Bardolf he assessed the tallage laid on Northumberland, Westmorland, and Lincolnshire in this year. As a first step towards his consecration as bishop he was ordained priest by Henry of Abergavenny, bishop of Llandaff, in Durham Cathedral on 15 June.[2]

Archbishop Hubert seems meanwhile to have made known to the king his indignation that his honesty and that of his subordinates should be questioned, for on 15 April Richard hastened to assure him that he had directed the enquiry to be made, not through base motives of cupidity, but so that he might know 'who has helped us in our need and by how much'. Richard went on to assure him loftily, and this must have been news indeed to the archbishop: 'By God's grace we have plenty of money, so that we do not need to try to get it by unworthy means.'[3]

The poorer citizens of London were particularly loud in their complaints against the heavy contributions that were being demanded from them. They had paid nothing as yet of the 1,500 marks that had been assessed 'as their gift for having the king's goodwill and for keeping their liberties and as their aid for the lord king's ransom' that had been levied in 1194 or of the £20 that they owed for the scutage of 1195. In 1196 they were assessed another £20 as scutage and an additional 500 marks 'as their gift as a present to the lord king'.[4]

The burdens of the king's unceasing demands for money bore particularly heavily upon the people because there had been a series of poor harvests in both England and Normandy. The famine began in 1193, and succeeding years added to the misery. By 1196 many of the poor were starving, and pestilence raged to such an extent that in many parts of England pits were dug in which to bury its victims.[5]

Even the reports of the cases heard by the itinerant justiciars,

[1] Newburgh, Vol. II, pp. 464-5; Howden, Vol. IV, p. 5.
[2] Chancellor's Roll 8 Richard I, pp. 96, 98, 251; Howden, Vol. IV, pp. 9-10.
[3] Diceto, Vol. II, p. lxxix.
[4] Pipe Roll 6 Richard I, p. 182; Chancellor's Roll 8 Richard I, pp. 295-6.
[5] Newburgh, Vol. II, pp. 484, 492; Howden, Vol. IV, p. 13.

which rarely include such details, show that in 1198 men were dying of hunger and exposure. In Chelmsford Hundred 'Robert son of Rannulf was found dead of hunger in the fields of Badow', and in Dunmow Hundred, 'in the village of Kenwell, William Hiche was found dead of cold'. These instances found their way into the rolls because in both cases the verdict was murder, and a murder-fine of 20s. was levied on the respective hundreds.[1] How many of the enormous number of murder-fines recorded in the Pipe Rolls were levied for deaths in similar circumstances one cannot even guess, but these two cases lead one to believe that many murder-fines originated in just such deaths from hunger and cold.

Richard son of Nigel, whom we have met in these pages as bishop of London, defines murder as 'the concealed death of a man at the hands of an unknown slayer', and in a famous passage he explains the origin of the murder-fine:

> In the period immediately following the Conquest what were left of the conquered English lay in ambush for the suspected and hated Normans and murdered them secretly in woods and unfrequented places as opportunity offered. Now when the kings and their ministers had for some years inflicted the most severe penalties on the English without effect, it was finally decided that the hundred in which a Norman was found killed, without his slayer being known or revealing his identity by flight, should be mulcted. . . . For that reason whoever is found slain nowadays, the murder-fine is exacted, except in cases where there is definite proof of the servile condition of the victim.[2]

In practice, however, the murder-fine was extended to all deaths, including death by misadventure, when no-one could be found responsible for the death and the victim could not be proven to be English by 'presentment of Englishry'. In each of the following cases the verdict was murder:

> The jury say that John son of Leven and Alice daughter of Siward were drowned in the mill-pond of Eswell and Englishry was not reasonably presented.
>
> The jury say that a certain woman was found dead in the fields of Erdele and it is not known who she was and no-one is suspected.

[1] *Rotuli Curiae Regis*, Vol. I, pp. 202–3; Pipe Roll I John, p. 101.
[2] Richard son of Nigel: *Dialogus de Scaccario*, pp. 52–3.

A certain man was found slain in the fields of Clahull and no-one knows who killed him.[1]

On the other hand, if the victim could be proven to be English the hundred escaped the murder-fine, as in the following instance:

A certain girl ten years old was drowned at Stanton in a well and Englishry was presented.[2]

Sir Francis Palgrave, commenting on the cases in which the murder-fine was levied when the victim is stated to have died of hunger or cold, remarks:

Since the hundred was thus subjected to a mulct, if the man died for want of the necessaries of life, may it not be inferred that the inhabitants were bound to provide those necessaries—food and raiment:—and that, consequently, the principle of a legal provision for the poor was recognised by the common law?[3]

His conjecture is strengthened by the fact that in the case of William Hiche the serjeant of the hundred attached 'four neighbours for the death of this man and brought four men who were not attached'.[4] The murder-fine, as we have seen, was originally levied in order to punish the hundred for not apprehending the slayer of a Norman. By the end of the twelfth century it was being levied with great frequency on the inhabitants of any hundred in which any death took place that could not be ascribed to natural causes, in which case a priest would presumably be present at the death-bed, or to homicide by someone who could be named, even though he might have fled, or to cases in which the victim could be proven to be English. It is difficult to see how the hundred could be held responsible, although it obviously was, for deaths by misadventure such as drowning, but if the many cases of an unknown person found dead really represent death of starvation and exposure, as one is strongly inclined to believe, then the hundred is clearly held responsible. While this may not imply a formal organisation for the relief of the poor, it points to one of the most striking features of English life of this time: the extensive structure of accountability for each

[1] *Rotuli Curiae Regis*, Vol. I, p. 159.

[2] *Three Rolls of the King's Court in the Reign of King Richard the First, A.D. 1194-1195*, ed. F. W. Maitland, p. 102.

[3] Introd. to *Rotuli Curiae Regis*, Vol. I, pp. xxxiv-xxxv.

[4] Ibid., Vol. I, p. 203.

member that one finds in the tithing and the hundred. If a man commits a crime and flees, the tithing to which he belongs is fined; if a man dies of want, the hundred is fined: not merely because a man died of want, but because the hundred allowed him to die of want.

In these hard times of want and famine, the common citizens of London declared that the whole burden of taxation was being shifted onto their shoulders by the richer men, who refused to pay their share. They found a champion and spokesman in one of the magistrates, William son of Osbert, called William Longbeard. Roger of Howden, the only writer of the time who shows any sympathy either for the Londoners or for William, describes him as 'a man learned in the law, fired by zeal for justice and fairness'.

William had an elder brother, Richard, who belonged to the ruling clique that was oppressing the poor and whom William had accused of treason. According to his deposition:

> He heard, in Richard's stone house where they were discussing the aids given for the lord king's ransom, Richard say that with the forty marks that the chancellor had taken from him in the Tower of London he would like to buy a chain with which to hang the king and his chancellor. . . . And Jordan the Tanner said: 'May the lord king always stay where he is now.' . . . Robert Brand was there, too, and they said: 'Come what may, London will never have any other king than the mayor of London.'[1]

William Longbeard, according to William of Newburgh, enrolled 52,000 of the poorer citizens in a conspiracy against the richer ones with the aim of forcing the rich to agree to a more equitable distribution of the burden of taxation, and crossed the Channel to present their demands to King Richard. The king sent him back to the chief justiciar, who became so enraged at having his integrity questioned that he forbade the Londoners to leave the city and threatened to seize any that were found outside the walls as 'enemies of the king and the realm'. This was no idle threat, for at mid-Lent some London merchants were seized at Stamford Fair at the chief justiciar's orders.

Since William did not cease haranguing the citizens on the injustices under which they were suffering, Hubert Walter sent

[1] *Rotuli Curiae Regis*, Vol. I, p. 69.

some of the leading Londoners to arrest him and bring him before the chief justiciar. William resisted arrest and in the course of the scuffle killed a member of the party named Geoffrey. With some of his followers he then took refuge in the church of St. Mary-le-Bow and barricaded the doors.

The archbishop of Canterbury, as chief justiciar, ordered that the church be set on fire. When William was at last driven out of his sanctuary by the smoke and fire, on Saturday, 6 April, he was stabbed, but not fatally, in the belly by the son of that Geoffrey whom he had killed. He was taken to the Tower and there condemned to death. He was dragged at a horse's tail through the streets of London and then hanged, together with eight or nine of his leading supporters. With their leaders thus disposed of, the danger of an uprising by the poorer citizens was dispelled. To make sure of their good behaviour in the future the chief justiciar took hostages from many of them.

Unfortunately for Hubert Walter, the church of St. Mary-le-Bow belonged to his own monks of Canterbury, and they were loud in their complaints against his conduct. For the archbishop of Canterbury, even though he was acting as chief justiciar, to disregard the rights of sanctuary and to set fire to a church in order to drive out of it a man who had taken refuge there was so flagrant a violation of the rights of the Church that the monks complained to the pope about it. They were the more inclined to find fault with their archbishop because he was beginning at about this time to revive his predecessor's plans for founding a college of canons at Lambeth.[1]

When King Richard learned what his chief justiciar had done to put down this disturbance, he wrote to express his approval and thanks. He turned then to the matter that was uppermost in his mind. Although he and King Philip had made a truce at Louviers in January 1196, it had brought little more than a lull in the warfare between the two. Philip soon broke the truce by taking Aumale and Nonancourt, and Richard wrote to Hubert Walter that 'we think we are more likely to have war than peace from the king of France'.

In order to prepare for the inevitable resumption of hostilities, Richard directed that all barons who had their chief estates, the

[1] Howden, Vol. IV, pp. 5-6, 48; Gervase, Vol. I, pp. 532-4; Newburgh, Vol. II, pp. 466-73; Diceto, Vol. II, pp. 143-4.

'heads' of their baronies, in Normandy should cross over without delay, for they would be the ones most concerned to repel Philip's attacks. All others who owed military service in England, except those charged with guarding the Welsh marches, were to go to Normandy by Trinity Sunday, 'with horses and arms, ready for our service, and let them come prepared to stay in our service for a long time'. Richard directed that they were to come prepared for serious fighting and hence were not to bring a numerous following more suited for display than for business; each baron was limited to a retinue of seven knights.[1]

Richard relied upon mercenaries for the body of his troops and called upon his knights and barons to serve mainly as castellans and as captains for his army. The forms were carefully preserved, however, for by calling upon 'all those who owe us knight service in England' Richard could avail himself of the services of those whom he wanted as fighters and at the same time exact scutages from the rest, with which to pay his mercenaries. As F. W. Maitland puts it: 'Military tenures still supply an army, though chiefly by supplying its pay.'[2]

The Pipe Roll for this year shows that 'the third scutage of the army of Normandy' was levied at the regular rate of 20s. for the knight's fee and that, as usual, tallages and aids were imposed on the towns. John of Wick was paid one mark 'for carrying the king's summonses concerning aids and hidages and tallages throughout England' and 12d. 'for wax that he found for sealing the aforesaid summonses', and Thomas, the clerk of Hugh Peverell, was paid 2s. 6d. 'for his livery for six days in which he wrote the aforesaid summonses'.[3]

A new feature appears in the scutages levied in 1195 and 1196. For the first time, some tenants-in-chief, in addition to their regular scutages, offered or were assessed fines in order that they might not be obliged to cross over to Normandy. For the lay tenants, this meant that the payment of scutage relieved them only from the necessity of sending their quota of knights to the king's army; the fines were to purchase their own exemption from military service. Ecclesiastical tenants-in-chief apparently

[1] Howden, Vol. IV, pp. 3-5; Diceto, Vol. II, p. lxxix.

[2] Sir Frederick Pollock and Frederic William Maitland: *The History of English Law before the Time of Edward I* (2d ed., 2 vols., Cambridge, 1899), Vol. I, pp. 252-3.

[3] Chancellor's Roll 8 Richard I, p. 290.

were forced to pay in order to escape personal service on the part of their knights.[1]

These fines to avoid crossing over to Normandy bore most heavily upon ecclesiastical tenants-in-chief. The largest fine levied upon a layman was that imposed upon Hugh of Bayeux, who was assessed 60 marks for leave not to cross over and to collect the scutage from his 20 knights, in addition to his scutage of £16 18s. The abbot of Peterborough, on the other hand, was assessed £60 at the regular rate as scutage for his 60 knights and an additional £100 as his fine to avoid crossing over and for permission to collect the scutage from his knights to reimburse him for the £60.[2]

The abbot of Abingdon, in Berkshire, owed the service of 30 knights, but he paid 100 marks as his scutage and to avoid crossing over. The abbot of Evesham owed 4½ knights, but he paid £10. The abbot of Hyde, owing 20 knights, was assessed 50 marks. The bishop of Chichester, on the other hand, owing 4 knights, paid only £4 as both scutage and fine. The bishop of Hereford paid only £15 for the second scutage in 1195, but in 1196 he paid £20 for both scutage and fine. In Gloucestershire the abbot of Winchcombe paid a fine of £10 and the abbots of Gloucester and Tewkesbury each paid a fine of 10 marks to avoid crossing to Normandy. Even the abbess of St. Edward's, at Shaftesbury, was assessed £20 as scutage for 7 knights and 'that she may not be obliged to cross over to Normandy'.[3]

That Richard should now impose such fines upon some of his ecclesiastical tenants-in-chief shows not only his great need for money but also a feeling of resentment against the Church for not giving him greater help in his struggle against Philip. That feeling was brought to a head by his quarrel with Walter of Coutances, archbishop of Rouen, over Les Andelys. In order to protect the lower valley of the Seine and particularly Rouen, Richard began building the greatest and most costly castle in western Europe, Château Gaillard, above Rouen at Les Andelys, which belonged to the archbishop of Rouen.

Walter of Coutances, instead of co-operating in the work which would defend Rouen from attack by Philip or of trying to

[1] A. L. Poole: *Obligations of Society*, pp. 40-3.
[2] Chancellor's Roll 8 Richard I, pp. 40, 45, 247, 249.
[3] Ibid., pp. 11, 16, 81-2, 85, 108-9, 226.

arrive at a compromise with the king, laid the whole of Normandy under interdict in order to punish the king. Richard considered this action both base ingratitude and sheer treachery, and his attitude towards churchmen whom he considered to be refusing to bear their fair share of the cost of defending Normandy hardened considerably.[1]

Archbishop Hubert Walter found his position becoming more and more difficult, placed as he was between the king, with his demands for more and more money, and the people of England, who found the king's demands more and more irksome. They had responded generously to the appeal for the king's ransom, but the demands for money with which to prosecute the war in Normandy, coming year after year, became more and more onerous, particularly since they did not benefit from these expenditures. Those barons who had lands to defend in Normandy were in most cases fighting beside King Richard; the barons who had no lands in Normandy and the common people on whom the king's demands fell most heavily had no interest in the matter and probably cared not a whit whether Richard or Philip had control of the duchy.

The archbishop frequently begged the king during this year to accept his resignation as chief justiciar, since it was more than one man could do to rule both the kingdom and the Church in England. When Richard at last showed signs of acceding to Hubert's request, the archbishop changed his mind. He had 'inspected the writings' and audited the accounts, he told the king, and had found that during the past two years he had collected and sent to him a hundred thousand marks of silver from the realm of England. This sum is impossible on the face of it, but it is evident, on the other hand, that money was being collected and shipped across the Channel in amounts larger than had ever been known before. Hubert Walter withdrew his resignation, and the king was of course happy that he did so.[2]

Archbishop Geoffrey, meanwhile, at last appeared in Rome to answer the charges that had been brought against him. He defended himself so well that his enemies admitted that 'they did

[1] Howden, Vol. IV, p. 14; Kate Norgate: *Richard the Lion Heart* (London, 1924), pp. 308-13; Sir Maurice Powicke: *The Loss of Normandy, 1189-1204* (2d ed., Manchester, 1961), pp. 115-17, 190-6.

[2] Howden, Vol. IV, pp. xc-xci, 12-13.

not wish to assume the burden of proof', a tame ending indeed to the accusations they had been making. The pope was so impressed by his defence and by the inability of his adversaries to substantiate their charges that he restored Geoffrey to his see and ordered the clergy of York to show him 'due reverence and obedience in all things'.

King Richard was drawing such a handsome profit from the confiscated estates of the archbishopric, however, that he countermanded the pope's order and directed his officers in Yorkshire not to allow either Geoffrey or his officials to administer the diocese. The king continued to reward his friends with the plums that fell into his hands through the enforced absence of Geoffrey, who returned to Rome when his brother refused him permission to go back to his see. Bourchard of Le Puiset, treasurer of York, died in this year, and the king gave the post, as well as the archdeaconry of Richmond, to Master Eustace, his seal-bearer and vice-chancellor, who was already dean of Salisbury. Likewise when Peter of Ros, archdeacon of Carlisle, died, the king rewarded his faithful friend Philip of Poitiers, bishop of Durham, by making Philip's nephew Aimeric archdeacon of Carlisle, and Philip added to Aimeric's dignities by making him archdeacon of Durham also.[1]

Richard had, at some time previous to this, given Adam of Thornover the archdeaconry of the West Riding, although Archbishop Geoffrey, before he left England, had appointed Peter of Dinan to the post. The dean and chapter of York, it will be remembered, had protested against Peter's appointment, claimed the right of naming their own candidate, and appealed, with Hubert Walter's permission, to the pope. Richard had intervened and settled the matter to his own satisfaction by naming Adam of Thornover.

Peter, however, had powerful friends in Brittany who used the young Duke Arthur, Richard's nephew, as their mouthpiece. Because of their representations, the king allowed the rival candidates to reach a compromise, the first evidence of any commonsense or willingness to settle matters peaceably that had been shown by the chapter of York since the beginning of the squalid troubles there. According to this ingenious agreement, the dean and chapter received Peter as archdeacon of the West Riding and

[1] Howden, Vol. IV, pp. 7-8, 14; Gervase, Vol. I, p. 543.

gave him his stall in both the choir of the minster and the chapter-house. With his rights thus recognised and his pride assuaged, Peter then turned over his post to Adam in exchange for a yearly pension of 60 marks, with the agreement that if Adam died before Peter, Peter should succeed him as archdeacon of the West Riding. If both of them meanwhile should happen to be in York at the same time, they agreed to occupy their joint stall on alternate days.

Shortly after Archbishop Geoffrey had succeeded in vindicating himself before the pope, one of his clerks, Ralph of Wigtoft, who had been looking after Geoffrey's affairs at Rome, fell gravely ill and confessed before the pope and all his cardinals that he had had letters forged in Rome, the centre, no doubt, of a thriving trade in such commodities, pertaining both to Geoffrey's affairs and to his own, and had already sent them off to England. The pope sent word to Archbishop Hubert Walter of Ralph's confession and ordered him to seize any letters pertaining to Geoffrey's affairs that might arrive in England and that looked suspicious to him.

Hubert Walter's agents seized a certain clerk, Roger of Ripon, who was bearing letters entrusted to him by Ralph of Wigtoft, and found that as well as the letters he was carrying a quantity of poison that he said Ralph had given him, to be used upon Master Simon of Apulia, dean of York, and a number of the canons of York. Master Simon was summoned to London, and the poison, together with a golden ring and a handsome belt, both said to be poisoned, was turned over to him. In the presence of a large crowd Master Simon cast the poison, the ring, and the belt into the flames at Tothill, and thus they were reduced to ashes. Geoffrey's enemies, says Roger of Howden in concluding this improbable tale, imputed the responsibility for all this to him.[1]

Although King Richard, before his departure on the crusade, had made peace, after a fashion, with the Welsh, the Lord Rhys, prince of South Wales, had for the last few years been pushing his way eastward, and successive Pipe Rolls tell of the expenses of expeditions, usually on a small scale, to contain him. Hubert Walter had had his hands too full with other matters to devote much attention to Welsh affairs, but in September 1196 the situation on the Welsh border became so critical that he was forced

[1] Howden, Vol. IV, pp. 8–9, 15–16.

to lead, in person, an expedition against the Welsh. The danger came, not from the Lord Rhys, who was nearing the end of his life and was beset by quarrels amongst his sons as to the succession, but from Gwenwynwyn, lord of Powys, who had succeeded his father shortly before this time and had immediately launched upon a series of attacks on the English border.

The preparations for this campaign were made carefully and well in advance. The Pipe Roll compiled at Michaelmas 1196 lists expenditures of £260 12s. 3d. 'for the king's affairs in Wales and in the Welsh Marches and for keeping knights and soldiers there in the king's service', a payment to Hubert Walter of £237 18s. 8d. 'for strengthening the king's castles and taking care of other of the king's affairs in Wales and in the Marches of Wales', and a further payment of £213 6s. 8d. for the same purpose. The magnitude of these sums would indicate that the operation was on a large scale.[1]

Hubert Walter led his army to Gwenwynwyn's castle of Pool (Trallwng) and laid siege to it. With a skill and determination worthy of his master, he undermined the walls and captured the castle. After concluding a treaty with the Welsh he allowed the garrison to depart peacefully, perhaps in the hope that his clemency would move the Welsh to keep the treaty.[2]

When he returned from his expedition he summoned a meeting of the Great Council on St. Edmund's day, 20 November, at Westminster. There he published the Assize of Measures, providing for the use of uniform measures and weights throughout the kingdom. That some attempt to enforce uniform standards had been made for a number of years is evident from the many entries in the Pipe Rolls of amercements laid on men who sold wine or corn 'contrary to the assize'.

Hubert Walter took practical steps to ensure uniformity. At a cost of £11 16s. 6d. he had 'measures and gallons and iron rods and beams and weights' made 'to be sent to every county in England'. He directed that four or six law-worthy men in each city, borough, and county be assigned as inspectors of weights and measures. Violators of the assize were to be imprisoned and their chattels seized, and they could be released only at the order

[1] Chancellor's Roll 8 Richard I, pp. 17-20.

[2] Gervase, Vol. I, p. 543; J. E. Lloyd: *History of Wales* (2 vols., London, 1948), Vol. II, p. 583.

of the king or the chief justiciar. As for the inspectors, negligence or fraud on their part was to be punished by the forfeiture of all their chattels. The assize was to become effective at Candlemas 1197, with a special provision for the measure and quality of cloth. Beginning with the great mid-Lenten fair at Stamford, all cloth was to measure two yards from selvage to selvage and was to be of uniform quality throughout the bolt. The 'iron rods' mentioned above were no doubt to be used as yardsticks.

In the provisions of this assize, clear, practical, and specific, we see an excellent illustration of the character of Hubert Walter, hard-headed, fair-minded, practical, and down-to-earth. The assize remained in effect till 1201, when the merchants at St. Botolph's fair offered King John a large sum of money in order to be allowed to fleece their customers at their pleasure.[1] It was so necessary for the orderly conduct of trade, however, that at the baron's insistence it was again put into effect by Chapter 35 of Magna Carta.

[1] Howden, Vol. IV, pp. 33-4, 172; Pipe Roll 9 Richard I, pp. xxi-xxii, 160.

IX

1197

WALTER of Coutances, archbishop of Rouen, had laid the whole of Normandy under interdict, it will be remembered, as a protest against Richard's building his great fortification of Château Gaillard at Les Andelys, on land belonging to the archbishopric. Since the king apparently could not make the archbishop see reason about the matter or engage in any sort of arbitration, Richard sent his chancellor, William Longchamp, bishop of Ely, William of Ruffière, bishop of Lisieux, and Philip of Poitiers, bishop-elect of Durham, to Rome to lay the matter before the pope.

When the party reached Poitiers, William Longchamp fell ill, and he died there on 31 January. 'England rejoiced at his death, for the fear of him lay heavy upon her', says William of Newburgh. 'The nobles of England greatly feared him when he was alive, and few wept for him when he was dead!'

After the funeral, William and Philip went on to Rome. Pope Celestine and his cardinals, 'realising the damages and perils that would befall Normandy unless Andely were fortified', sided with King Richard and ordered Archbishop Walter to agree to Richard's proposals for compensating him. After this matter was concluded, the pope consecrated Philip of Poitiers bishop of Durham on 20 April 1197.[1]

Archbishop Hubert Walter meanwhile was embarking on a year of great diplomatic activity. The death of the Lord Rhys, prince of South Wales, on 28 April 1197, called for a decision as to which of his sons should be his successor, and it is evidence of the power and importance of the chief justiciar that he was able to settle the matter peaceably. Hubert Walter went to the Welsh border, made peace between the heirs, and secured the recognition of Gruffydd as Rhys's successor.[2]

[1] Newburgh, Vol. II, p. 490; Howden, Vol. IV, pp. 16–18.

[2] Howden, Vol. IV, p. 21; Lloyd, op. cit., Vol. II, p. 584.

Around the middle of June King Richard summoned Hubert Walter to Normandy to help him with the diplomatic exchanges by which he hoped to weaken King Philip's position. As a warrior Richard had no equal, but he had little taste for the time-consuming niceties of diplomacy, as he himself admitted.[1] Hubert Walter, on the other hand, was an experienced negotiator, and Richard turned to him as the most influential and respected churchman in his realms. Walter of Coutances was still sulking over the matter of Château Gaillard and had not yet obeyed the papal mandate to arrive at a compromise with the king; as a negotiator he would be of no use whatever.

Richard's chief aim was to secure an alliance with Baldwin IX, count of Flanders, who had succeeded his uncle, Count Philip, after the latter's death at the siege of Acre. King Philip was Baldwin's overlord, but the count had no use for him, for Philip had taken Artois and Péronne from him in 1191. The kings of England had regularly paid a pension to the counts of Flanders to maintain the friendship of so valuable an ally, but when Baldwin had seemed indecisive and had even entered into a brief alliance with King Philip, Richard cut off the pension. Richard now won Baldwin over by paying up the pension, three years in arrears,[2] and by a gift of 5,000 marks, and Hubert Walter's persuasions induced him to sign a treaty of alliance with Richard against Philip. Baldwin attempted to regain his lost territories and acted with such vigour that he almost succeeded in capturing King Philip. Pushing his advantage and with Hubert Walter acting behind the scenes, Baldwin succeeded in bringing Richard and Philip together for a conference.

Richard meanwhile had been buying the support of various French nobles who were lukewarm about Philip's scheme to conquer Normandy. The Bretons, who had been rebelling periodically against Richard, at last accepted his overlordship and joined him against Philip. Backed by the support of these allies, Richard was in a strong position when he met the French king near Les Andelys on 17 September. Largely through the mediation of Hubert Walter, it would appear, the two kings, since they could not agree to a lasting peace, consented to the terms of a truce to run till Hilarymass, 14 January 1199.

[1] Richard of Devizes, p. 83.

[2] Pipe Roll 9 Richard I, pp. xxii-xxiii, 164.

As a climax to his diplomatic triumphs, Hubert Walter succeeded in persuading Walter of Coutances to obey the pope's orders and agree to an exchange of lands with King Richard. The agreement was made on 16 October, and Walter gave the credit for the success of the negotiations to Archbishop Hubert, John, bishop of Worcester, and Eustace, the king's vice-chancellor and dean of Salisbury, whom Richard had nominated to the see of Ely to succeed William Longchamp.[1]

Hubert Walter returned to England early in November and issued the summons for a meeting of all the tenants-in-chief at Oxford on 7 December, to gain their consent to a new proposal for supplying military aid to the king. Such conflicting accounts are given by contemporary chroniclers of what happened at the council and such varying interpretations have been placed upon those accounts of what Bishop Stubbs calls 'a landmark in English constitutional history',[2] that it may be well to summarise each of the contemporary narratives.

Roger of Howden seems to place the meeting early in 1198; Gervase of Canterbury gives a definite date, 7 December 1197.[3] According to Howden, 'Richard, king of England, through Hubert, archbishop of Canterbury, asked that the men of the realm of England find him 300 knights to remain with him in his service for a year, or that they give him such a sum of money that he might thereby keep 300 knights in his service for a year, that is, to each knight 3 shillings a day in English money for his wages'. All the members of the council were ready to agree to this proposal, 'not daring to resist the king's will'. Bishop Hugh of Lincoln alone declared that he would never agree to it, both because in the course of time it would work harm to his church and because he would set a bad precedent for his successor, and he concluded by rebuking the archbishop for the shameful way in which he was acting. Howden does not state the outcome of the discussion.[4]

Gerald of Wales, who was in Lincoln from 1196 to 1199 and may therefore be presumed to know Bishop Hugh's side of the story, tells how King Richard laid such heavy exactions upon the

[1] Diceto, Vol. II, pp. 152-9; Howden, Vol, IV, pp. 19-21; Newburgh, Vol. II, pp. 495-6; Gervase, Vol. I, p. 544.

[2] Preface to Howden, Vol. IV, p. xcii.

[3] Howden, Vol. IV, p. 40; Gervase, Vol. I, p. 549.

[4] Howden, Vol. IV, p. 40.

Church that the clergy met to consider what measures they should take to resist them. The clergy elected Bishop Hugh as their spokesman because he was universally respected for his sincerity and the holiness of his life, and he expressed, presumably at the meeting of the Great Council, their determination to resist these impositions and to uphold the freedom of the Church. When this was reported to the king he vented all his wrath upon Hugh, ordering that 'his whole barony, which the royal officials call "regalia" ', be confiscated and that his servants be persecuted in every way possible.

Against the advice of all his friends, Bishop Hugh crossed over to Normandy to confront the king. He found Richard hearing Mass in the chapel of his new castle at Roche d'Andely. The king drew back from him at first, but Hugh insisted that Richard kiss him. Hugh then took his place in the choir, and at the pax the king came down from his stall, went to Bishop Hugh, and gave him the kiss of peace. Richard followed this up by sending the bishop, who did not eat meat, a large pike for his dinner, and thus Hugh was restored to the king's goodwill.[1]

Adam of Eynsham, who became Bishop Hugh's chaplain shortly before this time, greatly expanded this account in his life of St. Hugh. According to Adam, Archbishop Hubert summoned a meeting 'of all the great men of the whole of England' at Oxford one year and four months before King Richard's death, which would place it in December 1197. The archbishop explained that the king, 'although inferior in resources and fighting men, was fighting against a most powerful king who was bending every effort to deprive him of his inheritance and work him harm'. Hubert Walter therefore asked the members of the council what aid they proposed to give their lord in such straits. Adam explains that the king's counsellors had already agreed that 'the barons of England, amongst whom the bishops were included', should furnish the king with 300 knights and pay their expenses for a whole year.

Both Archbishop Hubert, who probably originated the plan in consultation with the king, and Richard son of Nigel, bishop of London, who as dean of the province of Canterbury spoke next after the archbishop, announced that they were ready to do

[1] Gerald of Wales: *Vita S. Hugonis*, ed. James F. Dimock, in *Opera*, Vol. VII, pp. 103-6.

as the king asked. Bishop Hugh then reminded the assembly that he had come to England as a foreigner and that he had been raised to the episcopate from a simple Carthusian hermit. In the thirteen years that he had been bishop he had set himself to learn about 'the customs and dignities, the dues and burdens' of his see.

'I know that the church of Lincoln is bound to furnish military service to the lord king, but only in this country', he said; 'outside the boundaries of England she does not owe it.' Rather than relinquish the ancient immunities of his church and subject it to new burdens, Hugh declared that he would go back to his native land and his hermit's life.

At this refusal Archbishop Hubert, his lips trembling with anger, turned to Herbert, bishop of Salisbury, a son of Richard of Ilchester, bishop of Winchester, and a man thoroughly versed in legal and financial matters, and asked him what help he intended to give the king.

'It seems to me', Herbert answered, 'that I cannot, without great damage to my church, say or do anything more than I have just heard the lord bishop of Lincoln say.'

Faced with the opposition of two such influential men, the archbishop upbraided Bishop Hugh in the most bitter terms, dissolved the council, and reported to the king that the matter had fallen through, thanks entirely to Hugh. The king in great anger then ordered that all the possessions of the two offending bishops should be confiscated. Bishop Herbert's property was seized, and in February 1198[1] he crossed over to try to make his peace with the king. 'After injuries, loss, vexations, and many reproaches, with great difficulty he bought back his peace and his possessions for a very great sum of money.'

No-one, however, dared lay a hand on any of Hugh's property, 'for they feared his curse as they would death'. Thus matters dragged on from the feast of St. Nicholas, 6 December 1197, till August 1198, with the king repeatedly ordering the confiscation of Hugh's possessions and the royal officials not daring to execute the sentence. At last the king's officials begged Hugh to deliver them from the intolerable position in which they found themselves, and the bishop crossed over to Normandy to see the king. Hugh found King Richard at Château Gaillard, hearing Mass, on the feast of St. Augustine, 28 August 1198. The king was in

[1] *Annales de Wintonia*, p. 67.

his stall near the door, with Bishop Philip of Durham and Eustace, who had been consecrated bishop of Ely on 8 March 1198 and appointed chancellor.[1]

When Bishop Hugh greeted him, the king turned his head away and would not reply. Bishop Hugh demanded, 'Kiss me, my lord king.' The king turned still farther away. Hugh seized him by the front of his robe and shook him. 'You owe me a kiss', he said, 'for I have come a long way to see you.'

'You don't deserve a kiss', the king replied.

Shaking the king soundly, Hugh said, 'Indeed I do. Now kiss me.'

Laughing at the bishop's persistence, Richard kissed him. Hugh then took his place in the choir and followed the Mass with his usual devotion. Richard gave him the kiss of peace. At their interview later, when Hugh rebuked the king for being angry with him, Richard laid the blame on Archbishop Hubert, who was still smarting from Hugh's reproaches. Richard was completely reconciled with the bishop, gave him rich presents, and entertained him at Château Gaillard. The whole matter of the aid that Richard had demanded from his barons was apparently not mentioned.[2]

The last account to be considered, that of Jocelin of Brakelond, differs considerably from the others, although it is clear that he is telling the same story from still a different angle. Without giving any dates, he says: 'King Richard gave orders to all the bishops and abbots of England that out of every ten knights one should be chosen, and that those thus chosen should forthwith come to him in Normandy, with horses and arms, to help him against the king of France.' Since St. Edmund's Abbey owed the service of 40 knights, although 52¾ were actually enfeoffed, Abbot Samson called his knights together, explained the king's orders to them, and asked that they choose four knights and arrange amongst themselves to pay their expenses.

The knights replied 'that they did not owe such service, and that neither they nor their fathers had ever served outside England, though they had sometimes paid scutage at the king's command'. The abbot, fearing lest the rights of his tenants might be infringed upon if he acceded to the king's demands and at the same

[1] Diceto, Vol. II, p. 159; *Annales de Margan*, in *Annales Monastici*, Vol. I, p. 23.
[2] *Magna Vita S. Hugonis*, pp. 248–54.

time fearing 'that he might lose seizin of his barony if he failed in the king's service, as had happened to the bishop of London and many barons of England', crossed over to Normandy to see the king.

Richard told Samson that 'he wanted neither gold nor silver, but he pressingly demanded four knights'. The abbot accordingly hired four knights and gave them 36 marks for 40 days' expenses, the usual period of service, at the rate of 3 shillings a day. Some of the king's household, however, warned Samson as to what he might be letting himself in for. The war against King Philip, they said, might well last for a year or more, and they implied that the king would expect him to pay the wages of the four knights for as long as Richard needed them. Samson went back to the king and, by paying him £100, reached an agreement that he would not be responsible for the knights after the forty days had elapsed. The king in turn gave him a writ authorising him to collect from his knights what he had paid the king on their behalf.

When Samson returned to England and summoned his knights, they told him that they were too poor to bear the whole burden and offered to pay 2 marks each. If, as seems likely, all the knights who had been enfeoffed contributed, rather than merely the forty who owed knight service, Samson would have collected 105½ marks, or £70 6s. 8d., whereas he had spent £124 first in hiring four knights and then in buying quittance from further service.[1]

Although these accounts differ widely, one can nevertheless piece together from them a probable picture of what happened. At the meeting at Oxford on 7 December 1197, Hubert Walter in the king's name demanded that all the tenants-in-chief, both lay and ecclesiastical, send Richard a force of 300 knights to serve for a year. Roger of Howden's further statement that Hubert Walter offered them the alternative of providing the king with enough money to hire 300 knights at 3 shillings a day does not accord with any other of the accounts, which insist on the king's demand for men, not money.

Many tenants-in-chief were already serving with the king in Normandy; others who were charged with guarding the Welsh Marches and the Scottish border would be excused from service

[1] Jocelin of Brakelond, pp. 85-7, 154-5.

in Normandy. One may hazard the guess that 300 knights would be roughly one-tenth of the total who were obliged to do service and were neither already doing so nor excused.[1] In the same way, a year may be taken as roughly equivalent to ten times the forty days that were customarily demanded as the normal term of obligatory service.

Richard's demands, as expressed by his chief justiciar, were logical in view of the situation in Normandy. The king realised that the war against Philip, although suspended occasionally by truces that the two kings kept only for as long as suited their convenience, would be a long-drawn-out affair involving the defence of the frontier not only in Normandy but in the whole of his continental domains. His defences were of course strongest in Normandy, but the whole border had to be defended by a string of castles, each requiring a permanent garrison under the command of reliable and experienced men. For such a purpose it would not be worth the trouble to call out the whole of the knight-service due from his English tenants-in-chief, transport them across the Channel (almost an impossibility in view of the shipping available), and assign them to their posts for only forty days. Richard wisely decided that it would be better to have three hundred knights for a year than three thousand knights for forty days, and his demand was a legitimate and sensible one.

This demand was opposed by Bishop Hugh of Lincoln on the ground that he was not obliged to furnish knights for personal service outside England. His example was followed by Bishop Herbert of Salisbury. In the face of this opposition, Archbishop Hubert seems to have dismissed the council and reported the matter to the king, who ordered the estates of the two bishops to be confiscated.

It is evident, however, from the account of Jocelyn of Brakelond that either at this meeting of the council or at a subsequent one the archbishop again presented the king's demands and gained the agreement of the tenants-in-chief to furnish the king with one-tenth of the knight-service at which they were assessed, with the understanding that each knight was to serve for a year.

The refusal of the bishop of Lincoln to furnish knights for service oversea was not based, as Bishop Stubbs maintained, on any constitutional principles. The constitution, whatever that might

[1] Doris M. Stenton: Introd. to Pipe Roll 10 Richard I, p. xxi.

have been, was not involved. The bishop based his refusal on what he considered to be the rights and immunities of his see. He was bound to pay scutage, he admitted (he could not well claim otherwise), but he was not bound to furnish knights for personal service outside England. The fact that the bishop of Salisbury sided with Bishop Hugh indicates that there may have been grounds for thinking that this exemption applied to all ecclesiastical fiefs. Whether or not the two bishops were correct in their contention there is simply not enough evidence on which to base an opinion.[1]

That not all ecclesiastics thought as the two bishops did is evident from the many fines levied in connexion with the scutage of 1196. Not only did a number of clerics pay the usual scutage, but, as has been noted previously, they paid an additional fine in order to be excused from crossing over to Normandy. It is obvious from these fines that the king considered that the knights of ecclesiastical fiefs, like all the others, were bound to serve in Normandy unless they both paid a scutage and paid in addition a fine to avoid the obligation of crossing the Channel. In 1197, for example the abbot of St. Albans paid 50 marks 'so that he need not cross over in the third army of Normandy and for having the scutage of 6 knights' and further 50 marks 'for his 6 knights': a total of 100 marks to discharge an obligation that would ordinarily be rated at £6.[2]

Furthermore, twelve heads of religious houses are recorded as paying 'gifts for knights' in 1198, usually at the rate of 5 marks on each knight's fee. As Lady Stenton points out, these entries 'can only represent financial bargaining by individual ecclesiastical tenants to avoid the production of knights'.[3]

Whether or not Richard was justified in making such a demand we have no way of knowing, and it is certainly not a question that would have interested the king. From his point of view it was justification enough that he should make the demand, of his own free will and pleasure, and that the tenants should heed it. That it may have been a new and thus, from the points of view of the tenants, an unwarranted imposition is per-

[1] Helena M. Chew: *The English Ecclesiastical Tenants-in-Chief and Knight Service* (Oxford, 1932), pp. 39-43.

[2] Pipe Roll 9 Richard I, pp. 73, 76.

[3] Doris M. Stenton: Introd. to Pipe Roll 10 Richard I, p. xxiii.

haps indicated by the opposition of the two bishops, the declaration of the knights of St. Edmunds, and the fact that a fine to avoid military service oversea, in addition to the normal scutage, is levied on ecclesiastical tenants for the first time in the scutage of 1196.

On the other hand, the fact that only two bishops opposed the imposition might indicate that the obligation was generally recognised. The whole matter rested upon the king's absolute will and upon custom, not upon written contracts. No body as a whole was so tenacious of what they considered their ancient rights and privileges and so vociferous in their protests when they imagined that those rights were being infringed upon as were the bishops. It is significant, then, that only two bishops protested against Richard's demands, and of those two, one was brought to an expensive submission, whilst the other escaped only because of the forcefulness of his personality.

Richard and his chief justiciar may have resorted to this added exaction in an attempt to force the ecclesiastical tenants to pay their fair shares of the heavy costs of the defence of Normandy. The clergy did not deny that they were liable for scutage, but they were more than dilatory in paying it. A review of the financial affairs of the three ecclesiastics with whom we are concerned may show why the king felt some impatience with them.

For the 'scutage for the lord king's ransom', which was counted as 'the first scutage of the army of Normandy' and was levied in 1194, the abbot of St. Edmunds was assessed £40 and paid the whole amount; the bishop of Lincoln was assessed £60 and paid £58; and the bishop of Salisbury was assessed £32 and paid £31. All these assessments were levied at the regular rate of 20s. for each knight's fee.[1]

For 'the second scutage of the army of Normandy', levied in the late summer of 1195, and the third scutage, of the spring of 1196, the three ecclesiastics were assessed the same amounts and had paid nothing at all by Michaelmas 1196.[2]

By Michaelmas 1197, after a year marked by Hubert Walter's strenuous efforts to collect outstanding debts, they had made a better but still not an impressive showing. The abbot of St. Edmunds still owed £40 each for the second and third scutages,

[1] Pipe Roll 6 Richard I, pp. 65, 119, 201.
[2] Chancellor's Roll 8 Richard I, pp. 137, 247, 29; 122, 247, 59.

but 'he has quittance by a writ of Hubert, archbishop of Canterbury'.[1] It is probable that when Abbot Samson made his bargain with the king in Normandy, Richard included this general quittance of past debts in the terms, so that Samson's payment of £100 included the £80 outstanding on the scutages. If this be the case, Samson made a good bargain with the king. The entry concerning his quittance was made after the roll was completed at Michaelmas 1197 but before the roll for Michaelmas 1198 was drawn up.

The two bishops, however, paid an instalment on their debts. Although he still owed the small amounts due on the first scutage, the bishop of Lincoln paid £51 on the second scutage, leaving £9 owing, and £31 on the third, leaving £29 owing. The bishop of Salisbury seems to have paid £30 on the second scutage, leaving £2 owing, and £26 on the third, leaving £6 owing. Although these payments were delayed, they are certain evidence that the bishops did not dispute their liability to pay scutage.[2]

All that this 'landmark in English constitutional history' amounted to was a refusal to grant the king something that the two bishops thought he was not entitled to demand.[3] A similar situation arose in 1166, when all the ecclesiastical and many of the lay tenants-in-chief refused to pay the extra scutage that Henry II thought he was entitled to under 'the new enfeoffments' reported in 1164. In that year, it will be remembered, Henry required that his tenants report to him how many knights they had actually enfeoffed. If the figure was higher than the number at which the tenants were customarily assessed, Henry used the higher figure as a basis for subsequent scutages and aids, the first of which was the aid for the marriage of his eldest daughter Matilda to Henry the Lion, duke of Saxony.

Henry was not successful in this attempt to increase his revenues. The lay tenants simply did not pay the increment; the ecclesiasti-

[1] Pipe Roll 9 Richard I, pp. 238-9.

[2] Pipe Roll 9 Richard I, pp. 101, 201; 109-10, 212-13.

[3] For general discussions of the Council of Oxford in 1197 and the issues involved, see Stubbs, Preface to Howden, Vol. IV, pp. xci-xcii; Kate Norgate: *England under the Angevin Kings* (2 vols., London, 1887), Vol. II, pp. 349-50; J. H. Round: 'The Oxford Debate on Foreign Service (1197)', in *Feudal England* (London, 1895), pp. 528-38; Sir James H. Ramsay: *The Angevin Empire* (London, 1903), pp. 355-7; Helena M. Chew, op. cit., pp. 39-45; Doris M. Stenton: Introd. to Pipe Roll 10 Richard I, pp. xix-xxiv; A. L. Poole: *From Domesday Book to Magna Carta*, p. 371; and H. G. Richardson and G. O. Sayles, op. cit., pp. 83-4.

cal tenants had their protests entered on the Pipe Rolls. Thirty years later, the Pipe Roll for 1196 still carries those debts with such entries as 'The bishop of Salisbury owes 13s. 4d. of the aid for marrying the king's daughter on account of the knights that he does not recognise'.[1]

If Richard's needs had been a little less pressing and if he had been convinced that he was getting the support he was entitled to as a crusader from the Church, he might, like his father, have let the matter rest with entering these new debts on the Pipe Roll for future collection. Richard was not content to do so. He had repelled Philip's attacks with notable success; he was building the greatest and most expensive fortress in western Europe to guard Rouen and the lower valley of the Seine from Philip's threats; he had garrisoned a string of castles to protect the whole Norman border; and he was even now engaged in building up a great confederation of allies against the French king that might break Philip's power once for all.

On his leisurely journey down the Rhine in 1194 he had made alliances with many of the nobles of Germany and the Low Countries. In the autumn of 1197 he had won the counts of Flanders and Boulogne and many French nobles to his side. The southern borders of his continental domains were made secure by his brothers-in-law, Sancho of Navarre, one of Richard's firmest friends, and the erratic Count Raymond VI of Toulouse, to whom Richard had married his favourite sister Joan, the widow of King William of Sicily, in 1196.[2]

Finally, the Emperor Henry VI died on 28 September 1197, and Richard set about securing the election of his beloved nephew Otto, whom he had made count of Poitou in 1196, as Henry's successor. Richard sent a delegation that included Philip, bishop of Durham, Eustace, bishop-elect of Ely, and Baldwin of Bethune, count of Aumale, to the meeting of the electors at Cologne. Their efforts were successful; Otto was elected emperor on 6 June 1198.[3] By his astute diplomacy Richard had succeeded in isolating Philip, who now had to reckon with a coalition that threatened him from every side. Richard was now at the height of his power and influence, the mightiest king in western Europe.

[1] Chancellor's Roll 8 Richard I, p. 25.
[2] Howden, Vol. III, p. 235; Vol. IV, pp. 13, 19-20; Newburgh, Vol. II, p. 495.
[3] Howden, Vol. IV, pp. 31, 37-8.

X

1198

HUGH of Nonant, bishop of Coventry and 'the special persecutor of monks',[1] had, it will be remembered, expelled the monks from Coventry in 1190 and instituted in their stead a group of secular canons as the cathedral chapter. Because their lands had been seized and they themselves forced to disperse amongst various religious houses that were willing to shelter them, the monks had neither the opportunity nor the means to prosecute their appeal to Rome immediately and effectively.

That they managed to preserve some sort of corporate identity is shown by the fact that their prior, Moses, in the autumn of 1194 brought a suit of novel disseisin against the canons who had supplanted them at Coventry, and he offered 600 marks for the restoration of the community's lands. The canons at the same time offered a like sum to be confirmed in their possession, and Archbishop Hubert Walter further confused the issue by claiming that the suit fell within the jurisdiction of the courts christian. Unfortunately we do not know how the suit was decided, although it seems probable that the decision, if there was one, went to the canons.[2]

When at last they were able to obtain a hearing at Rome, Pope Celestine III decided in their favour, on the ground that Bishop Hugh had obtained 'by false suggestion' permission from Clement III to eject the monks. The pope ordered Archbishop Hubert Walter, Bishop Hugh of Lincoln, and Abbot Samson of St. Edmunds to restore the monks to their convent and to make sure that all their possessions were returned to them.

The pope's letter was evidently shown to King Richard on its way to England, or at any rate he learned of its contents before

[1] Gervase, Vol. I, p. 550.

[2] *Rotuli Curiae Regis*, Vol. I, pp. 3, 66-7.

action was taken. When the parties assembled at Oxford, perhaps on the occasion of the meeting of the Great Council on 7 December 1197, they were given letters from the king, asking that they put off taking any action, although Richard gave no reason for making such a request.

Archbishop Hubert and Bishop Hugh were inclined to follow the king's orders, but Abbot Samson, zealous for the honour of his order, insisted that they obey the pope. They accordingly gave one of the monks of Coventry symbolic seisin of the convent and its lands, but they deferred the actual installation of the monks out of deference to the king's wishes.

Abbot Samson, to show his sympathy for the monks, opened his hospice to the fourteen monks from Coventry who had assembled in Oxford and gave a magnificent feast at which the monks and 'the masters of the schools' at Oxford were the guests of honour. 'Never in his life', says Samson's biographer, 'did he seem happier than he was at that time.'

Shortly before Hilarymass, 14 January 1198, Samson went to Coventry to meet the other two. Archbishop Hubert meanwhile had spent Christmas in the Welsh Marches in strengthening the English defences, gravely threatened by the disorders that followed the death of the Lord Rhys and the ensuing dispute between two of his sons over the succession. Hubert took the castles of Hereford, Bridgnorth, and Ludlow away from the castellans to whom they had long been entrusted and whose fidelity he was perhaps beginning to doubt, and turned them over to new men.

During the five days that he awaited at Coventry the archbishop's arrival, Abbot Samson entertained the whole monastic community, who did not as yet have a home, and their servants in his hospice. The three prelates formally re-installed the monks on 18 January and restored all their possessions to them.[1]

Bishop Hugh of Nonant, meanwhile, was still in Normandy and still apparently in the king's disfavour. He fell ill in the autumn of 1197 and lingered in great suffering all through the winter. Gerald of Wales paints a touching picture of the old bishop in seclusion at Bec Herlouin, devoting his last days to prayer, deeds of penitence, and almsgiving, and spending his

[1] Howden, Vol. IV, pp. 35-7; Jocelyn of Brakelond, pp. 94-5; Diceto, Vol. II, p. 159; Gervase, Vol. I, p. 550; Dom David Knowles: *The Monastic Order in England*, p. 324.

whole fortune on works of charity and in feeding the poor. 'He who had been the most bitter enemy of monks' was clothed with a monk's habit, so that, as Roger of Wendover explains, 'he might have as patrons in the life to come those whom he had persecuted in this world'.

He died on Good Friday, 27 March 1198, while the Passion of Our Lord was being read, and was buried in the monastic cemetery at Bec. The Winchester annalist, who was probably the same Richard of Devizes who recorded Bishop Hugh's persecution of his monks, writes with satisfaction, 'After a long illness and unbearable suffering he closed his miserable life by a well-deserved death.'[1]

Richard promptly gave the bishopric thus vacated to Geoffrey of Muschamp, archdeacon of Cleveland and one of Archbishop Geoffrey's persistent enemies. Archbishop Hubert Walter consecrated him bishop of Coventry at Canterbury on 21 June.[2]

The burden of taxation during the last few years had fallen most heavily upon the tenants by knight-service, who had been called upon either for personal service or for three scutages and fines to avoid service, and the cities and boroughs and the villages in the royal demesne, which had been tallaged heavily but in a curiously haphazard fashion.[3] The hidage of 1194 had brought in almost nothing, and no determined effort had been made to collect it on a wide scale. Hubert Walter, hard pressed by his master, now determined to turn again to that source of revenue, which had at least the merit of bearing fairly equitably upon all occupants of land.

Roger of Howden says that in the spring of 1198 King Richard 'took five shillings as an aid from each carucate or hide of land in all England' and that the tax was collected according to a new assessment, which he describes in great detail.

A clerk and a knight were to be sent from the Exchequer to each county. Together with the sheriff and an unspecified number of knights elected (again, we do not know just how these knights were to be elected or chosen) for this purpose and sworn

[1] Gerald of Wales: *Speculum Ecclesiae*, pp. 68-71; Howden, Vol. IV, p. 45; Gervase, Vol. I, p. 552; Ralph of Coggeshall, p. 80; Roger of Wendover: *Flores Historiarum*, ed. H. G. Hewlett (3 vols., Rolls Series 84, 1886-9), Vol. I, pp. 273-4; *Annales de Wintonia*, p. 67.

[2] Howden, Vol. IV, p. 45; Deceto, Vol. II, pp. 162-3.

[3] See Doris M. Stenton, Introd. to Pipe Roll 9 Richard I, pp. xiii-xvi.

'to carry out the king's business faithfully', they were to summon the stewards of the tenants-in-chief in the county; the lord or his bailiff, the reeve, and four law-worthy men, either free or villein, of every township; and two law-worthy knights of the hundred.

These men were to declare 'faithfully and without fraud how many wainages of ploughs were in each township: how many in the lord's demesne, how many in the villeins' holdings, and how many held by churchmen in free alms'. Each 'wainage of ploughs' was to be assessed five shillings, with the sole exceptions of 'the free estates of parish churches' and lands held by serjeanty, that is, in return for some special service other than regular knight-service.

These returns were to be written down in four copies, of which one was to be kept by the clerks and one by the knight from the Exchequer, one by the sheriff, and the fourth by the stewards of the tenants-in-chief. The tax was to be collected by two law-worthy knights and the bailiff or serjeant of each hundred. They were to turn the money over to the sheriff, who in turn was to account for it at the Exchequer. The whole survey was to be completed by 31 May 1198, at which time all tenants holding by serjeanty, whose names and holdings were to be recorded in the survey, were to present themselves in London 'to hear and do the lord king's orders'.

At first sight it would appear that the assessment was to be based on the simple process of counting the number of plough-teams, normally of eight oxen each, working on each manor and equating 'the wainage of ploughs' with the carucate or plough-land. Roger of Howden throws the whole matter into obscurity, however, by adding casually, at the end of his account, that by the estimate of law-worthy men a hundred acres was to be counted as 'the wainage of each plough'.[1]

Much has been made of the presence of the elected knights on the group of assessors. Bishop Stubbs says: '. . . the principle of representation for the purpose of assessment was fully recognised as applicable to real property, whilst the mention of the chosen knights, who in each county were to superintend the proceeding,

[1] Howden, Vol. IV, pp. 46-7; James Tait: 'Studies in Magna Carta. I, *Waynagium* and *Contenementum*', *English Historical Review*, XXVII (Oct. 1912), p. 722; Reginald Lennard: 'The Composition of Demesne Plough-Teams in Twelfth-Century England', *English Historical Review*, LXXV (April 1960), p. 194.

points to the speedy approach of a time when the ideas of representation and election were to be permanently united'.[1] 'The representative principle had now reached its fullest development in the financial administration of the shire', writes Miss Norgate.[2] Sir James Ramsay says: 'The appearance of the representative knights to superintend the process of assessment is the most interesting feature of the inquest.'[3]

It must be remembered, however, that the mission of the board of assessors, made up of a clerk and a knight from the Exchequer, the sheriff, and the elected knights, was simply to find out and record the number of carucates or plough-lands under cultivation and who cultivated them. As was the case in the compilation of Domesday Book, which this survey was intended to supplant, the facts could be gathered only from the men on the spot.[4] The testimony of these men was to be corroborated by the two law-worthy knights of the hundred. If the elected knights had any representative function, it would only have been to see in a general way that fair play was done; their main duty would have been to share in the drudgery of assembling all the interested parties and hearing their testimony.

Throughout the second half of the twelfth century the governmental machinery became more and more complicated, but the professional civil service, if one may call it that, to operate the machinery did not increase in proportion to the amount of business to be handled. The central judicial system had become enormously more complicated under Henry II and became even more so during the reign of Richard I as Hubert Walter increased its scope and importance. The financial system, likewise, was subjected to increasing demands under Richard as scutages, tallages, fines, amercements, gifts, hidages, and now carucages were piled on one after the other.

The solution was not to increase the number of professional officials who were wholly at the service of the judiciary or the Exchequer but to call upon the knights of the shire to assume more and more of the burdens of local government and tax collection. Of the board of assessors charged with levying this

[1] Preface to Howden, Vol. IV, pp. xciii-xciv.

[2] *England under the Angevin Kings*, Vol. II, p. 354.

[3] *The Angevin Empire*, p. 356.

[4] See V. H. Galbraith: *The Making of Domesday Book* (Oxford, 1961), pp. 37 et seq.

carucage, only three, the clerk and the knight from the Exchequer and the sheriff, could be considered as officials of the central government. Most of the drudgery of the assessment, one surmises, would have to be done by the elected knights of the shire and the knights of the hundred, and the even heavier drudgery of collecting the tax would fall on the two knights and the bailiff of each hundred.

Although there is no evidence that the carucage was collected on a new basis or at the rate of five shillings or that the survey as ordered by Hubert Walter was completed, the Pipe Rolls show that some of the justiciars in eyre during the autumn and winter of 1198-9 made a determined effort to collect a carucage from some of the counties they visited. The attempted levy of 1194 figures in the Pipe Rolls as 'hidage'; that collected in this year is called 'carucage'. There is no indication as to whether the carucage was considered as a belated attempt to collect the hidage of 1194 or as a new levy.

Richard, archdeacon of Ely, William of Warenne, and Osbert son of Hervey visited a group of eastern counties. In Northamptonshire the sheriff offered £100 on behalf of the county 'for staying the inquest of carucage', and Rutland offered 20 marks 'as the county's fine for the carucage'. In Cambridgeshire and Huntingdonshire and in Norfolk and Suffolk the justiciars levied the carucage at the flat rate of 40s. on each hundred.[1]

Geoffrey son of Peter headed a party that used London as its headquarters. They laid a fine of 40 marks on Hertfordshire and £100 on Essex 'so that the inquisition of carucage may not be made', and assessed Buckinghamshire and Bedfordshire 80 and 140 marks respectively 'for the carucage'. Surrey offered 40 marks and Berkshire 70 marks 'to be quit of the carucage'.[2]

Two members of Geoffrey's party, Simon of Pattishall and John of Guestling, together with Richard Fleming, served with Alan, abbot of Tewkesbury, in visiting the west country after John's accession. They taxed Gloucestershire 100 marks as 'quittance of the carucage', of which £4 5s. 2d. was contributed by Tewkesbury Hundred and £7 3s. 6d. by Thornbury Hundred 'as quittance so that the inquisition of carucage laid in King Richard's time may not be made'. They assessed Shropshire at

[1] Pipe Roll 1 John, pp. 16, 19, 157-9, 275-88.
[2] Ibid., pp. 98, 112-13, 58, 259.

£20, Worcestershire at 35 marks, Herefordshire at £20, and Oxfordshire at 80 marks 'for quittance', and Staffordshire paid £20 'for the carucage assessed in King Richard's time'.[1]

Although no evidence of the general survey beyond what has just been cited has survived, a survey of holdings by serjeanty exists for nineteen counties. The letter that the assessors in Yorkshire wrote shows that they were following the instructions as given by Roger of Howden.

> To their most excellent lord Hubert, by the grace of God archbishop of Canterbury, primate of all England, his devoted R[oald], prior of Guiseborough, and R[eginald] of Arundel, precentor of York, and Roger of Batvent, sheriff of Yorkshire, and William of Percy and Ralph of Bolebec and Geoffrey Baard and Geoffrey of Wells and Robert of Mayton send greetings and service both due and devoted in all things.
>
> We inform your excellency that while we were making our round in the North Riding in order to put the tallage on the wainage of ploughs according to your order, we were delayed by various affairs in Richmondshire and Cleveland and could not reach the Wapentake of Pickering before the Friday next after the Feast of the Holy Trinity. Therefore the serjeants of the lord king holding of the lord king by serjeanty will not be able to appear before us in London on the day we set for them, that is, on the octave of the Close of Pentecost. And because we cannot certify the value of their lands and the number of carucates unless they are present, we have set the day on which they are to be before us in London as the Sunday next before the feast of St. Barnabas the Apostle [11 June].

The return from Herefordshire is made by 'the sheriff of Herefordshire and his associates assigned to making the tallage of carucates'.

The returns list the names, the holding, its value, in some cases the service by which it is held, and in fewer cases the amount the tenants offer the king. Richard Engaine, for instance, holds his land in Gidding, Huntingdonshire, 'by the serjeanty of catching wolves and he does his service every day'. Roger of Liddington holds one carucate in Bampton, Oxfordshire, 'and it is worth 1 mark a year, for the land is very sterile; by falconry [that is, by keeping one of the king's falcons]. He offers the lord king one mark.'

The returns by serjeanty are obviously incomplete, either be-

[1] Pipe Roll 1 John, pp. 29, 36, 78, 84, 217, 227, 167.

cause they were not finished in the first place or because they have been lost. Forty-two tenants by serjeanty are listed in Wiltshire, for example, but only seven in Oxfordshire.[1]

Roger of Howden records that the clergy refused to pay the carucage, 'as the other men of the realm did', and that the king in retaliation placed them outside the protection of the law. No clerk could sue a layman or get any redress from him for any offence, but laymen on the other hand could bring suit against a clerk and compel him to make satisfaction. This placed the estates of the Church at the mercy of rapacious neighbours, and as a result of this state of virtual outlawry the clergy were at length compelled to pay.[2]

In reviewing the scattered evidence for the projected new assessment of carucage, one surmises that Hubert Walter, with a desire to put the taxation of land on a tidy and equitable basis, had undertaken a project too big and complicated for the means he had to carry it out. He had as many men at his disposal as did William the Conqueror when the Domesday survey was made, but the itinerant justiciars, the sheriffs, and the Exchequer officials all had their hands more than full in an effort to cope with the multitudinous concerns already in motion. The chief justiciar therefore was not able to complete so grandiose an undertaking as to re-survey all the land under tillage.

The carucage, like the scutages and tallages of which the Pipe Rolls give ample evidence, was a legitimate and customary tax. The novel feature of taxation during Richard's reign was not the kinds of taxes levied, although fines, in addition to scutage, to escape personal service overseas appear for the first time, but the frequency with which the king's agents exploited every possible, though legitimate, device for raising money.

In his desperate need King Richard now tried an expedient that had never been used before and that was most bitterly resented on that account. At some time between 7 January and 16 May 1198 he changed his seal and ordered that all documents bearing the old seal be renewed under the new seal in order to be held valid. He had evidently been planning this action for several

[1] *The Book of Fees*, ed. Sir H. C. Maxwell Lyte (3 vols., London, 1920-3), Vol. I, pp. 1-13; J. H. Round: 'The Great Carucage of 1198', *English Historical Review*, III (July 1888), pp. 501-10, and IV (Jan. 1889), 105-7.

[2] Howden, Vol. IV, p. 66.

years, for the Pipe Roll for 1195 records the payment of 2 marks 'to William the Goldsmith, who made the king's seal, to buy a robe and to pay his wages', and in the following year 'plate to the weight of 5 marks for making the king's new seal' was accounted for. Both entries probably refer to the same seal, for the one in the Roll for 1196 covers the period 'from the Feast of Pentecost of the sixth year [1194] to the Octaves of the Apostles Peter and Paul of the eighth year' [6 July 1196].[1]

The pretext Richard gave for this unprecedented action was that the Great Seal had twice been out of his possession and therefore the validity of all documents sealed with it was open to question. The first occasion was a brief period in 1191, when Roger Malchiel, the king's seal-bearer, was drowned off Limassol on the way to the Holy Land, on 24 April, with the seal in his possession. When his body was washed ashore, a peasant found the seal on the corpse, and the king bought it back from him.[2] The second occasion was during Richard's captivity in Germany.

Richard now required that all charters issued under the first seal, of no matter what date, be renewed. A charter that was issued under the old seal on 7 January 1198, for instance, was reissued under the new one on 22 August 1198. The real reason for this extraordinary decree, of course, was that a heavy fee was charged for the renewal. Philip of Poitiers, bishop of Durham and one of Richard's best friends, had to pay 100 marks for the renewal of two charters.[3]

Richard treated Bishop Philip less harshly, however, than he had Philip's predecessor, Hugh of Le Puiset. It will be remembered that Bishop Hugh had bought the manor of Sadberge with a promise of 600 marks, which he had never paid. Bishop Philip now bought the same manor, which had meanwhile escheated to the Crown, for only 400 marks, but the fact that he paid in ready cash rather than in promises may have had something to do with the reduced price.[4]

Bishop Godfrey of Winchester received much rougher treat-

[1] Pipe Roll 7 Richard I, p. 113; Chancellor's Roll 8 Richard I, p. 19.

[2] *Itinerarium Regis Ricardi*, p. 184.

[3] Howden, Vol. III, p. 267, and Vol. IV, p. 66; Coggeshall, p. 93; J. H. Round: 'Richard the First's Change of Seal (1198)', in *Feudal England*, pp. 539-51; Lionel Landon: 'The Seals of Richard I', in *The Itinerary of King Richard I* (Pipe Roll Society, New Series 13, 1935), pp. 173-83; Doris M. Stenton: Introd. to Pipe Roll 7 Richard I, p. xxix; Pipe Roll 10 Richard I, p. 145.

[4] Howden, Vol. IV, p. 55; Pipe Roll 10 Richard I, pp. 43, 145.

ment. He had already paid £3,000 for the manors of Meon and Wargrave and for his patrimony. He was now forced to pay a further £1,000 for the same purpose.[1]

The monks of Christ Church, Canterbury, in addition to their long-drawn-out quarrel with their archbishop over his projected foundation of a college of secular canons at Lambeth, had a particular grievance against Hubert Walter because he had violated the sanctuary of the monks' church of St. Mary-le-Bow when he had caused William Longbeard to be seized. They had complained to the pope, but Celestine III had paid little attention to their complaints.

The new pope, Innocent III, who had succeeded Celestine in January 1198, was a different type of man. According to Roger of Howden, he turned an attentive ear when a delegation of monks from Canterbury complained to him that their archbishop, 'contrary to his priestly order and dignity, was acting as justiciar of the realm, was passing sentences of blood [i.e., of mutilation or death], and was so wrapped up in wordly affairs that he was hardly able to govern his church'.

Innocent, one of the greatest canon lawyers of the Middle Ages, was keenly aware of the impropriety of such a situation. Until this time, Richard had had the Church in England almost completely under his thumb. He had directly appointed every bishop who was consecrated during his reign with the sole exception of Savaric of Bath, who had a blanket authorisation from the king to accept any position to which he might be elected. Richard had treated papal legates with a high-handed contempt that would have delighted his father, and no archbishop of Canterbury had ever been so completely the king's servant as was Hubert Walter. Until the accession of Innocent III Richard had had to deal with a succession of weak popes who were too impressed by him as the leader of the Third Crusade to object to his domination of the Church in England. It was intolerable to Innocent that the archbishop of Canterbury could so degrade his office as to serve as Hubert Walter was serving, and he directed King Richard, as he valued his soul's salvation, not to allow the archbishop to continue to act as chief justiciar. For this reason, says Roger of Howden, Richard dismissed Hubert Walter from his secular post.[2]

[1] Pipe Roll 10 Richard I, p. 26.

[2] Howden, Vol. IV, pp. 47-8.

Richard's letter, however, announcing Hubert Walter's resignation and dated 11 July 1198, says nothing of the pope's urging. In a gentlemanly tribute to a man who had served him with the utmost fidelity and devotion, the king recalls how Hubert had often begged him in the past to release him from his office as chief justiciar, pleading 'the weakness of his body, the multitude of his illnesses, and other pressing reasons. But we', Richard continues, 'for our own benefit and yours and for the tranquillity in which he kept the realm, would not listen to him. Considering, however, his illness and the intolerable burden of his labours and his own weakness, at his request we have released him from the office we committed to him.'[1]

Hubert Walter, by accepting the position of chief justiciar when he was already archbishop of Canterbury, had put himself into an almost impossible situation, and only a man of the most extraordinary abilities could have acted, for four years, both as chief justiciar, particularly at a time when the king's prolonged absence from the country made the chief justiciar virtually regent, and as archbishop of Canterbury. As archbishop and papal legate, Hubert Walter discharged his office with surprising efficiency; there is nothing to indicate that he did not rule the province of Canterbury as well as any of his immediate predecessors had done.[2]

As chief justiciar at a difficult period, Hubert Walter ranks supreme among the men, some of them highly able, who have filled that exacting office. Under him the position assumed its greatest importance. It had always, since its beginning under Henry I, been the most important lay office in the kingdom, for its holder was the chief administrative and legal officer in the kingdom when the king was in England, and in the king's absence the chief justiciar was his representative and ruled in his name, subject always to the king's direction.

Henry II had occasionally been out of England for periods almost as long as Richard's second absence. He was across the Channel from August 1158 to January 1163 and again from March 1166 to March 1170.[3] When he was absent, however, he

[1] *Foedera*, Vol. I, Part 1, p. 71.

[2] C. R. Cheney: *From Becket to Langton: English Church Government 1170–1213* (Manchester, 1956), pp. 32-41.

[3] Doris M. Stenton: 'England: Henry II', Chap. XVII of *The Cambridge Medieval History* (8 vols., Cambridge, 1911-36), Vol. V, p. 554.

had exercised a minute and continuing supervision of the acts of his chief justiciars and the course of government, whilst Richard, as far as we can tell, left Hubert Walter largely to his own devices and limited himself to unceasing demands for men, money, and supplies. The great administrative measures of Richard's reign are to be attributed wholly to the genius of Hubert Walter; King Richard had no part in formulating them.

Hubert governed England efficiently and capably; he contributed in no small measure to the development of the machinery that functioned smoothly and ably in administering justice, whether the king was there to direct it or not; and he succeeded as probably no other man could have done in exercising the most important and characteristic functions of a powerful government in preserving the peace, maintaining law and order, and collecting money and services from the king's subjects. This last he did on an unprecedented scale and yet without arousing the country to rebellion, for he was careful always to adhere to customary and recognised forms of taxation, although he pushed them to limits that England had not previously known.

Although Hubert was virtual ruler of England, he ruled always in the king's name; what authority he had, and it was great, derived from the king. Richard was content to give him almost a free hand, but the ultimate power was the king's; when the occasion arose Richard intervened and used that power as ruthlessly as any of his predecessors. By his mere word Richard could strip a man, no matter how great, of all his estates and power and leave him defenceless before his enemies.

Hubert's greatest strength lay in his realisation of the limitations of his power and of his office. In that respect he differed from William Longchamp, who sent out his orders under his own seal, affected to rule in his own person, and paid the penalty for his presumption. Hubert's exactions were far heavier than Longchamp's had been, but they were made always in the king's name and in the accepted traditional forms and were submitted to for that reason.

To take Hubert's place as chief justiciar Richard appointed Geoffrey son of Peter, the next most experienced and capable man in the kingdom. A man of modest origins, he had served Henry II in several capacities and had been sheriff of Northamptonshire during the last five years of Henry's reign. Richard, when he came to the throne, released Geoffrey from his crusader's vow, as had already been told, and named him as one of the justiciars who were to be associated with the chief justiciar in the government of the country. He was sheriff of Northamptonshire again from Michaelmas 1191 to Easter 1194 and of Essex and Hertfordshire from 1190 to 1193; he had served as an itinerant justiciar throughout the reign, and he had been chief custodian of the royal forests during both reigns. A prudent marriage enabled him greatly to increase his wealth and importance.

When William of Mandeville, earl of Essex and count of Aumale, one of the two chief justiciars whom Richard had appointed before leaving England, died childless late in 1189, the king gave William's widow, Hadwisa, and the county and title of Aumale to William of Fors. Hadwisa did not inherit Earl William's estates in England, which would descend to the nearest heir of the Mandeville line. The estates were claimed by two descendants of Beatrice, Earl William's aunt: Beatrice of Say, the elder daughter of Beatrice's elder son William, who was married to Geoffrey son of Peter; and Geoffrey of Say, the younger son of the elder Beatrice. These relationships are indicated by the accompanying table.

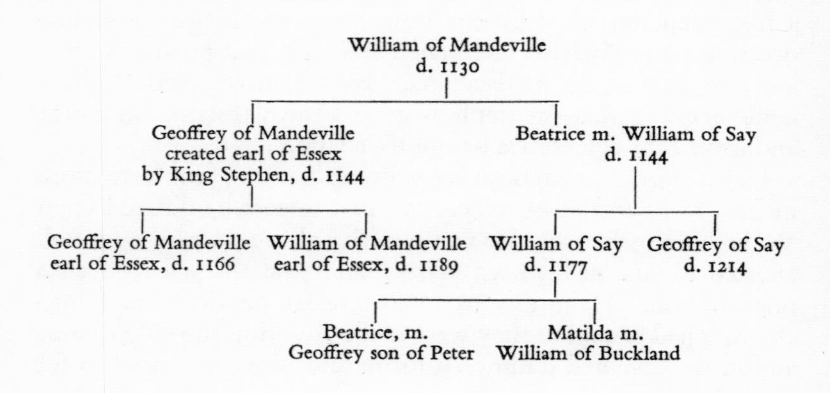

Geoffrey of Say offered 7,000 marks 'to have the land that was Earl William's'; Geoffrey son of Peter offered only 3,000 marks 'to have Earl William's land as the inheritance of Beatrice of Say, his wife, provided that he will be of such service to the lord king that it shall be in the king's pleasure whether he chooses to accept it or not'. Geoffrey of Say paid nothing, whilst Geoffrey son of Peter by Michaelmas 1190 had paid 900 marks. Needless to say, Geoffrey son of Peter was given possession of the land. Richard's charter, dated 23 January 1191, at Messina, gives Geoffrey son of Peter and his wife Beatrice, 'the lawful and nearer heir', all of Earl William's lands, thus ignoring the claim of Beatrice's younger sister Matilda, who was entitled to half the inheritance. In 1191 Geoffrey son of Peter paid 1,460 marks in discharge of his promise; in 1192, 140 marks; and in 1193, with unusual promptness, he paid the debt in full. Geoffrey received only the lands; although he had been receiving the 'third penny' normally given an earl from his county since Easter 1190, he was not formally made earl of Essex till John's coronation.[1]

The change of chief justiciars made no visible difference in the administration of the government. The two had worked closely together for many years, and the transition was so smooth and uneventful that one may assume that Hubert Walter, although he had relinquished the title, continued to exercise a great deal of power.

Shortly after he assumed office, Geoffrey issued a set of instructions for the itinerant justiciars that follows closely the articles of the eyre of 1194.[2] A few points, however, are worthy of notice. Chapter IX directs the justiciars to investigate 'concerning the ladies and the young men and the girls who are or ought to be in the king's gift, and the value of their lands; and if any of them has married; and let it be investigated to whom, by whom, and when'. The following chapter continues: 'And enquiry is also to be made as to what widows have not made fines for marrying, and let the fines be taken for the lord king's use.'

In the course of the eyre the justiciars, under the new chief justiciar, exploited to the full this source of revenue, which had been somewhat overlooked during the last few years. The Pipe Roll for this year abounds in fines from widows who want either not to marry or to marry at their own choice and from guardians of minors who want to profit from their wards' marriages. In Lincolnshire, for instance, Nicholaa, the wife of Gerard of Cam-

[1] *Ancient Charters*, pp. 97-9, 108-10; Pipe Rolls 2 Richard I, pp. 104, 111; 3 Richard I, p. 29; 4 Richard I, p. 171; 5 Richard I, p. 5; Howden, Vol. IV, p. 90.

[2] Howden, Vol. IV, pp. 61-2.

ville, promises 100 marks for leave 'to marry her daughter Matilda to whom she will, except the king's enemies'.[1]

Gerard of Camville and his family had felt the full weight of the king's displeasure for his share in Count John's rebellion. He was fined 2,000 marks in 1194 for his share in the rebellion and succeeded in paying off the debt by 1197; in payment of the last remaining £8 he gave the king two horses. As soon as that debt was settled, however, he was fined £100 'to have seisin of his land of which he was disseised because his knight was not found in the king's service' in Normandy. His wife, in addition to the fine recorded above, was still paying instalments on a fine of 300 marks she had incurred in 1194 for the marriage of Matilda's elder sister.[2]

In Lincolnshire, again, Cecilia of Crèvecoeur paid £13 6s. 8d. 'as her fine for marrying'. In Norfolk and Suffolk, Helewisa of Werres paid 20 marks not to be married, 'for she has taken a vow of chastity', and Matilda of Felmingham offered 5 marks 'to marry where she will'. Osbert son of Hervey paid £20 to marry Margaret of Rye 'by the lord king's grace', and Countess Gundreda, the widow of old Earl Hugh of Norfolk, who had died more than twenty years ago, promised £100 'so that she may not be married against her will, and if she wants to marry, this may be with the king's advice'.[3]

Chapter XIX of the instructions directs that enquiry be made concerning the assize of weights and measures, which shows that a determined effort was being made to enforce the assize.

Chapter XX provides: 'Enquiry is to be made in every county concerning the hides and carucates, and if the justiciars who were delegated for this purpose did their work well, and if they collected from everyone, and if they concealed anything.' This is further evidence that the survey ordered in the spring was carried out, at least to some extent, even though the results of the survey have not survived.

The justiciars were busy, too, in imposing tallages on the cities and boroughs, to accompany the payments 'to sustain the king's serjeants beyond the sea'. The sheriffs and the justiciars made every effort to collect as much as possible; old debts, some of

[1] Pipe Roll 10 Richard I, p. 63.

[2] Pipe Roll 6 Richard I, pp. 118-19; 9 Richard I, pp. 103, 114.

[3] Pipe Roll 10 Richard I, pp. 64, 93-4.

which had been owing for many years, were paid up, and an unusually large number of debts incurred during the year were paid in full. Geoffrey was proving to be even harsher and less scrupulous than Hubert Walter had been in raising money for his master. The revenue paid in or accounted for at the Exchequer rose from around £17,500 in 1197 to a little over £22,000 in 1198.[1]

'By these and other vexations, whether just or unjust, all England, from sea to sea, was reduced to poverty. But even before these things were ended another kind of torment was added to the confusion of the men of the realm by the justiciars of the forest.' Geoffrey son of Peter, who had acted as chief of the forest justiciars under Henry II, issued in the king's name a new Assize of the Forest that was an expanded version of the Assize of the Forest that seems to have been enforced throughout the reign of Henry II.[2]

The forest laws, for the protection of 'vert and venison', that is, both standing timber and the beasts of the chase, had been strictly and ruthlessly enforced by Henry II, both as a source of revenue and for the preservation of the game that he dearly loved to hunt. Richard had had almost no opportunity to hunt in the English forests and apparently had little interest in preserving game, and no forest eyres had been held during his reign. Geoffrey son of Peter and Hugh of Neville, who succeeded Geoffrey at this time as justiciar of the forests, now carried out a forest eyre, largely, one assumes, for the sake of the money collected in fines and amercements. Before Michaelmas they visited seventeen counties that lay in a compact group ranging from Lincolnshire in the north to Sussex in the south and from Essex in the east to Warwickshire in the west, and made a brief excursion into Cornwall, Dorset, and Somerset.

In spite of the repetition in the Assize of 1198 of the ferocious threats of the earlier enactment that those who offend against the forest laws will lose their eyes and their testicles, there is no record that such punishments were inflicted. The Pipe Roll records many amercements for such offences as keeping hounds

[1] Sir James H. Ramsay: *A History of the Revenues of the Kings of England, 1066–1399* (2 vols., Oxford, 1925), Vol. I, p. 227.

[2] Howden, Vol. IV, pp. 62–6; *Gesta*, Vol. I, pp. 323–4; Richardson and Sayles, op. cit., pp. 444–9.

within the forest, which seems to have been a particularly common offence in Cornwall, where 49 men were amerced sums ranging from half a mark to 20 marks. Thirteen townships in Wiltshire paid half a mark each for waste, or destruction of the forest; men were amerced half a mark for taking venison. Assarting, or bringing part of the forest under cultivation, reflects the pressure of a growing population on the supply of arable. Roger of Torpel in Northamptonshire, for instance, paid £8 to be allowed to assart 12 acres 'and have them by hereditary right as his right and inheritance', and a number of men in the same county paid to be allowed to assart their own woods, which happened to be within the limits of the royal forest.[1]

During his first summer as chief justiciar, Geoffrey son of Peter was called to the Welsh Marches by a fresh outbreak by Gwenwynwyn, prince of Powys. In July the Welsh besieged Painscastle, or Maud's Castle, as the English called it, in what is now Radnorshire, which was held by William of Braose. The chief justiciar raised a large army and went to William's relief. In a pitched battle before the castle on 13 August he utterly defeated the Welsh, killing great numbers of them and putting the remnant to disorderly flight. Ralph of Diceto puts the number of Welshmen killed at more than 3,000; Gervase of Canterbury at more than 5,000, and Roger of Howden says that 3,070 were killed, as well as many more who were fatally wounded but who managed to escape from the battlefield. Only one Englishman was killed, he adds, accidentally slain by an arrow that one of his comrades had carelessly loosed.[2]

Hubert Walter, with his experience of Welsh affairs, was of course associated with Geoffrey son of Peter in this expedition. Gervase of Canterbury, indeed, says that Hubert inflicted the defeat on the Welsh and then returned to London. Having summoned the Great Council, he laid his resignation of his secular office before it and was succeeded by Geoffrey son of Peter in August. Against this must be considered the facts that Richard's letter announcing Hubert's resignation is dated 11 July and that Ralph of Diceto says that the Welsh were defeated 'on the feast-day of the holy martyr Hippolytus', 13 August. Roger of

[1] Pipe Roll 10 Richard I, pp. 174-6, 187, 107.

[2] Diceto, Vol. II, p. 163; Gervase, Vol. I, p. 572; Howden, Vol. IV, p. 53; Lloyd, op. cit., Vol. II, pp. 585-6.

Howden attributes the victory to Geoffrey son of Peter, after he became chief justiciar.

Gerald of Wales, who would be particularly well informed concerning Welsh affairs, says that while Hubert Walter was still 'justiciar of the realm and a public official', he collected an army 'to show off his great power and his hatred' for the Welsh and led them to the relief of a castle, obviously Painscastle, that the English had built, 'not within the borders of England but rather in Wales, in order to take their lands away from them', and that the Welsh were besieging.

Hubert Walter did not direct the battle but contented himself with excommunicating the Welsh. He received the news of the English victory, in which 3,000 Welshmen were slain, at Bridgnorth, in Shropshire, on the day after the battle and had all the bells in the town rung and the *Te Deum* sung, 'giving thanks as a good pastor of God', Gerald adds bitterly, 'that the souls of so many of his parishioners were sent to hell in one day'.[1]

This confusion as to whether or not Hubert Walter was still chief justiciar in mid-August may well indicate that Hubert's part in public affairs was little less active after he had gone through the motions of resigning his office than it had been before.

King Richard, meanwhile, scored an equally spectacular success against the French. On 28 September, with only a small force, he put the French utterly to rout near Gisors, in the Vexin. Philip, mounted on a ten-year-old horse named Morelle, led the flight across the River Epte. The bridge broke under the weight of the French knights; Philip himself 'drank of the river', as Richard wrote in triumph to his friend Bishop Philip of Durham, and was hauled out of the water by his heels, and twenty of his knights were drowned. Richard himself unhorsed and captured three French knights. The bag ran to 130 knights, 200 warhorses, and more common soldiers than Richard had time to count.[2]

[1] Gerald of Wales: *De Invectionibus*, ed. J. S. Brewer, in *Opera*, Vol. III, p. 25.
[2] Howden, Vol. IV, pp. 55-60.

XI

1199

RICHARD'S victory over the French at Gisors in September 1198, although it was a total rout of King Philip and his forces, was little more than a skirmish; it was not a pitched battle that resulted in an overwhelming defeat for Philip, which alone would force him to abandon his designs on Richard's continental possessions. It was, however, a severe set-back for Philip, who narrowly escaped being captured, and probably caused him to take stock of his position. In addition to Richard's blazing determination to defend his lands with all the resources at his command and with that skill that made him the greatest soldier of his age, Philip had to consider not only the strength of the coalition that Richard had succeeded in building up against him but also the determination of the new pope, Innocent III, to force the two kings to make peace, so that all Christendom might unite in the new crusade that he was planning.[1]

These considerations led Philip to heed the urgings of Cardinal Peter of Capua, whom the pope had sent to make peace between the kings. Richard and Philip met between Vernon and Les Andelys on 13 January 1199 and agreed to a truce for five years. Richard then set off for Poitou to reduce that perpetual rebel, Adhémar, viscount of Limoges, who had revolted against him and entered into an alliance with Philip. In Richard's absence his representatives worked out with Philip the terms of a lasting peace, to be based on the marriage of Richard's niece, Blanche of Castile, with Philip's son and heir, Louis, and the return by Philip of all the territory he had taken since hostilities had begun.[2]

While he was in the south, Richard accused Viscount Adhémar of refusing to turn over to him, as rightful overlord, a treasure-trove that had reportedly been found at Châlus. Richard be-

[1] Howden, Vol. IV, pp. 70-5.
[2] Howden, Vol. IV, pp. 79-81; Ralph of Coggeshall, p. 94.

sieged the castle and on 26 March was wounded by a crossbow bolt that entered his left shoulder at the base of the neck and penetrated deeply into his left side. Concealing his injury, the king went into his tent and pulled out the bolt, which broke off and left the iron head, as long as a man's palm, in the wound. The crude attempts of a surgeon to remove the head made matters worse; the wound became gravely infected.

Richard met his death like a man. He summoned his mother, who was at Fontevraud, but Eleanor could not reach him before he died. He nominated his brother John as heir 'to the realm of England and all his other lands' and had all his followers swear fealty to John. He left all his jewels and three-fourths of his treasure to his favourite nephew, the Emperor Otto, and directed that the remaining fourth be distributed amongst his servants and the poor. He made his confession and received Holy Communion and the last anointing. Then, on Thursday, 6 April 1199, 'as the day ended, so ended his last day'.[1]

The only claimants to the throne were Count John and Arthur, duke of Brittany, the twelve-year-old son of John's elder brother Geoffrey, who had died in 1186. The Bretons in 1196 had placed Arthur under the wardship of King Philip, who had him brought up with his own son Louis. Richard of course did not even consider Arthur as a possible heir, for Arthur was completely under Philip's control.

In September 1197, on the other hand, Count John had made agreements with the counts of Flanders and of Namur, at his brother's direction, stating that in the event of Richard's death without issue, John would not make peace with the king of France without the consent of the two counts. The letters patent announcing these agreements, which implicitly recognised John as Richard's heir and assumed that he would succeed Richard as king, were witnessed by many of the leading men of both England and Normandy, including Archbishop Hubert Walter and William Marshal.[2]

The biographer of William Marshal tells of a debate between Hubert Walter and William Marshal when they learned of Richard's death as to whom they should support as his successor, with the archbishop favouring Arthur and William Marshal

[1] Howden, Vol. IV, pp. 82-3; Ralph of Coggeshall, pp. 94-6.
[2] Lionel Landon: *The Itinerary of King Richard I*, pp. 121-2, 207-8.

declaring for John. Apart from this, which contradicts the charter the two had witnessed, there is no indication that anyone in England seriously considered Arthur as a possible heir to Richard's crown.[1]

Richard, furthermore, on his deathbed had nominated John as his successor, and this would be the most telling factor in his favour. John was at least known, although probably not very favourably, in England, where he had at one time had a large following. Arthur, on the other hand, was unknown in England; he was not of age, and he was a ward of the king of France.

As soon as he was assured of the support of Archbishop Hubert Walter and William Marshal, John sent these two influential men to England to secure the adherence of the barons, to enforce peace and order, and to prepare for his coronation. John went immediately to Chinon and took possession of the treasure there. Robert of Turnham, seneschal of Anjou, acting on Richard's last instructions, turned over to John both the treasure and the castles of Chinon and Saumur. The counties of Maine and Anjou, however, declared for Arthur, and John devastated Le Mans to punish them.[2]

The news of Richard's death reached England on Saturday, 17 April. When the king died, his peace died with him. 'Everyone who had a castle, bishops as well as earls and barons, stocked it with men and victuals and arms', to be ready for the civil war that might attend a disputed succession. A wave of disorder swept over the country, and lawless men broke forth in depredations. Geoffrey son of Peter took immediate precautions, however; the Pipe Roll shows that repairs were made to many of the royal castles, and knights and serjeants, though never in large numbers, were posted in castles all over the country to keep these lawless men in check.

The firm hands of Hubert Walter, Geoffrey, and William Marshal soon restored order. They sent all over the country exacting oaths of fealty to John. At a meeting of the Great Council at Northampton they assured those from whom trouble might be expected that John 'would give each one of them his right, if they would observe fealty and peace to him'. At this

[1] *Histoire de Guillaume le Maréchal*, lines 11873-908; Richardson and Sayles, op. cit., pp. 140-1.

[2] Howden, Vol. IV, pp. 86-7.

assurance and under strong pressure from the archbishop, who pronounced a sentence of excommunication upon all disturbers of the peace, the barons 'swore fealty and faithful service against all men' to John.[1]

John meanwhile was invested as duke of Normandy by Archbishop Walter of Coutances at Rouen on 25 April. He landed at Shoreham a month later, went to London on the next day, and was hallowed and crowned king of England by Archbishop Hubert Walter in Westminster Abbey on Ascension Day, 27 May 1199.[2]

It is almost meaningless to say that Richard was a bad king; for all practical purposes he was king in name only. He never reigned over England, as his father had done and as his brother was to do, in the sense of directing the course of government, of contributing to the development of English laws and institutions, or of supervising and improving the workings of the English administrative system, which had been brought to a higher state of efficiency by Henry II and his helpers than that of any other state in western Europe.

Throughout the ten years of his reign Richard took little interest in England; he stayed in the country less than six months in all; he showed no knowledge of English institutions and no desire to learn about them. England gave him a crown, so that he could take his place amongst the rulers of the world; Richard repaid England by treating it as an inexhaustible source of money to finance his crusade, his ransom, and finally his defence of Normandy.

So Richard appears to us in the twentieth century. To the men of his time he was almost an ideal king, a perfect knight, a hero, bold, fearless, and courageous, a born leader of men in battle, quick to avenge an insult or to reward a friend, recklessly generous, wildly extravagant, dazzling in his person, and utterly tenacious in defending what was his. He covered himself with glory in the Holy Land and made every Englishman proud to be the subject of such a king. His duty lay where the danger was greatest, and after he returned from his crusade his duty kept him

[1] Howden, Vol. IV, p. 88; Ralph of Coggeshall, p. 98; Doris M. Stenton Introd. to Pipe Roll 1 John, pp. xiv-xv.

[2] Howden, Vol. IV, pp. 87, 89-90.

across the Channel, defending his lands, as a king should, against the aggressions of King Philip.

Richard's neglect was England's good fortune. Left almost to their own devices, with their king first at the other end of the world and then immersed in his preoccupations with his continental lands, the barons of England developed a sense of collective responsibility for the good governance of their country that would never have come into being if their king had been constantly amongst them, directing the affairs of the country with a strong hand.

In the deposition of William Longchamp early in the reign and in the orderly development of law and administration under the guidance of Hubert Walter, the barons of England showed a restraint and a sound commonsense that would have amazed their fathers. One has only to contrast the disorders, the lawlessness, and the brutal selfishness of most of the English barons during King Stephen's reign with the orderly, law-abiding, and responsible conduct of the barons during Richard's reign to realise how far the English nation had come along the paths of orderly government.

When William Longchamp showed himself a tyrant, the barons, acting under at least the pretext of lawful obedience to the king, deposed the man the king had put over them and, making the most of the king's contradictory orders, installed another man in his place. They had deposed the king's representative when they found his rule intolerable; it would be only a short step from that to bringing the king himself to account when they found his rule intolerable.

The meeting of the barons outside the walls of London in October 1191 was a rehearsal for the meeting of the barons at Runnymede in June 1215; what they learned at the one place they put into practice at the other. But for Richard's neglect, they might have been much longer in learning the lesson.

BIBLIOGRAPHY

Ancient Charters, Royal and Private, Prior to A.D. 1200, Part 1, ed. John Horace Round (Pipe Roll Society 10, 1888).

Annales Monastici, ed. H. R. Luard (5 vols., Rolls Series 36, 1864-9):
- I. *Annales de Margan.*
- II. *Annales de Wintonia.*

Charles Austin Beard: *The Office of Justice of the Peace in England in Its Origin and Development.* Studies in History, Economics and Public Law, Vol. XX, No. 1 (New York, 1904).

The Book of Fees, Commonly Called Testa de Nevill, ed. Sir H. C. Maxwell Lyte (3 vols., London, 1920-3).

C. N. L. Brooke: 'Gregorian Reform in Action: Clerical Marriage in England, 1050-1200', *Cambridge Historical Journal*, XII (1956); reprinted in *Change in Medieval Society*, ed. Sylvia L. Thrupp (New York, 1964), pp. 49-71.

C. R. Cheney: *From Becket to Langton: English Church Government 1170-1213* (Manchester, 1956).

— 'Legislation of the Medieval English Church', Part 1, *English Historical Review*, L (April 1935), pp. 193-224.

Helena M. Chew: *The English Ecclesiastical Tenants-in-Chief and Knight Service* (Oxford, 1932).

Conciliorum Oecumenicorum Decreta, ed. J. Alberigo *et al.* (Freiburg, 1962).

Alice G. Cramer: 'The Origins and Functions of the Jewish Exchequer', *Speculum*, XVI (April 1941), pp. 226-9.

Epistolae Cantuarienses, ed. William Stubbs. Vol. II of *Chronicles and Memorials of the Reign of Richard I* (2 vols., Rolls Series 38, 1864-5).

Foedera, Conventiones, Litterae, et Cujuscunque Generis Acta Publica, ed. Thomas Rymer and Robert Sanderson, rev. Adam Clark and Fred. Holbrooke (3 vols. in 6, London, 1816-30).

V. H. Galbraith: *The Making of Domesday Book* (Oxford, 1961).

Gerald of Wales: *Opera* (8 vols., Rolls Series 21, 1861-91):
- II. *Gemma Ecclesiastica*, ed. J. S. Brewer.
- III. *De Invectionibus*, ed. J. S. Brewer.
- IV. *Speculum Ecclesiae* and *De Vita Galfridi Archiepiscopi Eboracensis*, ed. J. S. Brewer.
- VII. *Vita S. Remigii* and *Vita S. Hugonis*, ed. J. F. Dimock.
- VIII. *De Principis Instructione*, ed. G. F. Warner.

Gervase of Canterbury: *Historical Works*, ed. William Stubbs (2 vols., Rolls Series 73, 1879-80).

Gesta Regis Henrici Secundi and its continuation, *Gesta Regis Ricardi Primi*, ed. William Stubbs (2 vols., Rolls Series 49, 1867).

Histoire de Guillaume le Maréchal, ed. Paul Meyer (3 vols., Paris, 1891-1901).

Margaret Howell: *Regalian Right in Medieval England* (London, 1962).

R. F. Hunnisett: *The Medieval Coroner* (Cambridge, 1961).

Naomi D. Hurnard: 'The Jury of Presentment and the Assize of Clarendon', *English Historical Review*, LVI (July 1941), pp. 374-410.

Itinerarium Peregrinorum et Gesta Regis Ricardi, ed. William Stubbs. Vol. I of *Chronicles and Memorials of the Reign of Richard I* (2 vols., Rolls Series 38, 1864-5).

Jocelin of Brakelond: *Chronicle*, ed. H. E. Butler (Nelson's Medieval Texts, 1949).

J. E. A. Jolliffe: *Angevin Kingship* (2nd ed., London, 1963).

Dom David Knowles: *The Episcopal Colleagues of Archbishop Thomas Becket* (Cambridge, 1951).

— *The Monastic Order in England* (Cambridge, 1940).

Lionel Landon: *The Itinerary of King Richard I* (Pipe Roll Society, New Series 13, 1935).

Reginald Lennard: 'The Composition of Demesne Plough-Teams in Twelfth-Century England', *English Historical Review* (April 1960), 193-207.

J. E. Lloyd: *History of Wales* (2 vols., London, 1948).

Magna Vita S. Hugonis Episcopi Lincolniensis, ed. J. F. Dimock (Rolls Series 37, 1864).

Materials for the History of Thomas Becket, ed. J. C. Robertson and J. B. Sheppard (7 vols., Rolls Series 67, 1875-85).

Kate Norgate: *England under the Angevin Kings* (2 vols., London, 1887).

— *Richard the Lion Heart* (London, 1924).

Henry Owen: *Gerald the Welshman* (2nd ed., London, 1904).

Sidney Painter: *William Marshal* (Baltimore, 1933).

The Peterborough Chronicle, ed. Cecil Clark. Oxford English Monographs (Oxford, 1958).

Pipe Rolls, 1 Richard I—1 John. The roll for 1 Richard I, ed. J. Hunter, was published by the Record Commission in 1844. The remainder were published by the Pipe Roll Society, 1925-33, ed. Doris M. Stenton, whose introductions are particularly valuable for a study of the period.

Henri Pierenne: 'Northern Towns and Their Commerce', Chap. XV in Vol. VI of *The Cambridge Medieval History* (8 vols., Cambridge, 1911-36).

Sir Frederick Pollock and Frederic William Maitland: *The History of English Law before the Time of Edward I* (2nd ed., 2 vols., Cambridge, 1899).

Austin Lane Poole: *From Domesday Book to Magna Carta* (Oxford, 1951).

— *Obligations of Society in the XII and XIII Centuries* (Oxford, 1946).

Sir Maurice Powicke: *The Loss of Normandy, 1189-1203* (2nd ed., Manchester, 1961).

Ralph of Coggeshall: *Chronicon Anglicanum*, ed. Joseph Stevenson (Rolls Series 66, 1875).

Ralph of Diceto: *Opera Historica*, ed. William Stubbs (2 vols., Rolls Series 68, 1876).

Sir James H. Ramsay: *The Angevin Empire* (London, 1903).

— *A History of the Revenues of the Kings of England, 1066-1339* (2 vols., Oxford, 1925).

The Registrum Antiquissimum of the Cathedral Church of Lincoln, Vol. I, ed. C. W. Foster. Publications of the Lincoln Record Society, Vol. XXVII (Lincoln, 1931).

Richard of Devizes: *Chronicle*, ed. John T. Appleby (Nelson's Medieval Texts, 1963).

Richard son of Nigel: *Dialogus de Scaccario*, ed. Charles Johnson (Nelson's Medieval Texts, 1950).

H. G. Richardson: *The English Jewry under Angevin Kings* (London, 1960).

— 'The Letters and Charters of Eleanor of Aquitaine', *English Historical Review*, LXXIV (April 1959), pp. 193-213.

— 'The Schools of Northampton in the Twelfth Century', *English Historical Review*, LVI (October 1941), pp. 595-605.

— and G. O. Sayles: *The Governance of Mediaeval England from the Conquest to Magna Carta* (Edinburgh, 1963).

Roger of Howden: *Chronica*, ed. William Stubbs (4 vols., Rolls Series 51, 1868-71).

Roger of Wendover: *Flores Historiarum*, ed. H. G. Hewlett (3 vols., Rolls Series 84, 1886-69).

Cecil Roth: *A History of the Jews in England* (Oxford, 1941).

Rotuli Curiae Regis, ed. Sir Francis Palgrave (2 vols., London, 1835).

J. H. Round: *Feudal England* (London, 1895).

— *Geoffrey de Mandeville* (London, 1892).

— 'The Great Carucage of 1198', *English Historical Review*, III (July 1888), pp. 501-10, and IV (January 1889), pp. 105-7.

Sir Steven Runciman: *A History of the Crusades* (3 vols., Cambridge, 1951-5).

G. V. Scammell: *Hugh du Puiset, Bishop of Durham* (Cambridge, 1956).

Doris M. Stenton: 'England: Henry II', Chap. XVII in Vol. V of *The Cambridge Medieval History* (8 vols., Cambridge, 1911-36).

— *English Justice between the Norman Conquest and the Great Charter, 1066-1215* (Philadelphia, 1964).

James Tait: 'Studies in Magna Carta. I, *Waynagium* and *Contenementum*', *English Historical Review*, XXVII (October 1912), pp.720-8.

Three Rolls of the King's Court in the Reign of King Richard the First, A.D. 1194-1195, ed. F. W. Maitland (Pipe Roll Society 14, 1891).

Walter Map: *De Nugis Curialium*, ed. M. R. James (Oxford, 1914).

William of Newburgh: *Historia Rerum Anglicarum*, in Vols. I and II of *Chronicles of the Reigns of Stephen, Henry II, and Richard I*, ed. Richard Howlett (4 vols., Rolls Series 82, 1884-9).

INDEX

Persons are listed under their Christian names
Places outside the British Isles are omitted